Twayne's Theatrical Arts Series

Warren French
EDITOR

Joseph Losey

Joseph Losey

Joseph Losey with Julie Christie on the set of *The Go-Between* (1971).

Joseph Losey

FOSTER HIRSCH

BOSTON

Twayne Publishers

1980

178635

Library of Congress Cataloging in Publication Data
Hirsch, Foster.
Joseph Losey.

(Twayne's theatrical arts series)
Bibliography: p. 229–230
Filmography: p. 231–48
Includes index.
1. Losey, Joseph.
PN1998.A3L564   791.43'0233'0924   80-14980
ISBN 0-8057-9257-0

Contents

About the Author

FOSTER HIRSCH received his B.A. degree from Stanford University (1965). His graduate degrees from Columbia University include an M.F.A. in Film (1966), and the M.A. (1967) and Ph.D. (1971) in English. From 1969–1971 he was a Lecturer on Drama at The New School. He is currently Associate Professor of English and film at Brooklyn College of the City University of New York.

A free-lance writer, Mr. Hirsch has published articles and reviews on literature, film, and theater in numerous publications, including the *New York Times, New Republic, Chicago Tribune Book World, Nation, Commonweal, America, Village Voice, Variety, Film Quarterly, Cinema, Film Comment,* and *Film Heritage.* He has written books on George Kelly. Tennessee Williams, The Hollywood Epic, Edward Albee, Elizabeth Taylor, and Edward G. Robinson. He is currently at work on a book on Woody Allen (for McGraw-Hill) and on a history of The Actors Studio (for W. W. Norton). His book on Laurence Olivier (for Twayne's Theatrical Arts Series) was published in 1979. A. S. Barnes will publish his study of Film Noir in 1981.

Editor's Foreword

WHAT WOULD the superstitious make of the disconcerting discovery that those three of this country's handful of imaginative and inventive film directors who were born within a few years of each other in the same chilly state of Wisconsin should have had the most discontinuous careers among their contemporaries because of the difficulties they had in getting their harshly critical, visionary projects funded?

Nicholas Ray, Orson Welles, and Joseph Losey have all sought with the overbearing zeal of Old Testament prophets to use the new art of this century to produce a modern equivalent of Ecclesiastes for our undisciplined, decadent society, and the society, from its sensationalist millionaires who control film production to the mindless audience gorging itself on Coke and popcorn, has responded by frustrating these missionaries' efforts to make thought-provoking pictures, eventually driving all of them into exile and silence.

Ray's and Losey's careers, however, have been quite different from Welles's, which, as he comments himself in *F for Fake*, started at the top and plummeted straight downward. Despite the offensiveness of *Citizen Kane* to some influential citizens, Welles never came under political fire; it was his expensive and egocentric methods that made him the scourge of the studio system. Even such a proper institution as the American Film Institute has seen fit to render him the highest honors; he just hasn't often been able to find work.

Both Ray and Losey had ideological difficulties with the political watchdogs that descended on Hollywood during the McCarthy era. Ray was never specifically blacklisted, but left Hollywood anyway in a kind of paranoid outrage. Losey was blacklisted and had to make a fresh start abroad—at first under assumed names—after

having enjoyed mild success in Hollywood with some social protest dramas that appear very heavy-handed today.

Ray, moreover, was able to return in triumph to score his greatest success in an increasingly daring Hollywood with James Dean in *Rebel without a Cause* in 1955. Dean's early, violent death was a blow from which Ray never recovered. Never really at ease within the studio system and never again able to strike up the kind of creative partnership that he had achieved with the cult idol, Ray finally walked out on Hollywood after squandering his talents on kitsch epics like *King of Kings* and *55 Days in Peking.*

Although a few years older than Welles and Ray, Losey had to wait almost another decade after Ray's major success to score his own in England with *The Servant* (1963), his first collaboration with playwright/scriptwriter Harold Pinter. So anglicized had Losey become by then that this brooding, baroque closet drama proved the classic study of the deterioration of British aristocracy that seemingly could only have been made by a product of the society (as Ray's *Rebel* was the classic study of the "absurdity," as Paul Goodman called it, of youth in America's suburban wasteland).

Losey went on to score his two other greatest commerical and artistic successes, *Accident* (1967) and *The Go-Between* (1971), also in collaboration with Pinter, during the period that also saw his direction of *Modesty Blaise* (1966) and *Boom* (1968), the most stylish achievements of this man whose rigid social conscience was complemented by a curious gift for creating films that resembled baroque paintings.

Like Welles again, like Ray, Losey was not able to continue to enlarge his reputation. His fourth project with Pinter, a film based on Proust's *Remembrance of Things Past,* the supreme literary embodiment of aristocratic decadence, has not found backers; and, although Foster Hirsch finds much to praise about Losey's latest pictures, they are almost unknown in the United States because of distributors' lack of interest in them.

Gone in these latest pictures is the lush decor and Byzantine plotting of *Secret Ceremony* and *The Go-Between.* In *The Assassination of Trotsky,* film versions of Ibsen's *A Doll's House* and Brecht's *Galileo,* and *Mr. Klein* Losey has returned to both the unremittingly stark and humorless style of *King and Country* and politically disturbing topics. French ciritics revere him, but such unrelievedly solemn and disheartening stories have never been ac-

cepted by American audiences in pursuit of magical escape. Small wonder that Foster Hirsch argues convincingly that Losey has become the most European of American-born directors, for Losey has even less in common with his countrymen than such celebrated literary expatriates as Henry James and Gertrude Stein. He does share with these predecessors, however, an increasing tendency to see human dramas in terms of abstract allegories and a lack of any sense of humor in dealing with the sordid spectacle of an increasingly closed society's inevitable self-destruction.

That Losey's greatest moments came in collaboration with Harold Pinter is not surprising, since he probably occupies a place among filmmakers very much like that of Pinter among playwrights. Both are artists of great sensibility, intensely admired by a small cult, but neurotically at odds with a preponderantly vulgar bourgeois society. Both also distrust, however, like T. S. Eliot, a degenerating aristocracy and a gross proletariat; and both produce cryptic, claustrophobic works that puzzle, bore, and finally antagonize a vast audience of thrill-seeking sentimentalists. They are, like Federico Fellini, but without his gargantuan sense of life, pioneers in bringing belatedly to film the "waste land" sensibility of Modernism. Perhaps, if the time is not lost beyond recapturing, they may crown their efforts by making a "living painting" of Proust's great novel.

W.F.

Preface

AT THE CENTER of the most famous shot in *The Servant*, Joseph Losey's most famous film, is a mirror with a curved, distorting glass. Changing the shape of the characters' faces and bodies, rearranging spatial proportions, the mirror provides a bizarre reconstruction of reality. This mirror is the film's main motif and symbol, its controlling metaphor, and, like the film itself (and beyond that, the entire Losey canon), it reorganizes physical reality in an elegantly stylized and thematically purposeful way.

Mirrors are part of the decor in almost all of Losey's films; they're one of the marks of his personal signature, one of the recurrent icons of the world that he creates on film. "Among filmmakers, Losey is the greatest poet of mirrors," Roger Greenspun has written, "greater even than Cocteau, because he knows they are environments in their own right, accepting, changing, and never quite giving back the world they reflect."[1] Included not merely for decoration or ornament, mirrors serve a variety of thematic and symbolic functions in Losey's work: they are sign and portent, reflectors and transformers of physical and psychological reality.

As mirrors in Losey usually have a metaphoric function, so can they be seen as the basic metaphor for Losey's work as a whole. A mirror reflects the scene that is placed in front of it. But even if a mirror is a faithful reproduction of reality, even if its surface does not disfigure space like the mirror in *The Servant*, it provides an image of reality rather than the thing itself.

A mirror has a frame whose shape limits the amount of reality that it can reflect. A mirror contains only part of a room, a space, a scene, rather than the whole: its reflection of reality is thus necessarily partial, fragmentary, selective, distanced. A film frame is very like that of a mirror. It too presents only a section of a scene, and it too is a copy rather than the original. Like mirrors as well,

the film image can portray reality through a variety of lenses and surfaces, from ones that are objective reproductions to ones that redesign spatial relationships. Mirrors are thus smaller versions of the "eye" of the camera.

Mirror shots in films enclose images in a frame within the frame, offering a kind of visual underlining or italics as they place the mirror image at a double remove from the original. Figures, objects, rooms which are reflected in mirrors in films are being singled out for special emphasis; they are being "framed" because they are of particular value or significance. Losey's films are filled with this kind of "pointing," in which objects like mirrors, and people and places that are reflected in mirrors, stand for something—have more than a merely literal signification.

Both the use and the "idea" of the mirror call forth many of the essential qualities of Losey's work: its treatment of objects as symbols; its selective and stylized recreations of reality; its aesthetic self-consciousness and its emotional distancing, as if the world in his films is being filtered through a mediating scrim. And the seeming omnipresence of mirrors suggests as well the interior spaces, the closed, limited settings in which Losey's films typically take place.

Losey's oeuvre can be seen as a progressive series of alterations of reality, from the muted stylization of his early social-consciousness dramas to the more intensively stylized collaborations with Harold Pinter to the allegorical abstraction that figures prominently in some of his films since the late 1960s. Although his work is rooted in a meticulous concern for realistic decor—for the rightness of the backgrounds in terms of story, characterization, and theme—Losey is at heart a symbolist, infatuated with moral and political metaphors. His tendency has always been to abstract from reality—to refine and to enhance it—in order to enforce a thematic point.

A brilliant stylist for whom mirrored impressions of reality are means to an end, Losey thus controls the real in order to make symbolic social statements. His films, a series of mirrors that refract, decompose, alter, and heighten reality, are an exhilarating mixture of art and politics: his elegant visual style transforms political realities the way his mirrors reconstruct the rooms in which his moral parables are enacted. "True art is the breaking down of reality," Losey has said, "and the reconstructing of it in a shape, in a form, to show people something in a way in which they wouldn't otherwise have seen it."[2]

Acknowledgments

PAT SHEEHAN and Joe Balian at the Library of Congress; the British Film Institute, Dean Street, London; the staff of the Theater Collection of the New York Public Library, Lincoln Center.

Photographic research by Bill O'Connell.

Chronology

1909   Joseph Losey born in La Crosse, Wisconsin, January 14.

1929   Graduates from Dartmouth.

1930   Graduates from Harvard with M.A. in English Literature; begins writing theater and book reviews for the *New York Times, Theater Arts Monthly, Saturday Review of Literature*.

1931   Stage manager of Charles Laughton's American production of *Payment Deferred*.

1932   Stages first variety show at Radio City Music Hall.

1933   Directs *Little Ol' Boy*, by Albert Bein, on Broadway.

1934   Directs *Jayhawker*, by Sinclair Lewis and Lloyd Lewis, on Broadway; *A Bride for the Unicorn*, by Denis Johnston, in Cambridge, Massachusetts; and *Gods of the Lightning*, by Maxwell Anderson, in Boston.

1935   Attends film classes conducted by Sergei Eisenstein in Moscow; stages English-language production of *Waiting for Lefty*.

1936   Directs *Hymn to the Rising Sun*, by Paul Green, at the Civic Repertory Theater in New York; directs various productions for the Living Newspaper, including *Triple-A Plowed Under;* also directs *Who Fights This Battle?*, by Kenneth White, and *Conjur Man Dies*, by Rudolph Fischer, for the Federal Theater in New York.

1938   Directs *Sunup to Sundown*, by Frances Faragoh, in New York.

1939   *Pete Roleum and His Cousins* (short film).

1940   *A Child Went Forth* and *Youth Gets a Break* (short films).

1940–   Stages various War Relief shows in New York, Washington,
1943   Boston, Philadelphia, Chicago, Detroit.

1943– Writes ninety half-hour programs for NBC and CBS, in-
1944   cluding "Worlds at War" and "Days of Reckoning" series.

1945   *A Gun in His Hand,* a "Crime Does Not Pay" short subject;
stages Roosevelt Memorial Show at the Hollywood Bowl.

1946   Stages Academy Award Show at Grauman's Chinese Theater,
Hollywood.

1947   Directs *The Great Campaign,* by Arnold Sundgaard, in New
York; directs *Galileo,* by Bertolt Brecht, in Los Angeles and
New York.

1948   First feature film, *The Boy with Green Hair.*

1949   *The Lawless.*

1950   *The Prowler* and *M.*

1951   *The Big Night;* leaves Hollywood because of the blacklist;
directs film in Italy, *Strangler on the Prowl;* settles in London.

1954   Directs *The Wooden Dish* on the London stage; *The Sleeping
Tiger* under the pseudonym of Victor Hanbury for British
film company.

1955   Directs *The Night of the Ball,* by Michael Burn, on the
London Stage; *A Man on the Beach* (short film); *A Finger
of Guilt* under a pseudonym, Joseph Walton.

1956   *Time without Pity,* first British film using his own name.

1957   *The Gypsy and the Gentleman.*

1959   *Chance Meeting.*

1960   *The Concrete Jungle.*

1961   *These Are the Damned.*

1961– *Eve.*
1962

1963   *The Servant.*

1964   *King and Country.*

1966   *Modesty Blaise.*

1967   *Accident.*

1968   *Boom* and *Secret Ceremony.*

1970   *Figures in a Landscape.*

1971   *The Go-Between.*

1972   *The Assassination of Trotsky.*

1973   *A Doll's House* (shown first on TV in the United States).

1975   *Galileo,* for the American Film Theater; *The Romantic Englishwoman.*

1977   *Mr. Klein* (in French).

1978   *Southern Routes* (in French).

1979   *Don Giovanni.*

1

Flight from America

JOSEPH LOSEY, SURPRISINGLY, was born in the American heartland, in La Crosse, Wisconsin, in 1909.[1] Except perhaps for the puritanical streak that remains a part of his work, there is very little in his films to indicate his middle-American roots. Blacklisted in the early 1950s, during the height of the Communist witch-hunt conducted by Senator Joseph McCarthy, Losey went to London, where he has been based ever since. His career thus parallels that of Jules Dassin, another American expatriate; and like that of Dassin, Losey's work reflects his absorption in another culture. Some of Dassin's most successful work (*He Who Must Die, Never On Sunday*) has a decidedly European rather than American texture. Losey's films likewise are noticeably "Continental"—in his recent *Mr. Klein*, filmed in France in French, there are no traces whatever of the director's American heritage. His original American puritanism—the attraction to absolutes that forms part of the fabric of his earliest work—is overlaid with increasing doses of European elegance and expressionism and with a European fascination with enigma and ambiguity. Moral and political values in his films become less clear-cut, less a neatly balanced matter of good against evil. Ironically, Losey's work gains in visual and rhetorical power as it becomes less "American" in setting and flavor.

The gradual erosion of an American "note" in his films echoes his rejection of his family and his early political idealism. At different points in his life Losey isolated himself from his quintessentially middle-American family and then from the Communist ideology to which he was drawn in the 1930s. Both his life and his career indicate a flight from America—from the right-wing Americana rep-

17

resented by his family, and from the left-wing groups that attracted American intellectuals during the Depression.

Losey comes from a wealthy family. His pioneer grandfather, one of the cofounders of La Crosse (the city has a Losey Boulevard) and of the Northern Pacific Railroad, was a prominent lawyer and political figure. His children—five daughters and one son, Joseph's father—were all educated abroad. This snobbish, anti-Semitic Wasp family provided a model of political conservatism against which Losey rebelled. "When my father died," Losey said, "I decided not to have anything to do with my family. I went to Dartmouth instead of Princeton, where my father had studied. At first, I was not interested in politics of any kind, because my family had been so involved in politics." Then, in the 1930s, "like all intellectuals, I was 'engaged.' After the war I was less so."[2]

During the Depression, separating himself politically and economically from his family, Losey came "in direct contact with political life. I had to work. I met *engagé* people, who told me: 'Do political cabaret, workers' theater. It doesn't matter that you are an Anglican snob from Dartmouth. If you do the theater you will become "engaged" and enter the Communist Party.' "[3] Though it took him many years to realize it, Losey had replaced one kind of tyranny with another. His belief in radical politics, like his upbringing in a severe Wasp family, was something he had to outgrow in order to claim his independence. "Once you became militant, it was almost impossible to re-establish an individual conscience, because you have abandoned it to collective conscience. Politics for me in the 30s took on a religious meaning, and I couldn't resist it. To get rid of that tyranny occupied all my years of maturity. . . . It is only in the last fifteen years that I have stopped having anything to do with all kinds of ideology."[4]

Although, at different stages of his life, he rejected his family's money and Communist idealism, both money and antiestablishment politics are continuing elements in his films. Many of Losey's films, in addition to *The Servant,* his most celebrated one, are about a struggle between masters and servants, between the privileged and the dispossessed, and Losey is typically critical of both sides of the class conflict, condemning almost equally unreasoned proletarian rebellion along with unenlightened and unearned despotism. Even as he attacks aristocratic privilege—and no rich person in any of the

films escapes censure—he is at some level seduced by the trappings of wealth, by the elegant rooms in which so many of his films are set—rooms whose occupants have the taste for, and can afford, the gilt-edged mirrors that line the walls. While his films attack the rich, they also reveal a distrust of "the people." Losey, in short, is a skeptic, poised uneasily between his attraction to the "Finer Things" and his disapproval of social and economic inequity. Losey is an earnest, though partial, rebel against the political status quo: he is a part-time Marxist and Socialist.

The negative tone, the doomsday aura, of much of Losey's work is but the reverse image of his initial political idealism. Losey is a disappointed radical who masks his hopes for social change beneath a cynical facade. Many of his films end in utter defeat, with neither the rebels nor the establishment figures able to claim a clear-cut victory. Losey's political pessimism contains a residual belief, however, in the possibility of change: if events are portrayed as so utterly gloomy, if the class conflict that surfaces in film after film is shown with such a bleak outcome, perhaps this will stimulate a desire for social progress, for a renovation of the corrupt and corrupting master-servant structure.

Losey has said in a number of interviews that he does not make films of social comment. "Because I was exiled doesn't mean that I am a social documentarian. . . . I am not particularly interested in social reforms, and I especially don't believe in message films."[5] But he does want his films to "show a sense of social responsibility," and it is clear that art, for him, remains a moral weapon, a means of isolating social issues for instruction and clarification and a way of provoking thought, though not a forum for providing easy, or even any, answers.

Losey instructs through negative rather than positive examples. There are no heroes in the old-fashioned mold in any of his films; there are virtually no heroes, in fact, of any kind in his work. Losey is attracted to victims, to characters closed in on themselves and in flight from a menacing social reality. Society in the films is invariably threatening, hostile to the concerns of the individual, positively dangerous to the potential or actual rebel. No character, in the mature Losey films, escapes the power of social forces: the image of the political world that appears in many of the films is evocatively symbolized in the hovering, omnipresent helicopter that

relentlessly pursues and finally overtakes the escaped prisoners in *Figures in a Landscape.* Political society in Losey always contains potential violence and the threat of annihilation.

Political Theater

Losey graduated from Dartmouth in 1929. In 1930, after he received an M.A. in English Literature from Harvard, he began writing theater and book reviews for the *New York Times, Theater Arts Monthly,* and the *Saturday Review of Literature.* In 1931 he was the stage manager of Charles Laughton's American production of *Payment Deferred.* In 1932 he staged the first variety shows at Radio City Music Hall. In 1933 he directed a problem drama on Broadway called *Little Ol' Boy* (which made Burgess Meredith a star) about a reformatory school. In 1934 he directed a political play by Sinclair Lewis called *Jayhawker,* which traced the career of a Kansas political mountebank who rode into the Senate in 1861. The play featured a virtuoso performance by the famed vaudeville monologuist Walter C. Kelly, an uncle of Princess Grace of Monaco and a brother of Pulitzer Prize–winning playwright George Kelly (author of *Craig's Wife, The Show-Off, The Torch-Bearers*). In 1935 Losey went to Moscow, where he attended film classes conducted by Eisenstein and staged a well-received English-language production of Clifford Odets's *Waiting for Lefty.*

In 1936 he was hired by the Federal Theater to direct several entries in the Living Newspaper series. The Federal Theater project (1935–1939), undertaken as a response to the Depression, was a unique episode in American cultural history, an attempt at a federally funded nationwide theater. Under the auspices of the project, and its energetic and independent director, Hallie Flanagan, the government sponsored a large number of plays in order to generate employment for theater people whose means of livelihood had been devastated by the Depression. As the most radical and explicitly political branch of the project, the Living Newspapers were investigated by the House Un-American Activities Committee, which accused Hallie Flanagan and her directors of being Communist inspired and infiltrated. Losey's association with the Living Newspaper productions was one of the reasons, a decade later, as his career in Hollywood was getting underway, that he was considered politically suspect.

In both its formal elements and its political posture the Living Newspaper was a precursor of Brecht's epic theater. Each play in the series was addressed to a particular social problem, usually a grievance of the working class. The politics of the plays were at least incipiently if not actually and fully Marxist, and the productions were designed to instruct Depression audiences and to encourage them to take action. The Living Newspaper dramas were then explicitly polemical—newspaper editorials brought vividly to life on stage. The problem that the play was intended to expose was dramatized in an episodic format, with rapid shifts of scene, and a succession of characters. The aggrieved workers were the heroes, thereby reversing the usual procedure of American drama and films of enshrining the individual hero. The Living Newspapers were invariably about oppressed groups rather than oppressed individuals.

Made up of comic and dramatic skits, of songs and dances, and using slides projected on a screen at the back of the stage, the productions were theatrical collages. "It was a popular theater, at popular prices," Losey said, "and we had extraordinary freedom. We used the circus, the music hall, the ballet, slides, music, but unified each time by a subject—the agricultural program of Roosevelt, trade-unionism. Unfortunately, the Federal Theater and its subsidy ceased before we were able really to create a style. But the methods and the very cinematic character of the Living Newspaper has had an incalculable influence on the American theater."[6]

Losey's production of *Triple-A Plowed Under*, a dramatization of the American farm problem 1920–1935, with a cast of 100, was commonly regarded as one of the strongest of the series. Briskly and forcefully directed, the production assaulted the audience with the message that "the farmer, the workingman and the middle-class consumer are the victims of capitalist speculators, of the system."[7] "This was Brechtian theater," Losey said about the Living Newspaper, "but I didn't know it at the time. Brecht saw it and adored it. And in spite of his austerity in matters of color, his preference for white light and neutral colors, he particularly appreciated the passage where I dressed my workers in fuchsia and rose."[8]

Because his acclaimed work for the Living Newspaper had stamped him as a political activist as well as an antirealist, Losey was chosen by Brecht to direct the American premiere of *Galileo* in 1947, in a production starring Charles Laughton, who had also

translated the play and urged Brecht to revise his original concept of the protagonist. *Galileo* was first produced at the Coronet Theater in Los Angeles in the summer of 1947 and then in New York the following December. In the interim between the productions, Brecht was investigated by the House Un-American Activities Committee—the production was considered politically suspicious not only because of Brecht's Communist sympathies but also because Losey was known to have had left-wing associations. Clearly, for Losey, his ability to work in America was going to be limited by his political activity during the 1930s; but before he was hounded out of America, he was able to direct five feature films between 1948 and 1951.

Working with Brecht on *Galileo* was one of the most important collaborations in Losey's career. Brecht's alienation theory, designed to prevent the audience from becoming emotionally involved with the characters, and his use of drama for polemical purposes,

John Carradine, Charles Laughton, and Joan MacCracken in Losey's authentically Brechtian production of *Galileo,* in Los Angeles (1947).

left a lasting impression on Losey. Absorbing the lessons of the playwright, Losey directed *Galileo* in a pure "Brechtian" style: cool, visually spare, precise, alienated. In a typical Brechtian ploy to dedramatize the action, Losey used placards to announce the idea of each scene in advance. The play's theme, then, was stressed more than the personal fate of Galileo. Losey directed Laughton to restrict his delivery to a dry recital quality, a detached monotone; and Laughton portrayed the scientist as a weak, self-indulgent, decidedly unheroic figure, as Brecht intended. Losey's famous production had the visual austerity and the didactic emphasis that many interpretations of Brecht aim for but miss.

With his taut production of *Galileo*, Losey's reputation as a director of experimental, antinaturalistic political theater was firmly established. The play's sold-out limited engagement in New York attracted the attention of Dore Schary, then head of production at RKO, who hired Losey to direct a political fable called *The Boy with Green Hair*.

Losey and Kazan in Hollywood

Losey's brief Hollywood career was confined to low-budget pictures at a time when they had real vitality, when formulaic material was embellished with personal style, when directors and screenwriters used well-worn movie stories to make insinuating or subversive statements about the escalating hysteria of contemporary politics. Losey's contributions to the B *noir* films of the period are not major pieces; none of his work has the solidity, say, of Nicholas Ray's *They Live by Night*, for example, or the idiosyncratic treatment of *noir* themes and settings of Ray's *On Dangerous Ground*. Losey's less flavorful work can more nearly be compared to that of Elia Kazan, also undergoing his movie apprenticeship after a long period in the theater. In problem dramas like *Boomerang, Gentlemen's Agreement, Pinky,* and *Panic in the Streets,* Kazan was working (although usually with A-film budgets) toward the explosive, stylized realism that erupted full force in the early 1950s in *A Streetcar Named Desire* and *On the Waterfront*. Kazan's work of the late 1940s, like Losey's, can be seen as a series of dry runs, of practical experiments in which the director was flexing his muscles, developing his feeling for the grammar of film. Kazan's sensibility, like

Losey's, is a dark one—his early social dramas present the American city as infested, as fatally corrupt, although Kazan believes more than Losey in the power of the noble individual to combat the plague (quite literally, in *Panic in the Streets,* where Richard Widmark as a dedicated medical officer tracks down a killer who has brought bubonic plague into New Orleans). The ultimate Kazan hero, Marlon Brando in *On the Waterfront,* single-handedly faces the corrupt labor boss. When Kazan's films have an upbeat ending, as in *On the Waterfront,* or even *East of Eden,* where father and son are reconciled, the optimism seems connected in organic ways to the preceding conflict. Losey's affirmative endings, in *The Boy with Green Hair* and *The Big Night* and *The Lawless,* on the other hand, seem imposed and unearned—Losey is clearly more comfortable with the devastation with which powerful films of his like *The Servant* and *These Are the Damned* conclude.

Kazan, that is to say, has a more popular sensibility than Losey. Losey's characters have never attained the powerful, charismatic appeal of the heroes of Kazan's strongest films; no figure with the mythic resonance of Brando in *A Streetcar Named Desire* and *On the Waterfront,* or James Dean in *East of Eden,* has emerged from Losey's work. Losey simply does not believe in heroes drawn in the popular American mold; and in the sense that his work undermines the power of individual initiative, and portrays circumstances in which the individual is controlled by forces outside himself, Losey's is a more subversive and negative cinema than Kazan's. With their neurotic characters and their preoccupation with the twisted family, Kazan's films are in fact very much in the American grain— American optimism ultimately triumphs in his work, and his movies end characteristically with a sense of renewal and affirmation. Losey's work, in this light, is decidedly "un-American," since his most representative characters are damned figures either condemned to endless repetition of defeat or else, having broken free of a conformist social mold, abandoned in a void.

It is not accident, or merely a question of political circumstance, that Losey's mature style was reached outside America and the major studio system while Kazan's greatest successes, for all their sexual kinks, were delivered, under contract, to Warner Brothers. From their associations with left-wing theater of the 1930s (Kazan worked with the Group Theater) to their delayed movie apprenticeship in the late 1940s, the careers of Losey and Kazan are re-

markably parallel. As they gained assurance in their use of film, as their work became more noticeably personal in the handling of actors and of mise-en-scène, their subjects were less about abstract social problems than about psychological conflicts within and between characters in limited settings. Their work, that is, became more purely private in focus, though always retaining connections between the personal drama and the larger social scene from which it evolved.

Significantly, both directors achieved full artistic maturity in their collaboration with major playwrights—Kazan with Tennessee Williams, Losey with Harold Pinter. Williams and Pinter released latent powers in the two directors. Williams and Pinter, so utterly different in style and tone, the one so deeply American, the other so fully and deliciously English, inspired the two strong directors, forceful personalities in their own right, to do their finest work. Williams, passionate, overwrought, with his poet's sense of image and rhythm, ignited Kazan's own high-powered direction of Method-trained actors and unleashed his explosive intensity—Kazan's direction of actors in films based on Williams material is among the most fevered in American movies.

Pinter's coolness, his utter ironic detachment from his characters, his dry wit, his love of nuance and innuendo, emphasized qualities that had been present in the Losey iconography from the beginning. Even in his early problem films, Losey was a more detached and objective director than Kazan, whose work always hinted at the sentimentality and emotionalism that were to be released at full steam in his work on Williams's plays. Losey's style, even in the 1940s, was dryer, more abstract, with a tendency toward lesson-pointing: his work always held intimations of a stern schoolmaster enforcing an important point to recalcitrant students. In his presentation of social and political issues there was a tendency toward demonstration that was part of the influence he absorbed from his work with the Living Newspaper and with Brecht.

Because of the political witch hunt of the early 1950s Losey had to wait more than a decade longer than Kazan to realize on film his full creative potential. Kazan's apprentice period dates from 1945, with his lovely film of *A Tree Grows in Brooklyn;* with *A Streetcar Named Desire,* in 1951, he became a major force in American films. Losey didn't "arrive" until his direction of *The Servant* in 1963.

After the blacklist forced him into exile, Losey was impelled by

economic necessity to direct a series of routine scripts for British film companies. The radical difference in the fortunes of Losey and Kazan during the 1950s was connected to their response to the House Un-American Activities investigation of Communist influence in the film industry. Disillusioned with Communism—or at least with the way that the party was run—and despising Stalin's dictatorship, Kazan cooperated with Senator McCarthy's committee by naming names. Kazan hated McCarthy and the repression symbolized by his committee, yet felt that people like himself had been duped by Communists and that therefore there was no reason to maintain silence. By cooperating, he hoped to rescue friends and former fellow travelers from what he considered was their wrongheaded loyalty not only to a lost but a corrupt cause. As a friendly witness, Kazan of course incurred the animosity of Hollywood's left-wing community—Kazan is still detested in radical circles to this day—but he did not, of course, damage his career opportunities. He was eminently employable, and the period of the early to middle 1950s, as the McCarthy witch hunt escalated, was Kazan's most productive, culminating in the brilliant *On the Waterfront,* which many critics have read as Kazan's self-vindication: the film's hero is a friendly witness for the committee investigating waterfront crime; Terry Malloy's testimony marks the beginning of a clean-up of the corrupt labor union that controls the longshoremen.

While Kazan had the best of Hollywood at his beck and call, while with each new project he was given increasing control, Losey, because he remained in exile after receiving a subpoena to appear before the House Committee as he was finishing a film in Italy, could not get work of any kind. He had to wait several years even to be offered such routine assignments as *Sleeping Tiger* and *Finger of Guilt.* He had, in a sense, to begin again, to start from the bottom. Biding his time, he was forced to discover, or to create, interesting elements in scripts that had few or none at all; he had to refresh stereotyped melodramas through mise-en-scène.

Losey's career has a lopsided, see-saw quality. He started high up on his first film, *The Boy with Green Hair,* for which he had a bigger budget than for almost any other project in his career. He was given smaller budgets and less artistic freedom on each succeeding film he made in Hollywood. He started at ground zero in England, gradually, painstakingly working his way up to a position of preeminent power and respect. His career, then, is filled with

contradictions, setbacks, studio interference, frustrated goals, mediocre scripts; and through it all he has managed to maintain his artistic integrity, to work honorably and with some sense of personal style in sometimes ignoble circumstances, turning out films of visual and even thematic interest even when all that was asked or expected of him was a standard formula melodrama. Against great odds Losey has carved out a distinguished career for himself; the effort, until the time of *The Servant*, to turn pulp into at least a semblance of art testifies to a remarkably secure ego, a great drive, and an enormous strength of personality.

2

Losey in Hollywood: The Manhunt Theme

LOSEY'S FIRST five films reveal a remarkable thematic and stylistic consistency. Completed within a four-year period, from 1948 to 1951, the films are all modestly budgeted didactic melodramas whose antiestablishment stance is both an echo and a continuation of Losey's work with the Living Newspaper. The films, like the plays he directed for the Federal Theater, dramatize a variety of political problems without offering any specific solutions: for Losey, *awareness* of issues is the beginning of social responsibility and social action.

Losey's narrative methods, like those of his mentor Brecht, are scientific—the characters and events of these early films are subjected to a kind of clinical laboratory analysis. The stories in these novice works are presented as a series of clear-cut test cases: good is neatly aligned against evil, the world is divided into victims and victimizers, oppressed and oppressors. The figure of the outcast haunts Losey's imagination. The worlds these films construct are dark, enclosed, claustrophobic, and the central characters, who are marked in some way as different or as antisocial, have little room to move or to breathe: they're outsiders on the run from an insensitive and monolithic social group. Losey's protagonists are maladjusted because, in some crucial way, they don't fit in, and yet they live in communities that demand conformity and that crush the aberrant individual.

The recurrent themes of conformist tyranny and the pursuit and punishment of transgressors link the stories to contemporary politics: the films contain metaphors for the House Un-American Activities Committee investigations. The political intransigence that shaped the appalling and ominous question, "Are you now or have

29

powerful image of entrapment in Losey's underrated M. *The sense of doom is created through skillful composition.*

you ever been?" hovers over Losey's early pieces. The films thus present a series of forceful images of American communities, whether small towns, as in *The Boy with Green Hair*, *The Lawless*, and *The Prowler*, or big cities, as in *M* and *The Big Night*, that will not tolerate difference or uniqueness.

The sense of imminent danger, the threat to personal liberty contained in the films, had more than an abstract social significance for Losey. Having been a member of the Communist party, Losey knew he was working in the film industry on borrowed time, and he completed these five films under the shadow of impending doom. Prophetically Adrian Scott, the producer of his first film, *The Boy with Green Hair*, was blacklisted almost as soon as production started. The project was finished in an atmosphere of political tension and a studio environment of escalating uncertainty. Losey's own political vulnerability, as well as his outrage against the kind of society which made him feel burdened and "accused" by his past, is absorbed into the tone of his work. The films forcibly dramatize their characters' loss of freedom as society closes in on them, insisting on punishment for past (actual or made-up) crimes.

Thematically and visually these early Losey movies are part of the postwar *film noir* tradition. Like the typical *noir* protagonists, Losey's characters seem to be hapless victims of fate, pursued into corners by a network of entangling circumstances. As in most of the *noir* films, the characters' options are ominously eliminated: the films portray a world in which there is no way out, and though there are provisionally happy endings in *The Big Night*, *The Lawless*, and *The Boy with Green Hair*, the tentative moral uplift goes against the essentially negative thrust of the films. The utterly damned characters of *M* and *The Prowler* are the ones Losey presents with the most conviction; the depiction of a gloomy, fatalistic environment, which mercilessly lays traps for the characters, inspires, in these early works, as throughout his career, Losey's most persuasive images. Losey is temperamentally attracted to prophesies of doom rather than to statements of moral affirmation or regeneration. The closed image of the circle is one that appears with obsessive recurrence in his work, whereas the Chaplinesque image of life as an open road holds no genuine appeal for him either aesthetically or philosophically. Losey's methods do differ somewhat from the prevailing *noir* mode, however, in that his films adapt *noir* techniques for social criticism—Losey stresses contemporary relevance, down-

playing the thriller elements that are part of his melodramatic stories and that are usually the focus of the *noir* movie.

Losey's command of film form is not fully developed at this period. Experimenting with the possibilities of camera movement, mise-en-scène, and the long take, Losey is plainly feeling his way in these novice undertakings. The technical flourish, the grace and fluency, that mark the mature Losey are nonetheless occasionally evident as the director manages to transform formulaic melodramas into social statements of some visual and rhetorical persuasiveness.

The Boy with Green Hair

Losey's first feature film is a naive pacifist fable. A war orphan arrives in a new town to stay with his grandfather. When the boy's hair mysteriously turns green, the townspeople, and the boy's fellow students, turn against him with fierce hostility. After he is forced to have his hair shaved, the boy runs away from home. He tells his story to the policemen who arrest him, and to a friendly doctor who encourages him to return to his town to explain the significance of his green hair to his tormentors.

"Green is the color of spring, the promise of new life to come," says Gramps at one point. His statement is later echoed by another war orphan who has green hair—"I have green hair because I am a war orphan," he explains to Peter, "and my hair is a reminder that there must not be another war. Our hair is a message for all of the people. If enough people believe you, there never will be another war."

The green hair is an unconvincing symbol, and a contradictory one as well, since the green hair is meant, on the one hand, as a reminder of the horrors of war and, on the other, of the promise of peace. The green hair is more persuasive as an image of individuality than as a pacifist sign. The film's insistent antiwar message is much less interesting, in fact, than its attack on a conformity-ridden small town. The war theme is really irrelevant to the film's satiric portrait of a representative American community that is seemingly benign but churning with repressed hostilities and violent xenophobia: the primal fear of difference which the film dramatizes has only marginal connections to the general issue of "war," but powerful links to the contemporary hunt for Communists.

There is no place for the outsider in this microcosmic American town. Even Gramps counsels Peter, "It's a dangerous thing to have green hair. . . . I want you to be happy and carefree like other boys your own age." What Gramps really means, of course, is that to be different is to be exposed and therefore to be utterly vulnerable.

The most evocative scene in the film is the one in which Peter's offending hair is cut off. Peter is seated in a barber's chair, as if waiting to be executed, as a group of townsmen, seated in a semi-circle, watch intently, seemingly poised for the kill. Outside the shop, kids peer tensely through the window. The haircutting is treated as a kind of initiation ritual, a ceremony for which the whole town has turned out. To underline Peter's shame and his isolation, the sequence ends with a long close-up on him.

As a story of insidious conformity, the film anticipates the imagery and the paranoid atmosphere of a fable of the 1950s like *Invasion of the Body Snatchers*, in which the people of another disturbingly

The hair-cutting scene in *The Boy with Green Hair*. Losey treats the event as a communal ritual.

average small town are overtaken by an alien force that erases individuality. As in that nightmare fantasy, Losey creates a seemingly bland environment which rumbles with menacing undertones. The sense of threat, and of imminent danger, is announced in the opening shot, where, from a distance and at an oblique high angle, we see a group of men standing in a tight semi-circle around Peter: the frightened child surrounded by powerful adults. Imagery throughout the film signals the fact that this is a town in which terrible things can happen. When Peter first arrives in town, we see a succession of houses which seem to stand in mute accusation as Peter walks past. Later, a visually tense high angle tracking shot as Gramps takes Peter to school anticipates Gary Cooper walking down the main street preparing to confront his adversaries in *High Noon*. When Peter takes a bike ride at night through the deserted streets of the town, the hovering shadows and the high angle shots underscore the mood of isolation and doom.

Losey realized that the look of the town was vitally important to his theme, but he was displeased with the patently studio quality of the film. "That particular RKO small town set was used many times before and many times after," he said. "It was, of course, very well done because a great deal of money was spent on it, but it was *any* American small town, and any American small town is not like any other. It is much too generalized."[1] Losey wanted to film on location, in order to capture the flavor of a specific community, but the studio did not want to incur the expense that that would involve.

In terms of the way the film is set up, as a series of contrasts between reality and fantasy, Losey's concern for making the town look as real and as solid as possible is certainly valid. At crucial points in the story, reality is "interrupted" by fantasy. At school, Peter looks intently at posters of war orphans; the scene of his absorption in the photographs is one of the strongest in the film, the sad children in the posters seeming to take on an individual identity as the camera lingers over them. The poster children "come to life" in a glade where they tell Peter about the meaning of being a war orphan. This glade figures later as the setting in which Peter's fellow students, led by a boy who wears thick glasses, and who is therefore himself "different," taunt and humiliate him. The glade then stands in opposition to the town as the place where fantasies are enacted—the glade represents a dreamlike environment in con-

trast to the reality of the town. Losey was also disappointed in the appearance of the glade, which he intended to look entirely different from the town, to stand apart from it as a background for both pacifist idyll and paranoid nightmare. Losey wanted the scenes in the glade to have the same relationship to the town as the color section of *The Wizard of Oz* has to the black-and-white opening: the glade, that is, should be a child's dreamlike transformation of reality. But the glade has the same studio quality as the town: both settings have the same degree of detachment from objective reality.

"What I wanted to get, in the scenes in the glade," Losey said, "was absolute horror, real terror, the kind of thing Joris Ivens and John Ferno did in their film of the Chinese-Japanese conflict, *The Four Hundred Million,* with that shot of the baby sitting on the railway track, bombed and with no clothes, desolate and crying. I wanted to get that kind of horror, that kind of reality; I wanted to get the pellagra stomachs of the Indian children, the dreadful starvation, the concentration camp feeling, into the glade. And I wanted to lead in to a completely idyllic glade, absolute beauty into absolute horror."[2] But Losey got no cooperation from RKO, and the sequence doesn't have the tension and the visual flair that would have set it off from the rest of the story.

The war orphans are frightening, though. Losey wanted them all "to be static and composed in ways that could be related to the war posters in the gymnasium."[3] The children look like zombies (another anticipation of *Invasion of the Body Snatchers* as well as the radioactive children in Losey's own *These Are the Damned*), and they speak, without using contractions, in flat, somnolent voices.

Losey would also have liked a more exaggerated color scheme for the fantasy scenes. For the realistic sequences he wanted, and for the most part attained, a muted, limited color range. "I wanted to use only neutral colors—the reverse of the usual use of color. One often loses reality with color, and very often, dramatically speaking, it is a disaster. Even if this isn't your intention, your film becomes unreal."[4] The soft, autumnal tones carefully avoid garish or deluxe quality—Losey didn't want the film to look like a big-budget project. But the mellow design of greens and browns is carried over into the glade sequences so that these don't have the sharp difference of texture that Losey intended.

Losey's use of objects as symbols is as awkward, and as technically immature, as his handling of the fantasy episodes. Peter keeps a

baseball bat near his bed, to protect him from the dark, and when he leaves Gramps's house he carries the bat with him. As a phallic symbol, an emblem of Peter's emerging maturity, the bat is obvious and forced. A poster of a circus lion hangs prominently in Peter's bedroom. Peter has a dream about being locked in a cage with a lion—a strained metaphor for his entrapment within the arch-conservative town. Losey's camera lingers on the poster of the lion as purposefully as it does on the posters of the war orphans. (Losey has retained an interest in artworks throughout his career, relying on paintings, sculptures, posters, and signs as a means of symbolic reinforcement.) Gramps has a green plant in the house, which, like Peter's hair, is a symbol of spring, of renewal and of life. There is an especially contrived scene in the town grocery, where a group of women, talking about war, take it for granted that people kill each other. Overhearing the thin, grating voices of the mean-spirited women, Peter spills a bottle of milk: is this the milk of human kindness? For the finale, as Gramps and Peter are reunited, they go upstairs singing as they turn on all the lights in the house.

Losey's visual signaling, then, is frequently overloaded, blunt, artless. But the film does demonstrate a genuine flair for the way ideas and states of mind can be communicated visually. And there are indications of the kind of composition and use of the camera that Losey will develop and refine in his subsequent work. The film features the long take and the roving, tracking, inquiring camera that will become Losey trademarks. In terms of its mise-en-scène, its mood of escalating danger, and its visual underlining of the boy's isolation, the film has many skillful moments. But it is seriously marred by the script's misguided insistence on using green hair as a symbol of peace rather than of individuality and by the folksy, upbeat ending in which Peter says he will spread the message of peace. Before he was killed in the war, his father had written Peter that "death is a sad thing because it takes away the gift of life but it need not be sad if the gift has been well used—it will have been fine if those who did not die do not forget: remind them, Peter, remind them." Peter says he hopes his hair grows back green, but that regardless he will speak about what he has learned from his father. Peter's symbolic force as a child of nature—"green is the color of spring"—is underscored by the theme song, "Nature Boy," which is smeared on in heavy doses throughout the film. (Under the titles, the song accompanies shots of pristine lakes and fields.)

The climactic optimism does not ring true. The town remains as potentially violent as the one in Shirley Jackson's *The Lottery* and as narrowly self-protective as the one in *High Noon.* Peter isn't a strong enough figure to be convincing as an apostle of change, so the film's mindless, sweet ending, with the boy enshrined as an inspired crusader, is pallid and simpering, partly a matter of the soggy script and partly a matter of Losey's temperamental distance from such unfounded moral affirmation. The sentimentality and the down-home folksiness that are part of the story are clearly alien to Losey, as the doom-ridden endings to most of his subsequent work attest. Losey's vision is darker, more brooding and complex, than RKO would permit, and as a novice contract director he had no choice but to turn out the simplistic, symbol-laden, pacifist allegory that was expected of him.

The Lawless

Losey's second Hollywood film, about race relations in another small, representative American community, is as didactic and as schematic as *The Boy with Green Hair.* "This is the story of a town," a prologue explains, "and of some of its people, who, in the grip of blind anger forget their American heritage of tolerance and decency and become the lawless." As in Losey's first film, group prejudice (with Mexicans replacing "green hair" as the catalyst) leads to violent group action. As in many of the films of the period the group is a mindlessly destructive force, fiercely resistant to any change or irregularity.

Losey is again dealing with material conceived in a simplistically moralistic manner. The story is built up of a series of neat contrasts. In *The Lawless,* as in many of his later films, Losey pivots one social class—one group or community—against another. Santa Marta, "the Friendly City," is divided by a bridge which separates the white side of town from the Mexican ghetto. The "other side of the tracks" is called Sleepy Hollow, a decidedly cleaned-up shanty town. As the idealized Mexican newspaperwoman (Gail Russell) explains to the journalist hero (MacDonald Carey), Sleepy Hollow has ridden itself of gang warfare. "Tell your readers to look across the tracks. We've erased juvenile delinquency over here."

The film compares the regenerated Mexican community to an

economically comfortable white community seething with repressed violence and race hatred. A chain of coincidences unleashes white rage. The film begins with a minor car accident between the two Mexican heroes, Paul and Lopo, and some vicious white kids, led by Joe Ferguson. The resentment engendered by the accident is rekindled at a Good Fellowship Dance, where Paul is accused of attacking a white girl. When Joe and his gang turn on him at the dance, Paul steals an ice-cream truck for his getaway. Through no fault of his own the police car that pursues him skids off the road, and the cops are killed in the ensuing explosion. Paul, now labeled a rapist as well as a cop-killer, becomes the object of a manhunt: as one overexcited reporter phrases it, "This is the greatest manhunt in the history of this lovely little town." Through the intervention of the liberal newspaperman, Paul is saved from a lynch mob and exonerated from the crimes wrongly charged against him.

Like the city of Santa Marta, the characters too are divided into "white" or "black" categories, right thinkers or wrongdoers, liberals or reactionaries. Typically for Losey, characters come in pairs, to provide pointed moral contrasts. Paul and his friend are compared as to their goals and expectations. Paul wants his own land, while his friend chides him for aiming too low; Lopo is more of a fighter than Paul, he's more willing to resist his white oppressors.

Paul's essential goodness, his little-guy decency, is offset by the spoiled white boy Joe, an aimless troublemaker. Paul's quiet mysticism is contrasted with Joe's brutish cynicism. As if to correct the racial imbalance, Joe's father is a deeply "concerned" liberal whose eyes are opened by his son's viciousness: "I didn't think it could happen here," he proclaims, at the end, speaking thereby for the reaction of American liberals to the escalating witch-hunt mentality of the period.

The characters are thus used emblematically, and it is part of the film's novice earnestness that they never transcend their racial and political labeling. They are masks in a deterministic morality drama, and they have no dimension apart from their usefulness to the film's moral diagram. *The Lawless* slants its case by making the oppressed characters noble sufferers and by rendering the oppressors (with a few notable exceptions) as unthinking conformists.

The rigid comparison-contrast method is carried over into the treatment of the two main characters, the Mexican newspaperwoman (named Sunny Garcia) and her "white" counterpart, Larry Wil-

der. The woman (played by a non-Mexican) is impossibly dignified, a forerunner of the perfect characters played by Sidney Poitier in piously "liberal" movies of the 1960s like *Guess Who's Coming to Dinner?* She is an idealistic crusader, a tireless propagandist for her people. It is her duty in the film to convince the hero to stay on the job even after racial violence erupts. The journalist is the only character who changes his political position; at first, he wants to abandon his newspaper. "I'm through with small towns," he announces. "They're not like I remember them. Do you know what it's like to have a bellyful of fighting?" he asks Sunny. "I had all that [the peaceful life] once, and I want it again." Like the townspeople in *High Noon*, he doesn't want to get involved. But when the inflamed mob attacks and destroys his office he decides to stay and to join forces with the Mexican newspaper, *La Luz*, while retaining the name of his own paper, the *Union*. In his movement from withdrawal to engagement, Larry Wilder is clearly designed as a representative figure, his actions intended for moral instruction.

Like *The Boy with Green Hair*, the film asks us to believe in the ability of the crusading liberal to rebuild society. The reformation here is as naively presented as in the earlier film. The group is vicious, unyielding, brutal, and yet, to supply the sort of moral uplift that the producers wanted, the story ends as Larry Wilder, his liberal conscience now fully awakened, berates the assembled mob for the destruction they have caused. The optimistic ending seems based on the premise that a good lecture can effect a moral transformation in a group of characters whose viciousness we have witnessed in full measure. After Larry appeals to the mob's sense of shame, the people look crestfallen, their hang-dog expressions meant to point a sharp contrast to their earlier blood lust. *The Lawless* is a well-meaning but naive political allegory.

Although both story line and character development are patently contrived, once again, as in his first film, Losey skillfully embellishes the film's threadbare ideology with his use of the camera and his choice of settings. Through editing and camera movement Losey quickly defines temporal and spatial, as well as political, relationships. The town's rigidly hierarchical social structure is forcefully conveyed through parallel editing. For the opening, Losey sets up a visual contrast between white privilege and Mexican poverty as Paul takes a shower in a flimsy outdoor structure while Joe showers in a clean bathroom of gleaming white tile.

Losey's command of film syntax is noticeably more assured in *The Lawless* than in his first film. The city of Santa Marta is the real thing rather than a studio recreation: it has a specific character as opposed to the slightly stylized, all-purpose small town that was used for *The Boy with Green Hair.* The distance from physical reality that defined the texture of the earlier film was not altogether inappropriate for its fablelike qualities, whereas it would have been false for the social realism of *The Lawless.* One setting in the later film is particularly well chosen. The manhunt takes place in a rock-filled, desolate landscape, a waste land that lies outside the town and that is a powerful reinforcement of Paul's mounting sense of terror and isolation. "The landscape I found at Grass Valley, the town where Bret Harte and Robert Louis Stevenson lived during the days of the silver rush. . .was the rubble of dredging for silver and gold. For miles and miles as far as you could see, the countryside was laid waste, the arable land swept to the bottom of the river and the rocks pulled to the surface. Here you saw something you just couldn't believe—a wilderness of rocks; and the sound of anybody being pursued across it was fantastic. There was no point in reproducing the sound literally, it had to be much bigger to create the full horror."[5]

The Lawless is a stronger piece than Losey's first feature. He is obviously more comfortable with the social realist mode of *The Lawless* than he was with the coy *fabliau* quality of *Green Hair.* The film was generally well received in America: "Mob violence has rarely been more vividly portrayed."[6] "It is no *Fury* or *Intruder in the Dust,* but it is a startling account of mob violence."[7] In France, like most of Losey's work, it was greeted with wild enthusiasm. "It is the most beautiful of films," wrote a critic in *Cahiers du Cinema.* "I breathe easier after each viewing. . . . It has the cleanest possible design. . . . It has a youthful tone, it is irresistible, like a morning swim."[8] In a delirious essay on the film, another French critic called *The Lawless* "the greatest western and even the only western ever made."[9]

M

Losey's version of *M* pursues themes and images given tentative articulation in his two preceding films. Again he is concerned with

the figure of an outsider, an outlaw who offends the standards of a tightly knit community. Again the town is presented as a group of witch-hunters, and the environment in which the drama unfolds is increasingly closed and threatening. Different from the earlier films, though, is the fact that the outcast here is a social danger, unlike the boy with green hair or the falsely accused Mexican. M is a child-murderer, and the town's well-organized pursuit of him is necessary both for its own self-protection as well as to save the criminal from himself.

The 1950 film is, of course, a remake of the 1931 German classic directed by Fritz Lang, with Peter Lorre as M. Losey has made conflicting statements about the degree of his fidelity to the original version. In 1961 he said that he did not think of the film "as a remake," although he admits to using "a couple of Lang's ideas."[10] He said at the time that he intended a different treatment of M, one that was more compassionate than Lang's interpretation. In an earlier interview with *Cahiers du Cinema* (September 1960), however, Losey regretted that he wasn't able to make more extensive changes in the material. "The producers had an agreement that the film respect the structure of the original. I had twice refused to direct it but finally my financial situation dictated my acceptance of the project. . . . I was constantly embarrassed by the enforced reliance on the original."[11]

Losey intended the film as another—his third—liberal social statement, a plea (this time) for humane treatment of the mentally ill and a criticism of an unfair system of justice. Losey regards M as needing help rather than criminal prosecution and designed the story to be read, on one level, as an attack of a social system that has no true understanding of mental disability. Losey's liberalism, however, is not so different from Lang's: both films regard the child-murderer as a victim, as someone more to be pitied (and helped) than convicted. And in both films the portrait of a vengeful society ruthless in its pursuit of a criminal is decidedly negative: in both versions group action is seen as ominous, robotical, annihilating to the individual. Both Lang and Losey had good cause to distrust the group and to fear mob psychology. In the Germany of 1931 and the Hollywood of 1950, a story of the pursuit and expulsion of an undesirable had terrifying associations.

Group action in Lang's *M*, as in many German films of the 1920s and 1930s, contained both visual and political anticipations of Fas-

cism. The group in many German films of the time was presented
as easily controlled by a tyrant figure and as capable of unleashing
great destructive forces. The mob in films like Lang's own *Metropolis*
offers a visual foreshadowing of the massed legions on ornamental display and controlled by a madman tyrant in *Triumph of
the Will*, Hitler's propaganda film made by the Nazi Leni Riefen-
stahl. In *M*, the roles of the group and the individual are reversed,
since here the mass turns on, and crushes, the aberrant individual
in the same way that, in *Metropolis* and the symptomatic archetype
provided by *The Cabinet of Dr. Caligari*, the individual smashes
the will of the group. In both instances, however, in either *Metropolis* or in *M*, the mass and the isolated individual are elemental
antagonists locked in a battle for survival.

Lang's treatment of the interaction between the group and the
individual had stunning social and political premonitions. In his
book *From Caligari to Hitler* Siegfried Kracauer vividly records the
decay of German society as it is reflected in the films of the so-
called Golden Age of German cinema. Kracauer sees the recurrence
in German films of the period of the mad tyrant figure, and the
increasing examples of the lack of will and helplessness of the group,
as alarming signals of a society poised for disaster.

For Losey, working two decades later in a different country,
intimidating mob action indicated the erosion of personal liberties
represented by the House Un-American Activities Committee investigations. As in his other films of this time, the group in *M* is
monolithic and institutional—mercilessly efficient in exorcising
alien elements from its midst.

The cynical treatment of the group in both versions of *M* is enforced by the fact that the police and the underworld combine their
resources to track down the child-murderer. Because M's continued
freedom is "bad for business," since in their search for him the
police disturb the workings of the criminal underground, the gang
cooperates with the police in the manhunt. The gang and the law
employ the same methods of detection, and both groups are rigorously organized in their strategies of pursuit and entrapment.
Their power spreads ominously throughout the city.

Because both films present group action in such threatening ways,
sympathy is thrown toward the object of their quest, so that, in
terms of narrative structure, M occupies the place of the traditional
heroic rebel, the loner who outrages the code of a deeply settled

and conformist community. The disapproval of group action is so strong in both films that the lone individual engulfed by its tentacles claims some audience empathy despite the fact that he is a psychopathic criminal. M is doubly pursued; he's cornered by mob action as well as by his own pathology.

Losey's film inevitably invites and suffers from comparison to the original. Lang's creation of atmosphere, his use of closed frames, his famous counterpoint between sound and image, are unsurpassed: his M is the work of a film master. His control over his material is absolute, whereas Losey's film, made early in his career, lacks the precision and authority of its predecessor. In his mature work, in the 1960s and 1970s, Losey's characteristic creation of a closed, dark world on film has many similarities to Lang's methods. Both directors are preoccupied with enclosure and entrapment; both share a deterministic world-view. A grim fate stalks Losey's characters as much as it does Lang's. The meticulously preplanned mise-en-scène of both directors allows no space for the spontaneous, the accidental, or the fortuitous. Their tight frames are rigidly ordered and symmetrical. At his most assured, in *The Servant,* say, or *King and Country,* Losey's work approaches the tautness of Lang's highest achievements. In 1950, however, Losey simply did not have the experience or the artistic freedom to compete with Lang—he was, after all, a contract director told to pattern his own design for the film by using Lang's work as a model. His assignment, unenviably, was to imitate the style of an acknowledged classic, so that many of the shots in Losey's film, though beautifully composed, merely echo the images from the earlier film. Losey wasn't permitted a truly original handling of the material.

Since Lang's film is so powerful as both an artistic and social statement, there was no compelling reason to undertake a remake except if transferring the story from 1930s Germany to 1950s America might reveal a new political dimension. It does not. The story and characters, in fact, are not really comfortable in an American setting: the gang seems especially out of place in the Los Angeles where the film is set. The kind of underworld that is portrayed in Lang's film, with its smoky, subterranean cafés, its network of beggars and peasants, its rigid chain of command with a Caligari-like kingpin in charge of all activities, has the ambience of Brecht's *Three-Penny Opera.* The dives and dens of this underground world,

which express the instability and decadence of prewar, pre-Hitler Berlin, have no visual or social equivalent in a sunny 1950s Los Angeles.

Losey, cleverly, tries to mask the iconographic inappropriateness of the gang by setting the film in old Los Angeles, in a deteriorating downtown section called Bunker Hill that no longer exists, having been demolished to make room for modernistic high-rise apartments, towering office buildings, and the Los Angeles Music Center complex. The old Los Angeles used in the film has the almost surreal desolation of the American cities in the paintings of Edward Hopper; its decaying, outmoded architecture and its empty streets provide something of the same distance from a real city that Lang achieved in his studio-created environment. Even with this visual "protection" of setting the film in an unfamiliar section of Los Angeles, the ganglord and his henchmen—his regiment of spies and beggars and cutthroats—are not convincing as part of an American scene.

Under controlled studio conditions, Lang creates a truly enclosed, alienated environment. The settings in his film are tighter and more claustrophobic than those in Losey's rendition, where even carefully selected locations let in more of the flow of reality than the material needs. The handling of space in Lang's *M* is more ominous: the empty, shadowed streets have no precise equivalent in the sun-drenched exterior shots in Losey's film, no matter how atmospheric and crumbling the downtown area is.

Losey's choice of settings is nonetheless shrewd. From the run-down apartment in which Elsie (M's first victim) and her mother live, to M's dark room with its maddening ticking clocks, its mirrors, and a rag doll, to a very European-seeming outdoor café, bordered by shrubbery, in which M has a cup of coffee, to a factory in which M is finally caught in a room filled with mannequins, to an underground garage in which M is tried by a jury of thieves and hoodlums, the sets echo, without actually imitating, those in the original, and Losey's use of them is purposeful. That M is trapped in a room with mannequins is an appropriately bizarre touch that visually underscores the character's sexual pathology. The garage, with its low overhanging ceiling, its harsh blank concrete walls, and its prominent sign, KEEP TO THE RIGHT, is especially effective as a backdrop for the "trial." M literally has his back against the wall. He seems oppressed by the heavy ceiling beam. "The decor of the garage is

a miniature of the city," suggests Paul Mayersberg. "It is an image of hell. The hero, now underground, can fall no further. The garage has a machine-age artificiality."[12]

Like his choice of backgrounds, Losey's use of objects enhances theme and mood. Objects associated with M call forth images of a desperate and perverted sexuality and create an atmosphere of escalating sexual tension. M plays a flute—he is a perverted pied piper, luring innocent girls to their death. In his room, he looks at himself in a mirror, as if trying to untangle a maze—he doesn't seem fully to understand his reflection. This is the first time in his work that Losey uses a mirror to suggest psychological doubleness and disorientation. M's sexual frustration is revealed when he strangles a doll; the scene, enacted in semidarkness, with a ticking clock as a tense accompaniment, builds to M's sexual climax. Like Lang's, Losey's M has a knife which he uses to stab and peel an orange—a scary portent of sexual penetration. When M and one of his intended victims look in a store window, they see a toy train passing under a bridge that raises and lowers itself in a parody of sexual intercourse; the image recalls the dancing arrow that pierces a circle in the window of a children's store in the original.

Losey's framing is almost as deliberate, and often as distanced, as Lang's. At the beginning, we're kept away from M, seeing him only from the back, or in silhouette. He occupies only a limited space within the frame as he's trapped into corners or seen at oblique angles in reflections in mirrors and store windows. In ominous visual foreshadowings, M and his intended victims are several times isolated in the same corner of the frame, enclosed within sections of windows. M appears to be caught behind the shrubbery at an outdoor café, visually imprisoned as he drinks a cup of coffee.

In his original version, Lang enforces an aura of entrapment and paranoia with his use of two motifs: an image of the circle that dominates the film, from the first shot of children playing in a circle (one of them, ominously, is eliminated from the ring); and high angle shots which peer down on the characters and which seem to flatten space. Though Losey stresses neither motif, circles and vertiginous angles do appear throughout, almost in homage to Lang's original concept.

Losey's sound track is much more modest than Lang's. Following Eisenstein's montage theory, Lang creates tension between sound and image to highlight key moments. The most renowned coun-

David Wayne and one of his victims in *M*. The careful visual balance and expressionistic echoes in this shot are typical elements of Losey's mise-en-scène.

terpoint occurs in the sequence where a worried mother calls out Elsie's name while we see a series of disconnected images: Elsie's empty place at the dinner table; a shadowed stairwell; a deserted garage; and, climactically, Elsie's balloon floating above a telephone wire. The repeated cry of "Elsie!" links the separate images and underscores the utter isolation that they contain. Lang's recurrent

use of a lone, mournful car horn is another haunting off-screen sound which enhances the mood of the image—that single horn emphasizes the emptiness of the city streets.

Lang's experimentation with counterpoint, with voiceover, and with overlapping (sounds are used to connect different locations and to compress time) helped to free the early sound cinema from a strict adherence to the idea that sound must simply proceed from, and imitate, the image. Since it suggested possibilities for visual and aural interaction that had not been perceived by other directors at the time, Lang's use of sound was of decisive historical importance. Losey could not, of course, contribute anything with such reverberating aesthetic impact, and his sound track—with exceptions such as the ticking clock, the scraping when M tries to break out of the room in which he's trapped, and one single contrapuntal "Elsie!" that functions as an homage to Lang—does not call undue attention to itself.

Also to avoid comparison with Lang's film, Losey deliberately cast M with an actor, David Wayne, who is very different from Peter Lorre. With his aura of a well-adjusted, desperately unimaginative Midwesterner, Wayne looks entirely ordinary. Losey relies on the discrepancy between Wayne's manner and the criminally insane character he is impersonating: casting David Wayne as a psychopath is like casting Charlton Heston as the devil. The tension between Wayne's persona and the character of M is effective. Inevitably, Wayne plays M in a softer register than Lorre; he makes M more immediately sympathetic. His final scene, as he defends himself against his captors, explaining that he is not responsible for what he does, that he is being controlled by a malevolent internal force, is powerful. His self-defense builds in intensity until M explodes in a torrent of tears and frustration, pleading to be helped and screaming at his unjust treatment. Filmed in a long take, from a deliberately uncomfortable low angle, Wayne's aria has chilling highlights. But behind it, and overshadowing it, is the indelible memory of Peter Lorre. Lorre plays M with a rage and energy that are truly frightening: his eyes popping madly, his voice rising shrilly, his hands performing their own macabre dance of dementia, Lorre is simply unforgettable. He creates an image of a man driven by devils, haunted by a relentless fate from which he pleads to be released. His ecstasy evokes associations of Orestes pursued by the Furies, of Satan expelled from heaven and suffering the torments of hell.

The Prowler

Losey regards *The Prowler* as the best work of his Hollywood period. He had more time for preproduction planning; he rehearsed his actors thoroughly before filming started; he worked closely with his designer, John Hubley (who later earned a considerable reputation for his experimental animated films); and he had a taut script by Dalton Trumbo, who was blacklisted and whose name could not be placed on the finished film. Losey liked the material. *The Prowler* is the most technically polished of his early pictures, the most fully rounded in terms of characterization and theme—a hard-edged murder melodrama, a tightly sprung *film noir* that offers an acid comment on American materialism.

Strongly reminiscent of *Double Indemnity*, the ultimate *film noir*, Losey's movie is about an extramarital romance between a two-timing wife and a supposed member of the establishment, a policeman, who is the social equivalent of the straight-seeming insurance man played by Fred MacMurray in Billy Wilder's 1944 film. The bored wife is a failed actress who feels trapped in a childless marriage to a radio interviewer. Since his show is on at night, she has only his voice on the radio to keep her company. She has no way to fill in the long, lonely evenings—her life seems to have nothing in it beyond the material comfort of her house. When she sees a prowler outside her bathroom window, she calls the police; one of the two cops who respond to the call is attracted to her, and to her house. At first she resists his attentions, but after a time she becomes more attached than her pursuer. She feels guilty, though, because she cares for her husband, despite his absence and their sexual incompatibility. The policeman arranges an "accidental" shooting in which he kills the husband; in the scuffle, he even shoots himself in the hand, to lend the plan an authentic touch: here is another perfect crime, as in *Double Indemnity*. But the calculating cop, who now has the money, the woman, and the status that he has lusted after, has been tricked by natural forces beyond his control as the woman is pregnant and the baby will reveal their duplicity since her husband was known to be impotent and the timing of the birth will expose their adultery. Though abortion seems the logical way out, the woman, who desperately wants the child, convinces her lover to let her have it. They decide to hide out, in the Mojave Desert, until the birth. The cop plans on delivering the baby himself, relying on what he learned in his police

training. When the delivery becomes too difficult, he's forced to call a doctor. He fears, however, that the doctor may have recognized them. When the woman finds out that the cop still carries a gun, she is worried about what he might do to protect himself, and she warns the doctor. As he tries to escape, the policeman is gunned down.

The Prowler is different in form and intent from Losey's early social dramas; it doesn't have the same opposition between the group and the individual as the others, nor does it reflect, either directly or metaphorically, the conspiracy mentality that figures so prominently in the other works, although it does end with a chase as the police pursue and kill the scheming hero. In its story development and its characterizations it is less typical of Losey's methods than the three films about group pressure and mob psychology; yet Losey's signature is evident in the absolute clarity and detachment with which the characters are observed: the coldness and the cunning deliberation of the protagonist are echoed by the director's own removed style. And, typically for Losey, the actions of individual characters point up general issues, so that a little story about crime and passion in which, in a traditional *noir* manner, sex leads to murder, becomes the launching pad for a more general condemnation of American values. The policeman is seen as a fatally misguided character who has been infected by the American itch for money and social position. That the character is a corrupt cop is, of course, a pointed statement in itself; while masquerading as its representative, he is a destroyer of law and order. Losey presents him without pity, observing the character's inevitable fall with unbending disapproval. And Van Heflin's strong, unsentimental performance underlines the character's thick-headed, brutish qualities. Heflin makes Webb insinuating and covetous, a lecherous man consumed by his shallow values.

The woman is more sympathetically treated. Susan takes no part in the murder; she is shocked and grieved by her husband's death and refuses to speak to Webb after it, although in time she allows herself to believe Webb's weak story that the shooting was an accident, that he was responding to a call about a prowler and that in aiming for her husband he thought he had found the criminal. In the performance of a lifetime, Evelyn Keyes plays Susan as a dim, vulnerable, lost woman, moving through her house like a zombie and grasping to find meaning and point to her life. She is

a born victim, allowing herself to go along with the desperate policeman because of her own desperation and her desire to have a child. Keyes expertly portrays Susan's hesitation, her developing passion for Webb, her loyalty to her remote husband, her essential emptiness. It is a stunning piece of acting, unforced and precise.

In a reversal of *noir* patterns, the woman is here victim rather than catalyst; this time, it is the man who schemes and who has the warped values. Despite the character's limitations, Susan is one of the most affirmative female characters in Losey's films. The entire concept and performance of the role is a refreshing variation on the spider-woman archetype in the *noir* thriller, and as such an example of the departure from genre conventions that is a recurrent feature of Losey's work.

The Prowler is a first statement of the intruder theme that Losey is often to be attracted to later in his career, and that has provided the basis of some of his strongest pieces *(The Servant, Accident, Boom)*. The conniving policeman invades the rich man's house with the intention of taking it over—he regards Susan as part of the furnishings as he cleverly goes to work on her insecurity, her loneliness, her attraction to him. In a nice visual touch early in the film, Heflin is identified to the audience as himself a prowler. In the haunting pretitle shot, the camera is placed at a low angle outside Susan's bathroom: the camera is the prowler, the audience is the voyeur. Our first view of Heflin is from the same angle, as he stands outside the bathroom, in the same position as the prowler, so that visually he is identified as a potential threat to Susan. That the original prowler is never discovered introduces a note of ambiguity: did Susan imagine she saw someone peering at her? Does she want to be "invaded"? Was her calling the police merely an invitation, a way of curing her boredom?

Typically, Losey uses settings carefully, as quietly symbolic backgrounds that reflect the characters' state of mind. The film has three main locations: Susan's Spanish-style house, a motel that Webb buys with Susan's money, and a cabin in the desert where the story concludes. The Spanish house, with its rough stucco walls and its many arched doorways that seem to imprison the characters, clearly belongs to people who are well off, but it also has an underlying emptiness. Although the rooms are filled with overstuffed furniture and with paintings and tapestries, the house looks somehow forlorn; it radiates an atmosphere of defeat. When Susan plans to leave it

after her husband's death, the house is stripped (it "dies," like several houses in later Losey films) and the literally bare rooms only reinforce the barren quality that emanated from the house when it was "full."

The motel which Webb buys and to which he and Susan go after their marriage has the same empty feeling as the house. The plain white walls of the motel room and its arched doorway, which repeats the dominant architectural motif of the house, provide a cold environment for the newlyweds. A flashing neon sign of "vacancy" in front of the motel is an appropriate indicator of the characters' own vacancy. The desert background for the finale deepens our sense of the characters' isolation. The shack in which Webb and Susan set up house has visual echoes of Susan's house and the motel; its barrenness is accented by the high contrast lighting that Losey uses for the final scenes. The harsh desert landscape recalls the rocky waste land of the chase scene in *The Lawless* (as well as the parched, cracked desert vistas against which the climax of *Greed* is enacted). The desert is a trap, as wide-open spaces often are in Losey's films. At the end of the chase, as Webb flees from the police, he climbs onto a mountaintop from which he is shot down; the imagery (an echo of Cagney on top of the world at the end of *White Heat?*) is the only forced visual moment in the film.

The sound track provides a tense and sometimes ironic counterpart to the images. Webb's courting of Susan is often accompanied by the sound of her husband's voice on the radio; her husband says "good night" to her on the air as she lies in Webb's arms. As she and Webb dance, a crooner on the record player sings that it is time to fall in love. A tape of her husband's voice surprises Susan and Webb in their desert hideaway, as Webb mistakenly puts the tape on the phonograph: the voice reaches out to accuse them, and to disrupt their idyll, reminding Susan of her suspicions about Webb. In the motel, as the two characters worry over whether the birth of the baby will expose them, the continual off-screen sound of traffic, a passing siren, and the car lights that flicker over them lend the scene a conspiratorial quality; as they crouch in the bare semi-darkness of the grim highway motel they look like fugitives. The raw, howling desert winds heard throughout the last section of the film corroborate the mood of alienation and desperation.

Typical of a *noir* pattern, Losey establishes a routine, everyday world against which the protagonist's criminality festers and swells.

Van Heflin and Evelyn Keyes in their desert hideaway at the end of *The Prowler*.

Losey populates the film with vivid minor characters, plain-folks types like the motel manager who chews gum, Susan's in-laws, and the chatty cop who is Webb's partner and whose very ordinariness underscores Webb's aberrations. Brilliantly acted, directed with a control and a feeling for atmosphere and detail that surpass Losey's other Hollywood films, *The Prowler* is a real beauty, a B *noir* that deserves to be rediscovered.

The Big Night

Losey's final Hollywood film is certainly his most modest. Losey made it quickly, and he left before final editing and mixing had been completed because he had a commitment to do a film in Italy. *The Big Night* offers no overview of Losey's American period, being in fact more narrow, and more purely private in thematic focus,

than any of the other films of this time. It is a low-budget melodrama constructed on a standard revenge theme, and alone among his early pieces it attempts no broad social statement about representative American groups. It is a simple moral fable in which a young man comes of age in one "big night."

George La Main (John Barrymore, Jr.) watches helplessly as a man comes into his father's bar and beats him up. The boy doesn't know the reason for the beating, but he vows to avenge his father and goes off into the nighttime city to hunt for his father's assailant. His search takes him through the big-city underworld where he meets up with an assortment of thieves, prostitutes, and nightclub entertainers; he goes to a prizefight, a bar, a tenement; he establishes a tentative relationship with a serious young woman who is much finer than her environment; he finally meets up with and kills his father's enemy—and the measure of his maturity is that he decides to assume responsibility for his act, instead of allowing his father to take the blame for the shooting, as he is willing to do.

The slight, formulaic story, with its blunt morality and its schematic construction, is typical of Losey's early work. Less typical, though, is the emphasis placed here on free will: the young hero matures in the course of his nightlong odyssey through the city, and so he is different from the trapped, doomed Losey heroes for whom the possibility of regeneration is withheld. Settings, even in this modest studio-filmed melodrama, are evocative, succinctly and vividly defining the characters of their inhabitants. The scenes in the prizefight arena and the nightclub—smoky, claustrophobic, darkly lit, crowded—are further evidence of Losey's skillful integration of characterization, setting, and theme: his fluent mise-en-scène.

Originally Losey intended the story as a flashback, a format he used in *The Boy with Green Hair* (and will use again in *Eve* and *Accident*). He wanted to reveal the end—the boy committing murder—in order to reduce the suspense element and to emphasize the boy's psychological awakening, his entrance into the adult world. Downplaying the thriller aspect of the material by giving away the ending at the start was typical of Losey's renovations of the often formulaic stories he was offered both in Hollywood and for the first decade of his career in England. Losey agreed to do projects like *The Big Night*, which held little intrinsic interest for him, because he saw in them opportunities for turning the generic material upside down and for creating atmospheric backgrounds. In a modest way,

he succeeded here in making something out of almost nothing: he gives a standard B-movie melodrama a strong sense of place and manages to create interest and shading in the flatly written characters. His producers scrapped the flashback framework, deciding to tell the story in conventional chronological order. In both his ability to recycle pulp and in the interference from producers, *The Big Night* was to be a forerunner of his work in England for the next ten years.

3

From *Stranger on the Prowl* to *Eve*: Genre Variations

WHEN LOSEY left Hollywood hurriedly, in 1951, before he had completed postproduction work on *The Big Night*, he did not know that he would never return, that for the remainder of his career he would be an expatriate, that, in a very real sense, he would be a man without a country. Losey has the ability, however, to blend in with his surroundings, so that his films, whether made in America, Italy, France, or England, don't look like the work of an alien.

Losey thus adapts himself to different national sensibilities. He "becomes" English or French in spirit, as London and Paris have become his adopted cities (he owns homes in both). But Losey carries over from film to film, and from country to country, a distinct personal style as he explores a limited number of formal and thematic concerns. The Losey canon, despite its dislocations of place, its financial restrictions, its often mundane scripts, reveals a remarkable consistency.

Losey originally left Hollywood in order to do a film in Italy with Paul Muni. Though he was subpoenaed at the time to appear before the House Un-American Activities Committee, he decided to remain in London. Because he was blacklisted in America, he had to start at the bottom of the British film industry. At first, he couldn't get any assignments at all. Then he was not allowed to sign his own name to his first two English films, *The Sleeping Tiger* (1954) and *A Finger of Guilt* (1955), because fear of the blacklist had penetrated the British film studios. Not until 1956, with *Time without Pity*, would English producers permit him to place his own name on the credits.

During this lean period of his career, when he was fortunate to

55

get any work at all, Losey was handed routine scripts, all of them decidedly in the B-picture category, all of them strident melodramas. It wasn't until 1962, with *Eve*, that Losey undertook a project with full enthusiasm—this was the first film that he genuinely wanted to make, because the story and characters had a personal significance to him. And it wasn't until the following year, with Harold Pinter's exquisite screenplay for *The Servant*, that he was given material that did not have to be extensively remodeled before Losey felt prepared to begin filming.

Remarkably, his early English period, while he was working without prestige, on pulp material, with stripped budgets, is more interesting and lively than it has any right to be. The films—which are a kind of bridge between the promise of the novice Hollywood movies and the fulfillment announced in *The Servant* (and continuing to the present)—demonstrate Losey's growing mastery of mise-en-scène. The British films, from *The Sleeping Tiger* to *These Are the Damned* in 1962, are dress rehearsals for the major Losey pictures of the 1960s and 1970s: Losey probably has had a longer period of dry runs and test cases than any other major director; his movie apprenticeship extends from 1948 to 1963, when, finally, with *The Servant*, he produced a film that will surely claim a lasting place in the international film repertory.

Two qualities of the early British movies are noteworthy: their regeneration of standard generic elements through vigorous camera work and evocative settings and their insistent use of parallels to enforce a moral or social point. During this period, then, Losey continued to develop stylistic tendencies that had already been evident in *The Boy with Green Hair*. These middle-period films share a characteristic visual energy—the roving, sometimes nervous camera lends animation to the routine characters and stories. It is in these films, where Losey did not feel thoroughly engaged by his subjects, that he began to develop what critics have labeled a "baroque" style, a preoccupation with decor, with symbolically charged environments, with elaborate camera movement and camera placement. Those who don't like Losey's work accuse it of being merely formalist, concerned with surface ornamentation, with manneristic effects that create a spurious illusion of meaning. Yet the films, for all their increasing attention to form, their compulsive visual heightening of formulaic material, are not giddily detached from the reality of their settings: form in Losey is always an attempt to complement,

rather than to obscure, content. In Losey at his best, style enhances meaning.

In his minor early British films, Losey refurbishes standard genre material not only by a calculated mise-en-scène but also by giving a significant thematic or social framework to basically melodramatic stories. Thus a domestic melodrama like *The Sleeping Tiger* becomes something of a case study of therapeutic transference and exorcism; a blackmail thriller like *Finger of Guilt* is linked to an autobiographical statement about the connections between film and reality; a crime drama like *Time without Pity,* built on the D. W. Griffith model of the last-minute rescue, supplies the foundation for a statement against capital punishment; a historical romance like *The Gypsy and the Gentleman* is turned into Losey's preliminary draft for his major English films on the corrosions of the rigid British class system; into a conventional murder mystery like *Chance Meeting* is channeled ideas about art and the artist, and about the dangerous differences between appearance and reality; a prison melodrama like *The Concrete Jungle* is a naturalistic study of the way environment both creates and entraps a criminal mentality; a science-fiction fable like *These Are the Damned* becomes a warning against atomic energy.

One of the main ways in which Losey reupholsters genre material is to set up his stories with parallels. Losey delights in the contrast-comparison method, pivoting two social classes, as in *The Gypsy and the Gentleman,* or two distinct environments, as in *The Concrete Jungle* and *These Are the Damned,* or dividing the film into specific visual textures, as in *Chance Meeting,* where light and dark, afternoon and evening, achieve symbolic significance. This "bifurcated" method, which is a narrative technique used in silent films such as Griffith's *Intolerance* and De Mille's *The Ten Commandments,* invites our moral responses to story and characterization: we are clearly meant to make connections between the contrasting places and character types, to see, for instance, the similarity between the functioning of the criminal underworld both inside and outside the prison in *The Concrete Jungle,* or the surprising connections, in *These Are the Damned,* between the world of the imprisoned radioactive children and that of the gang that terrorizes a seacoast community. Losey is an inveterate moralist, and to underline his message, to make us see the action in larger perspective, he needs the distance provided by breaking up his story into parallel

"texts"; the Brechtian abstraction and the tendency to generalization that are common elements in the films keep us focused on the ideas while discouraging emotional involvement with the characters or single-minded interest in the purely local significance of these stories of crime.

Stranger on the Prowl

Like the films themselves, Losey's early British period comes with its own "frame," since it begins with a movie made in Italy and ends with one, a decade later, made in both France and Italy. *Stranger on the Prowl* and *Eve* don't have the same atmosphere as the pictures made for British companies, just as the British films feel and look different from the earlier Hollywood ones. *Stranger on the Prowl,* made at the end of the neorealist revolution in Italian cinema, has the grainy texture and the naturalistic mood of a film by De Sica or Rossellini. Since it tells a story about a man and a boy, it contains echoes not only of Losey's *Boy with Green Hair* but, more significantly, of De Sica's *The Bicycle Thief.*

The film is set in the same world as De Sica's classic—the slums of a big city, where the simplest necessities are hard won, where poor and innocent people are victimized by circumstances and in turn victimize others in order to survive. The relationship that develops between The Man, who has no home and who wants to raise money to stow away on a ship, and The Boy, who wants money to be able to go to the circus, is the only uncorrupted one in the impoverished, cutthroat milieu the film vividly depicts. In order to make a moral point, the film cross-cuts between the activities of the man and the boy as they attempt to raise the money they need. When the man, in a rage, kills a mean store owner who begrudges him some cheese, the story turns into a manhunt, another recurrent Losey pattern. When he hears police whistles, the boy thinks he is the criminal, since he stole milk. At the end, the man risks his life to save his young friend; surrounded by the police, he jumps to his death from a rooftop. "Don't kill him," the boy pleads. "He just wanted something to eat. He had no place to go. He didn't want to kill anyone."

The film is set in the cavernous, bombed-out buildings of a severely depleted postwar Italian slum. Losey limits the backgrounds,

Paul Muni lost in a crowd in *Stranger on the Prowl.* The spontaneous and documentary-like quality of this shot captures the film's surprising neorealistic texture.

so that we never see the larger city within which this mutilated ghetto forms its own subcommunity. The people live in hovels, surrounded by reminders of their defeat; they are victims of a larger political group whose workings are felt but never seen. Losey's use of these limited, grim backgrounds is enhanced by crisscrossing patterns of natural light and shadow: the sun-bleached images contribute to the powerfully rendered atmosphere of wreckage and decay. As in the major neorealist films, Losey frames his action with a sense of the ongoing flow of life. The screen is almost always filled with background movement, as people go about the daily business of their lives: in scenes at a circus, and in an open-air market that is the center of the neighborhood, the passing life of the street encloses the action. In an unselfconscious way the film supplies the kind of openness and endlessness that Siegfried Kracauer suggests is the essential nature of the medium—Losey's film "redeems" physical reality. In its open compositions, its sense of life extending beyond the frame, the film is markedly different from Losey's usual

methods; the images don't have the calculatedly closed qualities of the director's customary mise-en-scène.

Despite the fact that the actors speak English and that the dialogue contains two self-conscious and intrusive parables that represent Losey's attempt to adapt his story to a preconceived moral purpose, *Stranger on the Prowl* has the texture of a traditional neorealist film. It creates an environment that seems more connected to the world of objective reality than the isolated and symbolic milieu typical of Losey: there are no symptoms of the director's baroque expressionism here.

Paul Muni, near the end of his career at the time, gives a wonderfully visual performance as the fugitive. Weather-beaten, his shoulders hunched over, his body slouching through the devastated streets and buildings as if he has no right to occupy them, he looks terrifically world-weary; his eyes have the hurt, bewildered look of a haunted man, and yet the character attains real dignity as he reaches out to the boy.

The film is rarely shown, and Losey is not at all attached to it. (Because of the blacklist, Losey wrote and directed the film under the name of Andrea Forzano.) Strikingly different from his other work, *Stranger on the Prowl* reveals surprising range and adaptability and deserves more attention than it has received.

Eve

Eve, which follows Losey's long "apprenticeship" period in England, is a film radically different from *Stranger on the Prowl*. In the earlier film, Losey tried for the objective, reportorial tone of pioneer neorealists like De Sica and Visconti. Amazingly Losey achieved something of the "invisible" style sought by the neorealists. With *Eve* Losey gives free play to his interest in baroque mannerism, and the focus of the film is the display of the director's temperament and sensibility—since the story and characters are so banal, the film really has nothing to rely on *but* the visual personality of its director.

An English screenwriter, living in Italy and mingling with international film celebrities, becomes obsessed with a "woman of the world." He betrays his loyal, high-strung wife, who kills herself. The two-timing writer is a professional as well as emotional fraud,

since the book that inspired the film that made him a rich man was stolen from his dead brother, who had entrusted him before his death to see that his manuscript was published. When he falls for Eve, who taunts him and remains maddeningly beyond his reach even when she finally agrees to sleep with him, he is "punished" for his betrayal of his wife and brother: Eve seduces and abandons him.

On the foundation of this routine romantic triangle, played out against glamorous settings, Losey constructed what was, to that point, his most personal and stylized piece. Here, in full array, we are regaled by Losey's infatuation with elegant decor, with elaborate paintings and tapestries and statuary, with ornate mirrors and ceilings, with all the trappings, in short, of Continental sophistication. In an interview in 1963 Losey dismissed the novel which supplied the film's basic framework as "too familiar and too hackneyed and too dreary and too dirty-sex. . . . We were interested in saying something that had a much wider application." Losey admitted that "the story could only be interesting in terms of its characters. . .in terms of the detail of character, the details surrounding the character, the atmosphere. . . . If that kind of mood film is tampered with and cut, you haven't got anything left. If you try to reduce it to its initial exploitation plot, you've got nothing."[1]

Just as *Stranger on the Prowl* borrowed its settings, characterization, and theme, and its journalistic visual style, from the neorealists, so *Eve* absorbs the stylistic preoccupations of the major Italian directors of a later decade. In its concern with a group of jaded rich people who move languorously through the baroque splendors of Venice, and in its lush, insistent symbolism and its cultivation of mood, manner, and atmosphere, the film echoes (in a distinctly minor key) Antonioni's *L'Avventura* and Fellini's *La Dolce Vita*. The film's big party scenes have the decadence and frivolity, the appalling insincerity, of the revels in other films of the period about "the sweet life." The Old World decadence of the rich earns both Losey's awe and condemnation; like Fellini, he is clearly drawn to the sensual surfaces—the opportunities for titillation and excitement—offered by the international jet set, and yet he exposes the excesses and the betrayals that he sees as an inevitable part of the luxurious life. Losey treats his protagonist with moralistic disapproval; like the crooked cop in *The Prowler*, Tyvian has all the wrong values, and he is severely punished for being seduced by

money, fame, and women. Losey's response to his "inauthentic" hero reveals a streak of American puritanism that distinguishes *Eve* from the other early 1960s dramas of Continental dissipation made by Continental directors.

The film is told, in flashback, from Tyvian's point of view, so that Eve is seen from a distance—she is an outsider. As in other Losey films *(The Gypsy and the Gentleman, Chance Meeting, The Servant, Accident)*, a woman is an amoral catalyst of male lust and insecurity; she is a remote *femme fatale* who wanders through the film creating havoc and then escapes untouched at the end, her own privacy unviolated. Tyvian is a hollow man, and in her perfect inaccessibility Eve is his true spiritual counterpart. Tyvian is a type that interests Losey (and the character is played by an actor, Stanley Baker, whom Losey used a number of times). Though the character is fatally misguided, the director clearly is drawn to him.

Tyvian is more complex than any of the characters in Losey's early social dramas, and *Eve* has a more private focus than any of the director's work up to this point; but Losey still proceeds from specific cases to general examples, enlarging the significance of character and story by embellishing them with a calculated pattern of symbols. To validate his "seriousness," Losey punctuates the film with biblical parallels, beginning, most obviously, with the name of his heroine. Raymond Durgnat writes that "the commentary and statuary relate the story to the biblical myth of the Fall—with money as the fruit, Venice as an ironic garden of Eden, and Eve as an ironic Eve."[2] Tyvian's opening narration recalls that he has played by the waters of Babylon (as we see him water-skiing in Venice). A prominently displayed tapestry depicts the scene of Adam and Eve's expulsion from Eden. At one point (Losey at his most obvious symbol-mongering), Eve eats an apple. Losey clearly wants to create surprising dissonances between the sacred and profane—between the worldly, jaded characters and the biblical associations that are introduced into their story. But Tyvian and Eve are too insubstantial to withstand the web of extracurricular parallels, and the film's symbolism is strained, inorganic, arty. Stanley Baker plays the part well, forcefully suggesting the character's obsession, his self-hatred, his desperate, coiled uncertainty, and Jeanne Moreau (though far too ravaged-looking to be the irresistible *femme fatale* that the script calls for) conveys her character's boredom and aloofness; but their doomed romance has a severely limited significance, unlike that of

the lovers in *L'Avventura* whose failure to connect illuminates the fabric of an entire society and world-view. The religious symbolism and the elaborate visual style seem far too grand a tapestry for the familiar characters. Durgnat's claim that "the style seems appropriate for the sumptuousness whose hollowness it exposes" is fanciful.

Despite its inflated imagery and its stubbornly routine story, the film is often wonderful to look at. As is usual in Losey, places become characters in their own right. Eve's luxurious apartment, Tyvian's country villa, with its stark white walls (à la Antonioni), and an elegant Venetian hotel provide richly detailed locations through which Losey's tracking, gliding camera takes evident delight in browsing. Eve's apartment is filled with different kinds of painted eggs. This veritable museum of eggs is a nice decorative touch, though it is certainly intended to "mean" more than that, to express something of Eve's sexuality. Since she remains an enigma, however, the eggs look more like an extension of the director's own quirky sensibility, just as her infatuation for Billie Holliday, to whose records she listens with worshipful and compulsive attentiveness, seems irrelevant to character but interesting in terms purely of atmosphere and texture.

Losey has a proprietary interest in *Eve*. He is probably more attached to it than to any of his other films, and, uncharacteristically, he has spoken about it at great length. His obsession with this minor, sour romantic drama is a result partly of the fact that he loved making it—the work has an exuberance and fluency, an exhilaration with the visual possibilities of filmmaking, that surpass his other pictures up to this point—and partly of the fact that his producers, the Hakim brothers, made substantial cuts. His original epic length of two hours and thirty-five minutes was progressively whittled down to one hour and forty minutes for release in England and to a puny 100 minutes for an American exploitation playoff (under the lurid title *The Devil's Woman*). The producers also tampered with the sound track, dubbing some of the actors (disastrously, in the case of Virna Lisi, who plays Tyvian's distraught wife) and adding what Losey felt was an inappropriate romantic score in place of the Billie Holliday songs he had used originally. It is hard to see how the film would really be any better at greater length—surely it would only be more self-indulgent and bloated, its thin story inflated to altogether unnecessary proportions.[3] Because Losey felt

so betrayed by the producers of *Eve*, he has since always fought for, and sometimes won, absolute control over his projects. He has insisted, even when working for major American studios (20th Century–Fox, for *Modesty Blaise*; Universal, for *Boom* and *Secret Ceremony*), on the freedom to make the film the way he wants it made, without compromise or capitulation to front-office insecurity. His bitter experience with *Eve*, coupled with his own independent temperament, insured that Losey would never hire himself out as a genial company man, or as a popular director of commodity material.

The Sleeping Tiger and A Finger of Guilt

Losey's first two British films are the least interesting of his entire career. At the time, Losey was anxious to work, and he accepted scripts that he did not respect in the hope that he would be able to improve them. To a modest extent, he succeeds, as both *The Sleeping Tiger* and *A Finger of Guilt* have a strong visual style and both create an illusion of dealing with significant issues. The films are confused melodramas in which Losey concentrates on characterization rather than the thriller qualities both stories contain. He manages in both pieces to work up a tense atmosphere by emphasizing the interaction—the struggle for power and dominance—among an enclosed group of neurotic characters.

The Sleeping Tiger, which Raymond Durgnat calls "an adept mixture of two genres, the 'young thug' story and the 'bad wife' story,"[4] is of interest principally because it represents an initial treatment of the invasion theme that is at the center of Losey's most forceful films. A psychiatrist invites a young criminal into his house with the intent of curing him. The young man—another Losey intruder—is attracted to the doctor's twitchy, neglected wife and thereby arouses "the sleeping tiger" in both her and her husband. The ensuing psychological and sexual contest between the two men—the rivalry over the woman, the cat-and-mouse games by which they taunt each other—is well acted (the psychiatrist is played by Dirk Bogarde, in the first of many appearances for Losey, and Alexis Smith performs the role of the pawnlike wife with nervous intensity). But the dialogue, and the narrative contortions that lead to the melodramatic climax, in which the wife drives her car through a huge billboard of a sleeping tiger (blatant Losey symbolism again), keep the material rooted at a mundane level.

A *Finger of Guilt* also suffers from a contrived story line. But again Losey manages to "rescue" from the project some striking images and the articulation of ideas of more than routine interest. Reggie Wilson (played by Richard Basehart, who has a general physical resemblance to Losey) is an American film director who has had to leave Hollywood because of a scandal (he was caught with someone else's wife). He has made his way in the British film industry by saving a losing studio with a hit picture and by marrying the boss's daughter. Now his new career is being threatened by letters from a woman called "Evelyn" who claims to be having an affair with him and who threatens to expose him if he doesn't support her. The blackmail angle, and its resolution, lack conviction: it turns out that the girl has been hired by a zealous employee of the studio who resents Reggie for having amassed so much power; the underling fears that Reggie will displace the boss, Ben Case, and to prevent this he tries to unseat Reggie by concocting the kind of scandal that had ended his career in America.

What is of primary interest here is the network of references to Losey's own career. The director has turned a corny crime drama into an autobiographical statement about his own exile and his own attitude toward his craft. The illicit sexual affair that destroyed Reggie's career in America has clear enough parallels to Losey's blacklisting and subsequent relocation in England. Reggie says at one point, in frustration, as he sees his kingdom about to crumble for the second time, "The past won't leave me alone. It's been coming at me from all sides." His wife tells him, "Father warned me that your sort of past wouldn't stay in the past." Losey felt too that the blacklist was continuing to haunt him even in England, its long arm forcing him into accepting scripts like this one and preventing him from signing his own name to his work (the credits list Alex C. Snowden as producer and Joseph Walton as director).

Beyond the personal allusions, the film contains some interesting insights into Losey's ideas about films, about the corporate structure of the film studio, and about the illusion and artifice on which the filmmaker inevitably depends. As an inside look into studio politics, and as a kind of self-referential piece on filmmaking, *A Finger of Guilt* has a genuine, if modest, appeal.

The story is told in flashback when the director, who feels he is cracking up, reveals his past to a psychiatrist. What he says to the doctor and, later, to his boss at the studio, about movies and the

process of making movies, has pointed relevance to Losey's biography. "Out of pictures, I was like a duck out of water, which is why I decided to come to London instead of going to New York. Here, I was given an ordinary picture but I had the story tight as a drum. . . . I've learned to live according to the law of the jungle that we call the picture business." The director talks with an almost mystical fervor about "the excitement in a projection room that people on the outside can't understand. You see your work and you say, this one, I like. I feel I'm the audience. When I laugh, they laugh." When the doctor recommends that he go away for four or six months, Reggie snaps, "I can't leave. You don't know this industry—I couldn't be sure of my job: what else have I got left?"

The climax, when Reggie learns who is responsible for the blackmail plot, takes place on a studio set where everything is fake, but where appearances nonetheless have their reality. Reggie hunts down "Evelyn," the fake girl, amid fake studio sets and a fake sky. She thinks at one point that soldiers are out to get her, but they are only extras in a film being made at the studio; she hears gunshots, which turn out to come from a film sound track. Studio artifice is enclosed by fences, doors, gates, as "Evelyn" is trapped within a place where illusion is manufactured. Make-believe also figures in the showdown between the director and his enemy: Reggie attacks Ernie within the circumference of light thrown by a studio spotlight, their shadows forming an eerie backdrop as they struggle.

Time without Pity

Once again, in *Time without Pity*, Losey is working on a manhunt melodrama played out against eccentric settings. A young man is sentenced to the electric chair for a murder he did not commit. His estranged father visits him in jail and vows to discover the murderer. He suspects his son's former boss, a powerful and power-hungry businessman, may be the one he is looking for, and with a grim determination he sets about catching him.

Losey underplays the thriller aspects of this familiar wrong-man story. He reveals the identity of the murderer in the prologue, where we see the crime for which the hero's son is wrongly convicted. Relieving the suspense about guilt and innocence allows Losey to construct the story as a manifold indictment—of capital

punishment, of a fallible system of justice, and (since the murderer is a tycoon who ruthlessly controls the lives of his family and employees) of the fascist tendencies of big business. The story's surface—a manhunt through an urban underworld—thus supplies the scaffolding for a conscientious social drama, a warning against the methods and the dangers of the justice system and of private enterprise.

Like so many of Losey's films, *Time without Pity* becomes a struggle for dominance between radically different personalities. Graham, the pursuer (Michael Redgrave), unlike Stanford, his quarry (Leo McKern), is a man who has lost control over his life. He drinks; he has been primarily an absent father and is now trying to atone by saving his son's life, even if it means risking his own. He knows Stanford is like a rabid dog, and yet, cunningly, he baits him, closing in for the kill. The contest of wills that takes place between them has premonitions of Pinteresque menace, but without Pinter's distinctive style to give it edge or complexity. And the climax is unconvincing. Racing against the clock (the "time without pity"), and fully appreciating his adversary's caginess, Graham concludes that he must sacrifice himself in order to save his son: he goads Stanford into killing him, thereby revealing Stanford's guilt and ensuring his son's release. The script does not make this noble, last-minute sacrifice credible.

Time without Pity tries to be too many things at once—a chase thriller, a psychological study of dominance, a statement against capital punishment—without having the force or clarity to treat any of its themes in depth. And yet Losey has managed to fashion a continuously interesting and occasionally provocative movie out of ordinary and underdeveloped material. The film is further evidence of his ability to enhance a basically undistinguished script through mise-en-scène.

Direction certainly transcends the material, but it cannot finally disguise its B-picture base. Yet French critics hailed the film with entirely unwarranted praise: "The decor. . . leaves no doubt that the word 'cosmic' is appropriate to Losey. We don't recall that another cineaste has brought as far the problems of dialogue, interpretation, decor, light, sound, music . . . all are integrated in the art of direction, and thus is projected a prodigious force that we have never felt before."[5] The sober response of the *Herald Tribune* reviewer is far more sensible: "This is not an unusual specimen of

this kind of picture; but it has been made with that patience in details that gives such British films, even when second rate, a note of chilling authenticity."[6]

Chance Meeting

Like *Time without Pity*, *Chance Meeting* is a thinking man's thriller. Its murder-mystery story is a frame for Losey's cynical statements about the British class system and about the closely linked theme of corruption and influence at Scotland Yard. The plot is as bare and as formulaic as that of *Time without Pity*, and Losey has said that he did not at all believe in it. "I had to try to make it look interesting and deceive the audience by making the characters interesting enough so that they'd forget that the story was a fraud. Content interests me more than subject. Here, the subject, that is to say the plot, didn't interest me at all, although I tried to give it some content in terms of the development of the characters and the background."[7] His "enrichment" of the trite story through characterization and decor is more persuasive than in *Time without Pity*.

A young man, a Dutch artist, goes to visit his mistress, for the first time meeting her at her apartment. When he arrives, he finds it empty. Two police investigators enter and charge him with the murder of his mistress, Jacqueline Cousteau. The artist reconstructs the story of his chance meeting with her at an art gallery and describes the course of their affair. The Inspector, a Welshman named Morgan, believes in the man's innocence, but is told by his superiors to convict him. The murdered girl was the mistress of a high-ranking diplomat, Sir Howard Fenton, and it would be indelicate and might even interfere with important political negotiations to open the case further. The surprise twist is that the woman Jan has thought was Jacqueline Cousteau was in fact Lady Fenton, who killed the real Jacqueline because she was planning to run off with Lady Fenton's husband. The shrewd Lady Fenton met and courted Jan in order to set him up as her fall guy, as the patsy who would take the rap for Jacqueline's murder.

What is most absorbing about the film is not so much the story of deception and masquerade, or the characterizations of the woman as fatal temptress and of the man as gullible victim, but the way in which Losey uses the settings. Jacqueline's apartment becomes a

full-fledged character. As Gilles Jacob has noted, "Losey deciphers an apartment just as one deciphers a human soul, but with such skill one can sometimes even sense the state of mind of the visitor. . . . The girl is dead and our only knowledge of her comes from the spiritual portrait gradually revealed by the apartment."[8]

The film opens with Jan's exploration of the apartment. He's delighted by its atmosphere of wealth and ease. He's amused by the sunken bathtub, by the mirrored boudoir, by the frilly ornamentation in the bedroom. As in many Losey films, we explore an environment along with a character, discovering in the decor important clues about the people who live there. Filled with ornate objects, with paintings and furniture and heavy velvet draperies that make a strong statement of social and economic status, the apartment is immediately established as a space that reverberates with symbolic meaning.

Inspector Morgan's response to the apartment is different from Jan's: there are, in this sense, "two" apartments, just as there are "two" Jacquelines, the real one and "Jan's" Jacqueline, who is actually Lady Fenton. "What kind of woman decorated this room?" Inspector Morgan asks disapprovingly; his tone implies that it is the kind of woman who ends up in the morgue. He looks with distaste at the striped wallpaper, the oversized bed, the frilly black lace underwear. To him this is the apartment of a prostitute. Yet Jan describes her as a woman of refinement, and the apartment does contain a few very valuable objects, including a Van Dyck portrait, that show genuine taste. The schizophrenic decor is the first clue that there may be "two" Jacquelines.

In addition to the apartment, there are two other important settings: Jan's studio, and an investigation room in the police station. In terms of light and texture, the two places are sharply juxtaposed, while the bareness and simplicity of both settings provide a strong visual contrast to the victim's cluttered apartment. The studio is brightly lit, its stark white walls intensified by the sun streaming through the skylight. The love scenes between Jan and "Jacqueline" all take place in the bright afternoon sun in Jan's studio. "I wanted the romance to take place during the day, never at night," Losey said. "We used a very pure white light . . . we wanted a very white light to be the decor for these scenes."[9] The clear light against which the romance is played and "Jacqueline's" duplicity would seem to point an ironic contrast: every date that Jan has with her is, in a

"Among filmmakers, Losey is the greatest poet of mirrors." (Roger Greenspun) This
mirror shot from *Chance Meeting* underscores the alienation of the hero (Hardy
Kruger).

sense, a "blind" one (*Blind Date* was the film's English title). And
yet the clarity of the images has an appropriateness, since Jan does
see one side of the woman ("What are you afraid will happen if you
really give yourself?" he asks); and he does manage to get through
to her more than she counted on.

The scenes in the police station between Jan and Morgan, as Jan
begins to clear up the mystery, are darkly lit, and filled with crisscrossing shadows. The bare inquisition room looks like a prison cell.
The "white" love scenes and the dark scenes of police interrogation
are typical of the visual irony and the strong chiaroscuro pattern
throughout the film.

Like many of Losey's British films, *Chance Meeting* is about the
class system. Jan is taken in by Lady Fenton's masquerade because
he does not understand the class code; he is seduced by her aristocratic bearing, her air of superiority: she can't possibly be other
than what she seems, he reasons. Morgan, a Welshman and there-

fore like Jan also an outsider, is at first duped by class as well: he is reluctant to attach any misdeeds to the prominent Sir Howard Fenton. In constructing her plan, Lady Fenton has in fact counted on the privileges of her class; she has assumed that her rank in society will remove her from suspicion in the murder of her husband's mistress, even if her husband's connection to the murder victim is revealed, which she doubts. Her assumptions are almost borne out when Morgan's associate tries to warn him against involving Sir Howard: "Rising to the top involves a sense of the deeper meaning of public service"—advice which Morgan has too much integrity to heed.

Class differences are underlined by the fact that Jan is the son of a coal miner and that he is working on a large canvas of a mining scene which he intends as a tribute to his proletarian origins. "It always amazes me about the rich," he tells "Jacqueline," "how mean they are." "The poor, how vulgar they are," she answers. Like many of Losey's characters, then—like the gypsy and the gentleman, like Barrett and Tony in *The Servant,* like the frustrated lovers in *The Go-Between*—Jan and Lady Fenton are representatives of different social classes whose encounter reflects a larger social conflict. Lady Fenton plays a cool Lady Chatterley to Jan's refined, though still passionate and natural, proletarian. His directness and sensitivity are a challenge to Lady Fenton—the brightness of his studio blinds her. "Damn you," she says to him at the end: not because she has been found out, but because Jan didn't play by the rules of the game. His openness and warmth disarmed her and exploded the class myth behind which she was trying to hide. Jan's vital honesty convicts all the characters who are ruled by rigid class considerations.

Losey has tried to underline the moral virtue of his hero by making him an artist. Often in his work Losey signals a serious intent by using paintings to comment on the action; and artists for him are characters with special insight. His treatment of the artist as mystic and visionary and his recurrent use of art objects to relate his stories to a large symbolic framework can be pretentious, as Losey's detractors have often pointed out. Here, Jan's aesthetic philosophizing introduces a kind of artificial high seriousness to the mystery-story format, and his inability to paint "Jacqueline"—she comes out flat, a stubborn, unyielding subject—is strained symbolism.

For all its forced attempts to add an intellectual dimension to routine genre material, however, *Chance Meeting* is a terse, clean-looking film. Its carefully balanced compositions, its long takes, its sedate camera movement, and its calculated variations of chiaroscuro are evidence of the director's growing control over his materials. The film reveals the poise and precision, the tact and sense of balance, that were to make Losey the ideal collaborator for Pinter.

The film received strong reviews both in England and America. It was with *Chance Meeting* that Losey's cult reputation in England began to develop. And in America, despite the fact that it was released as part of a modest double bill, the film earned praise for its visual as well as thematic regeneration of well-worn material. Eugene Archer, one of Losey's early American supporters, wrote that the director "proves himself a strikingly adept technician with an alert and caustic personal style. . . . No one is likely to deny his flair for visual movement, his neat sense of pace or the incisive cynicism of his approach to an overpopulated genre. . . . A fresh and ironic treatment to a flashback mystery."[10]

The Gypsy and the Gentleman

Despite their unpolished scripts, *The Sleeping Tiger, A Finger of Guilt, Time without Pity*, and *Chance Meeting* have at least a formal fastidiousness. Losey manages partial victories over his formula-ridden stories. But he is largely defeated by the preposterously antediluvian story line of *The Gypsy and the Gentleman*, a Regency horse opera conceived on the level of Georgette Heyer on a bad day. A conniving gypsy insinuates her way into a gentleman's house and makes rapid progress from the servant's quarters to the upstairs bedroom. After she becomes mistress of the manor, she discovers that her husband is besieged by creditors and that her only possibility of getting rich is by disinheriting her husband's sister. Plot contrivances—a battle over a will, complicated maneuverings with crooked lawyers and corrupt doctors, a last-minute rescue—push the film into old-fashioned melodrama and away from the serious character study in which Losey is really interested.

The material is played for story value in a way that Losey's other films of this period are not, and the director simply hasn't the temperament for stage-managing a pulpy Regency romance. He has

neither the humor to mock gently the improbable narrative conventions nor the patience to treat the coincidences and climaxes with proper respect. As the sprawling, shapeless story rushes toward the final showdown, Losey's direction grows noticeably less attentive. Characters are introduced and dropped in random fashion; an illustrious actress (played by Flora Robson), who has only a tangential connection to the main characters, materializes as a most improbable *dea ex machina*. "I quarreled terribly over the cutting," Losey said, "which I couldn't control."[11]

If Losey is indifferent to the story on the level of popular romance, he *is* attracted to the misalliance theme embedded within it. The affair between the aristocratic Sir Paul Deverill and the common gypsy Belle is his first treatment of the class theme that is at the center of *The Servant* and *The Go-Between*; and beneath the potboiler romantic saga he was hired to direct can be glimpsed a rough draft of *The Servant*. All of the characters in *The Gypsy and the Gentleman*, the outcasts as well as the aristocrats, are obsessed by "caste"—their lives are dominated by the strict gradations of the British social structure.

As an outsider himself, Losey was impressed by the powerful hold of the class system over English society, and it was this aspect of the material—the damaging effects of the idea of class—that he wanted, but was not permitted, to stress. Losey's tentative reading of the class theme, however, gives the film whatever interest it has. The debauched aristocrat, torn between allegiance to his family heritage and his passion for a gypsy, is a preliminary version of the effete, well-born Tony in *The Servant*. Like Tony, Sir Paul is an essentially weak character—easily seduced, and easily controlled. Like Tony, he is ripe for degradation. "I was half bad when I met you," he tells Belle. "Now I'm Satan's man." We first see him wrestling with a pig in a cellar tavern. Although he wants to dishonor his inheritance, he is too weak-willed to be an active rebel, and a sense of family pride restrains his nihilist impulses. Ironically, he forbids his sister to marry a doctor because such an alliance would betray their class status. In a strong scene, Sir Paul laughs manically at portraits of his ancestors; but his mockery is halfhearted because a part of him still believes in the traditional values he has so flagrantly polluted by marrying a gypsy.

Belle is the counterpart to Barrett, the sly, calculating servant in *The Servant*. Like Barrett, she sees that her master is someone

she can dominate. With her gypsy lover she sets out with fierce single-mindedness to dispossess Deverill of his money, his house, his social position, his manhood. She's like the grasping nouveau riche Natasha in Chekhov's *Three Sisters*—a social outsider who aggressively takes over a group of enfeebled gentry.

In the hands of another director, one with a more popular and less puritanical sensibility than Losey, Belle might well be treated as a vital figure, a kind of eighteenth-century Zorba the Greek. In the film's visual and symbolic scheme, she is clearly identified with the forces of nature: early in the story, in a typical sequence of Losey cross-cutting, Belle is seen in the forest during a rainstorm while Sir Paul is sheltered from the rain on his front terrace. After she has gained control of the house, she says, "I'm choked in that cold, glum house—I want to feel the forest and the wind." She is always dressed in shades of red—in rich purples and ruby—to set her off from the cool aristocratic characters, seen in pale blues, greens, and yellows. She is outlaw passion to their high-born pride. But Losey distrusts her "passion," sees it as destructive rather than liberating. She is a nasty character, a Regency *femme fatale*, rather than a vigorous and life-affirming natural woman. Her "passion" for Deverill is entirely manufactured, and, once she gains possession of the house, she apes the snobbishness of her betters by evicting her fellow gypsies from "her land." She is narrow, greedy, harsh, and is sexual only with her gypsy lover, whom she considers a real man and who slaps her and treats her with contempt.

Losey's evident disapproval of the character is emphasized in Melina Mercouri's garish performance. Losey clearly didn't know what to do with Mercouri, who works in an entirely different register from the director's stock company of subtle, modulated British actors like Dirk Bogarde and Stanley Baker. Mercouri is frankly gross. Her efforts to be sexy are exaggerated to the point of burlesque: she seems like a female impersonator. With her flashing eyes, her swiveling hips, her thick, ugly, cooing voice, her fake gleaming smile, she acts in a vaudevillian high camp style that is ludicrously inappropriate, and Losey has allowed her to sabotage herself as well as the film.

Losey thus remains detached from both groups of characters, maintaining the ironic distance and moral disapproval that is present, in a more mature and integrated way, in *The Servant*. The "good" aristocrats are either pale or psychotic; the commoners are

thoroughly vicious. The film pits proletarian evil against aristocratic weakness, with the disapproval apportioned equally between the "high" and "low" characters. This is a romance lacking a hero or heroine with whom the audience can identify. A moral fierceness radiates from Losey's depiction of the degraded protagonists, and his dark character study of corrupt sex and greed, and of aristocratic dissipation, is not adjusted to the superficial and plot-heavy narrative framework in which it is uncomfortably embedded. At the end, after a silly carriage chase that belongs to Victorian melodrama, Deverill and Belle drown—he kisses her as he holds her head under water. The last image is of her purple and green cloak floating away in the churning water. The echoes of Browning's "Porphyria's Lover" contained in the operatic conclusion—an obsessed lover killing his beloved in order to possess her ultimately and forever—is philosophically out of place as the coda to a rousing melodrama involving distressed maidens and stolen wills.

Despite the ghastly Mercouri, the lopsided plot, and the tonal imbalance, the film is beautifully designed. Losey and his production assistants consciously planned their use of color and their settings on Rowlandson prints to give the film an authentic flavor of eighteenth-century England. "I think it's largely a piece of junk that, on the whole, looks marvelous," Losey said about the film, accurately enough. "I made them show it without the sound track at a Losey festival in France. . . . It worked marvelously because the story tells itself without words."[12]

Losey is plainly attracted to the aristocratic world that Deverill Court represents. He disapproves of Deverill, at least in part, because he is irresponsible in keeping up the family tradition, and he despises Belle because she is determined to wreck Deverill Court altogether. When she first discovers that Paul is heavily in debt, she starts destroying the objets d'art with wild abandon—an act of desecration, according to Losey.

Like other houses in later films, Deverill Court becomes a central "character" in the action—the symbol of the family inheritance, as well as the prize possession in the contest between the aristocrats and the usurpers. Although it doesn't contain such a character, the film seems to imply that the true hero of the story would be the man or woman who has the integrity to preserve what is valuable about Deverill Court and is wise enough to be receptive to a few modern democratic notions. But this is the scenario for another

film, one that Losey would certainly much rather have made. Instead of that affirmative statement, in which the traditional and the modern, the aristocratic and the democratic, commingle in mutual enrichment, he has attacked an etiolated aristocracy and a destructive group of social outcasts. His indictment shoots in both directions at once, at the dark and sinister world of the forest and at the remote world of Deverill Court. But the film's sour tone does not entirely conceal Losey's aesthetic appreciation of true aristocratic decorum and "taste," and contained within the display of moral disapproval is a nostalgic evocation of a sylvan, aristocratic eighteenth-century England secure in its social hierarchies.

The Concrete Jungle

The Concrete Jungle is a B prison melodrama redeemed by Losey's skillful mise-en-scène. The hero (Stanley Baker again) is released from prison on parole. He falls quickly into his old way of life, plans and executes a bank heist, and buries the money before he is arrested. After he is once again paroled, he is killed in a climactic shoot-out among the dishonorable thieves. As a character study of an inveterate criminal, the film is certainly thin; the character is drawn more from other movies than from life. Brooding, hulking, shrewd, Bannion conforms to a stereotyped concept of a B-movie hood. He knows how to survive in the concrete jungle of the underworld both in and out of prison. A strong self-protective instinct and a hard-boiled environment have made him a total egoist. With women, as with every other aspect of his life, he takes what he can.

As in *The Gypsy and the Gentleman,* Losey is once again working on a story whose characters he disapproves of; and, as in many of his films, the world-view presented in *The Concrete Jungle* is deeply fatalistic. Losey records the criminal's inevitable doom with chilling detachment in a taut, clinical style. This is yet another Losey film, then, about both physical and psychological entrapment; the character has as little freedom outside prison as he does inside. He is condemned to reenact the cycle of parole from and return to prison over and over, until his death.

The entrapment of the cold-eyed antihero is ingrained in Losey's rigorously closed framing and in the deliberate repetition of camera

movement, as in the crane shot that is used whenever a former inmate returns to prison. The recurrent visual patterns in the "homecoming" scenes give the action a ritualistic heightening.

The prison setting itself, with its multiple levels of rows of identical cells receding into the distance almost as far as the eye can see, also contains repetition of visual motifs; and Losey's reiterative camera movement seems to lock the characters firmly within the cold, metallic environment. Losey's objective, rigorously unsentimental visual style emphasizes the utter impersonality of the prison background.

With its rising tiers of cells, its division between masters and servants, and its intense class-consciousness, the prison is a microcosm of the British class system. The social hierarchy within the prison is quickly outlined; we know from the opening card game who are the bosses and who are the followers in this rigidly stratified environment. The prisoners are as fiercely jealous of social rank and privilege as any of the characters in Losey's collaborative efforts with Pinter. The opening action concerns the return of a former inmate who is a marked man among his fellows. The details are sketchy, to enforce the general and typical nature of the situation, but the terror of the returned man, and the vengeance that unites the other prisoners against him, are powerfully rendered: we feel strongly that the men are acting in accord with a specific code that the guilty newcomer has in some way outraged.

In its broad outlines, the prison sequences are iconographically reminiscent of all prison movies; but in its selection of details, its level of performance, its creation of a tense atmosphere that hovers on the verge of violent explosion, and its sustained use of the prison as a metaphor for society, the film overcomes its formulaic elements and achieves an individual distinction.

Losey strictly confines the number of settings outside the prison so that Bannion's life seems as constricted and bounded as it is when he is locked up. Bannion's cramped apartment, in contrast to the dark prison, has glaringly white walls. He lives in a playboy pad, with pin-ups of models on the walls and a jazzy modern bathroom. It's a rugged man's environment. Although the decor expresses Bannion's hulking, macho personality, the rooms are small, and the ceilings seem almost to be closing in on him. The character is too big to be comfortable in such a tight space, and the recurrent low angle shot of the large-framed actor in his apartment suggests his

entrapment. The physical tension between character and setting has the effect of making Bannion appear to be less at home when he is home than when he is in prison.

The film's third major setting—an empty, snow-covered field where Bannion hides the heist money—provides a strong visual contrast. The white open expanse is a refreshing departure from the cityscapes and interior scenes that comprise the usual crime-film milieu; but the whiteness of the landscape contains its own terror; it too is a threatening rather than nurturing environment, and it is here, against the icy, impersonal whiteness, that the criminal is killed. In Losey's films, even open spaces are traps (as in *Figures in a Landscape*). Visually, the climactic shoot-out in a snowy wilderness anticipates the finale in *Shoot the Piano Player*, François Truffaut's homage to and satire of the American B crime film, of which *The Concrete Jungle* is a deft, "straight" British adaptation.

These Are the Damned

These Are the Damned is the most thematically ambitious film of Losey's early English period. For the first time since his departure from America, Losey felt challenged by a large-scale theme: "*The Damned* [the British title] is an emotional plea against the destruction of the human race," Losey said. "I don't have an answer. I've tried to unsettle people, to force them to think."[13]

A demented scientist has organized a secret, subterranean school of children who have been made radioactive so that they will survive after an atomic holocaust. The scientist, controlling the lives of the children and creating an underground world on the basis of his paranoid fantasies, is a tyrant in the Caligari mold; he remakes the world according to his own hallucinatory vision. The children's cavernous underground school is one of the most startling images of entrapment in Losey's work, and the scenes of the children's highly regulated lives are managed with a chilling and seemingly documentary authenticity. As in *The Concrete Jungle*, Losey is once again expert in dramatizing the dynamics of a severely enclosed society.

Because the children are contaminated, no one enters their sanctum unless masked, so that the visiting adults look like robots in the presence of the children. Isolated from the world in this awe-

somely controlled environment, receiving their lessons by remote control, the children have an eerie and almost otherworldly quality, reminiscent of the war orphans in *The Boy with Green Hair:* they seem like imitations of children.

Losey compares the children's world with one that is "socially distinct but paradoxically similar":[14] scenes in the school are cross-cut with life in a seaside town. But unlike the symbolic correspondences between settings and character groups in films like *The Concrete Jungle* and *The Gypsy and the Gentleman,* the terms of the equation are here vastly unequal in scale and significance, so that the film's moral statement becomes seriously unbalanced. The town and the underground school are not convincing as parallel environments. The town is threatened by a group of motorcyclists whose anarchic violence both recalls that of the gang that terrorizes a sleepy American town in *The Wild One* and anticipates the roving band of hoods in *A Clockwork Orange.* Throughout the first part of the film, Losey cross-cuts between the radioactive children and the violent rockers, though the connections between the two groups, and the two settings, are not precise: the rockers' tyranny over the resort and the gang leader's pathological overprotectiveness of his sister, on the one hand, and the scientist's control over the children, on the other, are not really thematically parallel. The rockers are too small scale to withstand Losey's heavy symbolic intentions. The scientist's manipulation of the children has cosmic dimensions, while the gang's violation of the town seems more a matter of local concern.

The school and the town, which at first seem remote from each other in time and space, are eventually linked through the figure of a journalist who is on vacation. Playing essentially the same character that he did in *The Lawless,* MacDonald Carey is a reporter who doesn't want to get involved. Though he is terrorized by the gang, he is drawn toward the group leader's sister, whom he wants to set free. As the two make their escape from the town, they come upon the entrance to the children's school. The journalist gradually understands what has been done to the children, and he attempts to rescue them. But his humanitarianism proves powerless against the greater force of the scientist and his masked emissaries. The crusading writer and his new girl friend are destroyed by the scientist's avenging helicopter. The film ends with a shot of the vast, empty ocean ("the omnipresent sea represents the destiny of the

characters"),[15] with the voices of the imprisoned children crying for help providing a grim aural counterpoint. Like several other Losey films, *These Are the Damned* concludes on a note of utter hopelessness: the contaminated children are condemned to their prison, "the damned" victims of a paranoid overreacher.

Losey underscores the disturbing triumph of science by including an idealistic sculptress—another of his saintly artists—among the "good" and vanquished characters. Losey introduces the character as a counterpoint to the doomsday scientist: "I wanted to tell a simple parable about a man who had a deep conviction about life but whose conviction was one that led me to believe that he was more interested in death than in life. I wanted to counterpose against that a woman who, without ever stating it philosophically, in what she did had a belief in life."[16] Freya's abstract sculptures of birds in flight, or birds struggling to fly, stand proudly on the grounds of her hilltop cottage. In the film's symbolic scheme, her art is a denial of the scientist's negative vision, despite the fact that she too is killed by the scientist's attacking helicopter. The sculptress is not believable as either a realistic or symbolic character, and, like the gang, she seems to belong to some other film.

Despite its forced parallels, its blatant symbolism, its imprecise message, and its glib fatalism the film has powerful moments, and it is splendidly designed. The restless, craning camerawork in the opening section, along with the disorienting angles, and the blaring rock music that identifies the rockers and suggests their brutal and aggressive sexuality, creates an atmosphere ripe with danger and poised for explosion. The towering rock cliffs in which the children's school is hidden are a powerful image: barren, craglike, intimidating, this is a landscape that positively forbids approach. Offering no shelter or comfort, the stark, sheer faces of the cliffs look like a vision of a postholocaust world.

Modesty Blaise

Although it was made in 1966, after *The Servant* and *King and Country* gave Losey two international successes, *Modesty Blaise* belongs, in spirit, to the director's experiments with genre in the 1950s. In films like *The Concrete Jungle* and *These Are the Damned* Losey takes a serious attitude to the conventions of the prison movie

and those of the science-fiction thriller at the same time that he is working variations on them. *Modesty Blaise,* however, is designed from first to last as a send-up of a popular genre of its period, the James Bond films, with their male-chauvinist ethic, their infatuation with gadgetry, their depersonalization, their evident and even self-glorifying delight in violence, and their complicated story lines. Losey's film is a burlesque of the form, made as a criticism of the vulgar materialism and the blunt comic-strip style of the audience-pleasing Bond fantasies.

The narrative details, based on the famous cartoon, make little sense. Events, changes of fortune, alliances and disagreements among the villains, occur so rapidly as to defy comprehension. The broad outline of the plot—Modesty and her partner, Willy, are hired by the government to recover stolen jewels—is of course familiar from the Bond movies. The story, with all its twists and reversals, unfolds basically as a series of chases which take place in outlandish and bizarre settings. To parody the exotic locales in the Bond adventures, Losey gives the film a lurid op art design; the zig-zag patterns, the brilliant anti-naturalistic colors, and the strong-ly molded shapes of lines and circles turn the settings into a garish fantasy landscape. At one point in the action, Modesty's jail cell is painted in a vivid op art red and green pattern. The oil wells in the last sequence look like huge op art sculptures painted in wild colors. The villain's luxurious villa has dizzying wallpaper and a patio dec-orated with purple and white circles. Cars emit green and yellow fumes. The exaggerated decor becomes a comment on the shallow-ness of the characters—the op art configurations reveal their heart-less chic, their obsession with glittering surfaces.

Modesty Blaise is a film of instant transformations. In a flash of the editor's scissors, Modesty changes clothes and identities throughout the film, remaking herself to help her in her assignment to recover the jewels. In one of the first scenes, set in a strange alleyway, a man in clown makeup turns a glove into a cane; when the man rings a doorbell, the house explodes. The film thus sets up what is for Losey a strange new world, one in which magical transformations, instant appearances and disappearances, are im-mediately available. Places, people, objects are devious, unstable; nothing is what it seems to be—and the "magic" is created through Eisensteinian montage which rearranges real space and time.

Objects, which are always important in Losey's work, here assume

diabolic proportions, since they are neither what they seem to be or are meant to be. Umbrellas are really guns; a belt becomes a bow and arrow; a mechanical bird speaks; a fake pigeon is used to carry a message. Wineglasses are long stemmed to the point of giddiness. Dolls in a fun house, where one of the numerous chases is set, take on an eerie life of their own: the inanimate springs to life, while people, in the film's topsy-turvy mise-en-scène, are reduced to ornaments. The juxtaposition of objects and things frequently attains surreal dimensions, as when a fish appears suddenly in a wineglass.

Losey burlesques his own reputation as a "baroque" director. Angles and placement of the camera are sometimes wildly arbitrary; foreground objects obscure our view, while important action is filmed through distorting mirrors or glass. The compositions are overly elaborate, the frame packed with visual embellishments. The film assaults our senses in its riot of vivid colors, its hallucinatory decor, its crowded framing.

Twentieth Century–Fox gave Losey the largest budget he has ever had—over $6 million—and of course tried to sell the film as "the real thing," as a female version of the Bond epics rather than a parody of them. The film became a cult favorite among college students, although it never achieved the wide popular success that the studio had envisioned. For what they wanted from the material, Fox of course hired the wrong director. Losey turned a Bond fantasy, a comic-strip caper, into a visually sophisticated and bitter satire of itself, and, along the way, of a number of other things as well—violence, government hypocrisy, heroism, and even sex. It is a mordant film, and a heavy one: Losey has none of the light-heartedness that a straight version of the material would require; he has little of the exuberance that, say, Richard Lester would have brought to the script. Losey's formal self-consciousness counters the producers' desire for a free-form "Hellzapoppin," a rip-roaring popular entertainment. Losey has no patience or ability as a director of big action scenes; his last-minute rescue sequence is a parody of the form, and not a well-managed one at that, and his irony cuts into the erotic aspects of the material.

The film is cold, strangely asexual: Modesty and Willy never have sex; the closest they come to it is when they sing a duet as Modesty licks an oversized ice-cream cone. The characters (including the fey

villain Gabriel) are antisex, and their essential heavy-heartedness is enforced by the casting of Monica Vitti and Terence Stamp. Vitti, a veteran of Antonioni's angst-ridden dramas, carries her existential despair into this film, and she makes the most plodding of super-spies. With her downcast features, her heavy, lidded eyes, and her thick Italian-accented English, she is disastrously miscast: did Losey use her deliberately, to undercut the pop thrust of the material, to play against its naturally light-fingered texture by offering us this most dour and unaccommodating of high thriller heroines? And Stamp, too, trained in an entirely different kind of film, is almost equally uncomfortable. He is plainly happier playing the enigmatic Billy Budd or the equally mysterious and ineffable intruder in Pasolini's *Teorema*. When Vitti and Stamp, both so serious and downbeat, are made to sing and dance, the results are embarrassing rather than comic: the dissonance between actors and roles works against the material.

Only Dirk Bogarde, with dyed gray hair, in a high camp performance as the outrageously effeminate villain, seems to be enjoying himself. It is a broad vaudevillian turn, at the opposite end of the acting spectrum from his customary subtlety and understatement. He plays the comic homosexual sadist with the zest and abandon that Vitti and Stamp, as well as Losey, lack.

Modesty Blaise is not a successful film on any level. Losey hasn't the temperament to make a light satire, or to sustain a staccato rhythm throughout, or to stage big-action set pieces; and his interest in decor almost overwhelms the film. As Penelope Houston commented, "The mood is that sort of interior decorator's sophistication which has allowed itself to lose sight of any relationship between purpose and effect."[17] Losey hasn't managed to coordinate the film's various levels so that it can be enjoyed at once as a sexy thriller and as a self-conscious satire of the Bond capers. His evident disapproval of the genre gets in the way; he isn't relaxed enough, or good-natured enough, to let audiences simply have fun with a stupid action story on its own terms. "At his Cannes press conference," Penelope Houston reported, "Losey seemed to want to be sure we all realized there was more to *Modesty Blaise* than met the eye. But what more? And for that matter, in this inescapably flimsy context, why more?"[18]

The film is an anomaly in the Losey canon. Losey lost control of

his material in a way he never has elsewhere. The failure of *Modesty Blaise* is proof positive of his unwillingness to turn himself into a genial, popular craftsman, a genre director able efficiently and selflessly to follow the orders of a front office demanding a blockbuster delivered to formula.

4

The Servant

LOSEY'S COLLABORATION with Harold Pinter occurred at precisely the right moment in his career. In 1963, when the director
and the playwright began work on the first of their three films
together (to date), Losey had been in England for over a decade,
during which time he had had to reconstruct his career. His growing
reputation in Hollywood erased by blacklisting, Losey had arrived
in England as an unemployed and virtually unemployable exile.
Gradually, through persistence and skill, he began to carve out a
place for himself in the British film industry as a director of stylish
melodramas. He gave strong visual treatment to scripts burdened
with generic conventions. In the minor formula films of this period,
Losey's mise-en-scène both enhances and creates meaning. Working on pulp, Losey demonstrates a growing command of filmic
means of telling a story and of portraying characters. *Eve,* made
immediately before *The Servant* and a culmination of Losey's visual
experiments of this period, is strikingly designed, its luxurious form
almost giddily detached from the film's ordinary romantic triangle
plot. *Eve* represents Losey in the unenviable position of being all
dressed up with nowhere to go.

In most of his work, formal considerations are adjusted in some
measure to content, whereas with *Eve* his interest in visual texture
escalates to self-infatuated proportions: here is the display of form
for form's sake that Losey's critics often unfairly accuse him of; here

87

he famous mirror shot (with Dirk Bogarde and James Fox) in The Servant. *The
mirror's distorting lens symbolizes a transformation in the master-servant relationship.*

is self-indulgent artiness that is more an example of the director's preoccupation with the materials of his craft than a purposeful harnessing of manner to matter. What Losey's elegant mastery of mise-en-scène in *Eve* indicates more than anything else is the need for a good strong script—and in Harold Pinter's adaptation of Robin Maugham's novella, *The Servant*, he found one.

The sensibilities of the director and the playwright are ideally matched; Pinter's style released and refined aspects of Losey's. Pinter, in 1963, had only recently established himself as a preeminent British dramatist. His one-acts—*The Room, A Slight Ache, The Dumb Waiter*— and his two full-length pieces—*The Caretaker* and *The Birthday Party* —were linked to contemporary experiments in theater of the absurd while claiming a distinctive voice of their own, one that critics very quickly (and to the playwright's displeasure) labeled "Pinteresque." The Pinter play, at any rate, has several particular trademarks. The action is confined to a single room which, at first, seems like a realistic space: the plays begin, typically, with small talk among ordinary-seeming characters in a nondescript environment. The space, invariably, is invaded, and the ensuing confrontation between the original occupants of the "room" and the newcomers assumes symbolic significance. The "room" in Pinter, which the characters at first cling to as refuge and shelter, becomes the arena wherein their deepest fears, guilts, and paranoia are exposed.

The playwright's characters use language to mock and to punish each other. Language is a means of invasion. Isolated words and questions, spoken with insidious repetition, acquire an accusatory edge and become the chief weapons in the psychological warfare that is at the center of each of the dramas. Though the character's mutual baiting is nasty, fiercely aggressive, it is almost always indirect. The combatants do not threaten and goad each other in head-on collisions as, say, in Strindberg or O'Neill, but in devious and subtle ways; their animosity, often ferocious, potentially violent, is nonetheless muted, evasive, and therefore all the more dangerous. The real dramatic conflict in Pinter is not so much between characters as in the tension between what the characters say and what they don't say, between statement and implication.

Pinter's indirect method has been compared to Chekhov's. Although the tones of the two playwrights differ—Chekhov's objective compassion for his characters is in striking contrast to Pinter's mock-

ing superiority toward his creations—their writing shares a throbbing subtext. In Pinter, as in Chekhov, what the characters say often masks their real feelings: underneath bland conversation about the weather lives may be falling part. In Chekhov, the foreground action, the private drama of misalliance and unrequited love, represents a larger social framework, the passing of an era, the erosion of a class and a way of life, whereas Pinter's work isn't attached to such a large social canvas; its frame is much more circumscribed; the direction of the drama is inward, toward psychological exposure rather than outward, toward society and politics.

Beneath the deceptively naturalistic echo of their chit-chat, their badinage, Pinter's characters are engaged in fierce power struggles as husbands and wives, parents and children, lovers and friends enact allegories of dominance and submission: the master-servant theme is a recurrent motif in the plays. To achieve mastery of the "room," the characters perfect a vocabulary of intimidation. Victimizer and victim square off against each other, poised either to attack or to be attacked as the plays become charades of sadomasochism.

Pinter dramatizes these struggles for control in a style distinctive for its own control. The language in the plays is as lean as their stories. Plot and dialogue are elliptical, "mysterious." Since details about character and situation are calculatedly withheld, the action seems curiously suspended in time and place: the "room" becomes microcosm and metaphor; the stories, related in such skimpy detail, take on allegorical dimensions. Though the speech teases us with naturalistic overtones, it is a mockery of the way real people speak. The bare, allusive dialogue is as surreal as the stark narrative development and the emblematic characterizations. Pinter mimics the way people hide behind words; since confusing the opponent is one of the chief weapons in the characters' verbal assaults on each other, the adversaries refuse to communicate clearly and directly.

Pinter confines his work to a limited range of human experience. In the world of the Pinter play there are no large emotions presented in a vigorous forthright manner. His deeply ironic vision of human interaction is narrow; his presentation of the way people relate (or fail to relate) is expertly controlled and stylized. There is no spontaneity in Pinter, and certainly little joy (though much grim humor); his characters are thrust into an environment in which all their fantasies of paranoia and entrapment are realized, as in a nightmare. The simple diction, marked by its repetitions and fragments, its

jabbing questions, has a ritualistic aura. The ceremonial quality is
enforced by calculated use of silences and pauses. Silences, for the
most part, are used to mark the end of a verbal sequence; pauses
indicate a silence that occurs within a question-and-answer passage.
Pinter's placement of these "intermissions" of dialogue is a large
part of the precise verbal rhythm of the plays, and the most attentive
directors of Pinter, like Peter Hall of the Royal Shakespeare Company, have been known to hold rehearsals in which the pattern of
silences and pauses is precisely calibrated.

Pinter's writing is thus meticulously "scored." Each verbal effect
is carefully orchestrated. His self-conscious and mannered style is
of course susceptible to self-parody and repetition. In the late 1960s,
in chamber plays like *Landscape* and *Silence*, Pinter narrowly skirt-
ed disaster. These dramas for disembodied voices consist of a series
of contrasting monologues. The writing attains a precious lyricism
that threatens Pinter's integrity—these mood-memory pieces have
a starched, recital quality in which Pinter's customary starkness
reaches self-defeating proportions. Recent pieces like *Old Times*
and *No Man's Land*, for all their formal elegance, lack the impact,
the quality of surprise, of his earlier work: the Pinter world has
become predictable in its charged air of mystery and menace, its
nasty wit, its dry sardonic humor (although it has escaped so far an
absolute dead-end self-imitation).

Pinter's temperament thus parallels Losey's. Both seek absolute
control of their medium. Both are calculating stylists who return
again and again to the same kinds of settings, stories, and characters. At the time they began their collaboration both had completed
a body of work that consisted of a set of maturing variations on a
limited number of themes. Both have a predilection for symbol and
allegory, so that the often confined surface of their work rumbles
with levels of meaning. Both avoid direct emotional conflicts—the
tone they aim for is cool, rigorously unsentimental, alienated: their
work is decidedly not intended to warm the heart. They discourage
conventional audience involvement and identification. They do not
respond warmly to their characters; they share (at least in their
work) a distrust of women and of sex and beyond that they seem
to have a negative view in general of human nature. Perhaps because
of this, their work is concerned with fatalistic themes of enclosure
and entrapment. As image and symbol, the "room" is as important

to Losey as to Pinter; characters in Losey are as locked into confined spaces as the people in Pinter's menacing bounded environments. The rooms and houses where people live often attain in Losey's work the status of a character in the drama.

The portrayal of the "room" in the work of the two men differs according to their medium. Pinter's rooms are semiabstract, more bare than in real life. The living room in *The Homecoming*, for instance, resembles a cave, big and dark and threatening and as such reflective of the strange and almost barbaric family of men that inhabits it. The decor of Pinter's rooms is as stark as the language his characters utter. Because he is working in a basically realistic medium—movie audiences expect to see real rooms, or rooms that approximate reality—Losey offers more detail in his rooms; the rooms are filled with objects, and they occupy realistic spatial dimensions, whereas the Pinter rooms belong to the closed space of theatrical convention.

Losey's films often address themselves to a specific social evil or injustice, whereas Pinter's work never includes a direct social consciousness. Losey inherited from Brecht an interest in joining art and politics, and many of his early films, like Brecht's plays, are designed for the moral and political edification of their audiences. In his earliest pictures, Losey's didactic impulse dominated: the world was divided into forces of good and evil, and characters and situations were presented in simplified, boldly outlined terms. This blatant desire to instruct his audience has never been entirely erased from Losey's work, although his collaboration with Pinter has certainly softened and "corrected" it. Pinter released Losey's latent fondness for ambiguity and nuance, and kindled his enjoyment in not simply handing the point to his audience but in cleverly obscuring it. After his experience with Pinter on *The Servant*, Losey is never again as baldly polemical or as direct as he tended to be in the late 1940s and throughout the 1950s. From Pinter Losey took his feeling for mystery and shading, and his work becomes noticeably more subtle. Losey, on the other hand, helped place Pinter in closer contact to the world outside his rooms.

Losey's work is not, to say the least, rich in humor; his own dour temperament is evident in all of his films, but his collaborations with Pinter retain the playwright's distinctive mordant wit: there are things to laugh at in the Pinter-Losey pieces, as there are almost

no such opportunities in any other Losey film (including the one movie designed, more or less, in a comic vein, the deadly *Modesty Blaise*).

Losey's three films with Pinter—*The Servant, Accident, The Go-Between*—represent his most assured, his most expertly controlled, and his most resonant work. They are brilliant pictures that show a surprising range of texture and theme. *The Servant* and *The Go-Between* dramatize class struggles between masters and servants, aristocrats and commoners. *The Servant* has a contemporary setting, while *The Go-Between* takes place in 1900. In both stories, the notion of class hovers dictatorially over the characters, forcing them to act unnaturally. In both films, class considerations—the idea that some people are better than others, have more rights and privileges than others—smash personal relationships and ultimately destroy lives. The two films address the class question from different angles, but in each the rigid structure of British society is condemned as antinature and antilife. The two films admit more of the social world than is customary for Pinter: the struggles among the characters are enacted against a palpable social framework, a world governed by graded separations among social ranks. *Accident* has a smaller compass than *The Servant* or *The Go-Between*. The theme, though, as in *The Servant*, is the Pinteresque one of the invader: an enigmatic young woman who comes to study at Oxford stimulates male insecurity and competitiveness among dons and students.

Of the three films, *The Servant* most nearly approximates the "baroque" label that is often attached to Losey's work. It contains the greatest stylistic range, moving by subtle degrees from daydream to nightmare. *Accident* is the most subdued of the trio, a miniaturist examination of middle-aged malaise. *The Go-Between* is the quintessence of the Losey-Pinter style, representing the most synchronized union of form and content among their collaborative efforts.

Working in an essentially realistic medium, Pinter makes only minor adjustments in his stylized dialogue. His characters retain the clipped utterance, the veiled insinuations, the arch ironies and repetitions familiar from his plays. The film characters live in a realistic environment, yet they speak in the same deceitfully "real" way as the characters created for the closed frame of the theatrical proscenium. The Pinter people on film say even less than their stage counterparts—they are given no long speeches, as in the

climactic moments of *The Birthday Party* and *The Caretaker*, and no lyrical flights. The language, if anything, is even leaner than that in the plays. Confrontations often consist of isolated phrases and brief, stabbing questions. Revelations of character and theme are transmitted with marvelous economy. As a screenwriter Pinter conserves energy, using as few gestures as possible.

In the plays Pinter organizes the action, more or less, as a series of duologues, the beginnings and endings of which are indicated by thunderous silences. For his screenplays, Pinter's structure is more varied, to accommodate the greater number of locations and the more complex time span that are possible in films. The overall structure of the films, though, like their dialogue, is elliptical: transitions of time and place are curt, so that the films have an unusual, arhythmic movement. Quick cutting from scene to scene is analogous to the syncopated rhythm supplied solely by language and silence in the plays.

For all its deceptively dictaphonic ring, language in the screenplays is stylized—and it requires the subtly stylized framework that Losey gives it. An absolutely straightforward rendering of the Pinter dialogue would betray its ironic and astringent spirit, its cultivated manner. Losey's calculated compositions, his purposeful placement of actors within the frame, lend sturdy visual support to the droll, rhythmed language.

For each assignment, Pinter was adapting a novel, transforming someone else's idea into his own distinctive mold. In each case he had to change the novel's point of view. The three stories are supervised by first-person narrators whose perspectives are not readily available to the filmmaker. Pinter discards the narrator of Robin Maugham's *The Servant* altogether, while he retains the narrators of *The Go-Between* and *Accident* as participants in the action. Except briefly for *The Go-Between*, Pinter avoids the voiceover technique that would tie the action to the point of view of a specific character. The subjective and introspective methods of the novels are thus transformed into the objective presentation of events that is more congenial to film.

His achievement is considerable. In the case of both *The Servant* and Nicholas Mosley's *Accident* he was adapting mediocre material; only with L. P. Hartley's *The Go-Between* was he faced with the responsibility of adapting work of genuine literary distinction to a new medium. In each case, he follows the main narrative thrust of

the novels and even retains isolated chunks of original dialogue. As
case studies of how to adapt novels into films, the three screenplays
are exemplary. Pinter is able to convey the essence of pages of
novelistic exposition in a single brief scene or a charged interchange
between characters. He knows how to select action and dialogue
that will be comfortable within the film frame.

Pinter was drawn to the three novels because they express themes
and, beyond that, a world-view he finds compatible. He has had
the tact to respect the novelists' original concepts and the skill to
give the unmistakable Pinter touch to their material. And Losey has
respected Pinter's brilliance without subduing, or denying, his own
particular gifts. The result of these three-way collaborations are
three remarkable films rich in mood, atmosphere, and sensibility.

The Servant

The apparent simplicity of *The Servant* is as deceptive as the title
character. This story about the relationship between a man of prop-
erty and his manservant reverberates with social and psychological
implications. Using a fable about class antagonism as their base,
Losey and Pinter have constructed a multi-layered allegory, a richly
textured tragicomedy whose pertinence extends beyond the British
social system which provides its foreground setting.

Tony, a man of "class," advertises for a gentleman's gentleman.
Barrett, with many years of experience in service, answers the ad.
The two set up house in a building Tony has just bought. There are
two female visitors to the house. The first is Tony's fiancée, Susan,
a girl very much of the proper class. The second is Vera, who is
introduced as Barrett's sister, though in fact she is his fiancée. Both
women disrupt the male household. Susan is jealous of Barrett, and
resents his growing control over Tony's house and life. With Barrett's contrivance, Vera also separates the two men when she succeeds in seducing the master. When Tony discovers that Barrett
and Vera have been enacting a masquerade, he expels them from
his house.

Left on his own, Tony is helpless. The house gets messy. Dishes
remain unwashed. His bed is unmade. He is unshaven. He with-
draws further than ever from Susan. Through a chance encounter,
he meets Barrett in a pub. Barrett pleads to be allowed to return,

claiming that he didn't intend to betray Tony but that he was "besotted" by Vera, who has left him for another man. Tony takes him in again. But this time their relationship has little of the decorum—the respect for class differences—that defined it the first time around. Barrett talks back to Tony and treats him, in fact, with open scorn, while Tony responds to Barrett more and more as a buddy, as one of his own. Susan and Vera make one final visit each to this den of masculine competition and understanding. Vera comes to ask for money; Susan, to stake one final claim on Tony's attention. Her appearance coincides with a party the two men are having with some bizarre-looking women. Barrett expels both Susan and the invited guests, leaving him and an inebriated Tony in sole possession of the house.

The plot is constructed with elegant economy. Character, action, and setting operate simultaneously on realistic and symbolic levels. The emblematic characters—the "master" and the "servant"—are also fully convincing as individuals. Tony is thus the type of the British master class and a complex individual character. He is a spoiled, weak-willed young man who has been protected all his life, without ever really knowing it, by class privilege. Never having questioned his inherited code of conduct, he is vulnerable to his servant's subversive use of the class system.

Barrett both conforms to and departs from the traditional servant "type." He is deferential, glad to be of use (like Eliot's self-effacing J. Alfred Prufrock), circumspect. His mask of politeness, however, his seeming acquiescence to the class code, covers terrific resentment. Like a caged animal he lies in wait, ready to attack his master at the earliest opportunity. Unprotected by social privilege, he takes risks, he defies social convention, as he subtly and resourcefully undermines his employer. Barrett attacks Tony in two ways: by making Tony so dependent on him that the master cannot fend for himself, cannot run his house or his life without his trusty manservant, and by disrupting Tony's alliance with Susan. Barrett introduces Vera as both a diversion and a snare—in succumbing to her sexual invitation, Tony loses further self-respect. His infatuation with her erodes his power. In his strategies to unseat his master, then, Barrett is shrewdly manipulative. On one level, his Mephistophelean campaign against Tony can be seen in specifically social terms, as the revolt of the mistreated peasant against an inept master, as an attack on the rigidity and exploitation that define the

British social structure. In this political context Tony's passiveness might be read as an indictment of an entire class whose power is based on an outmoded and inequitable social system. Tony has not earned his position, his power derives from an inheritance rather than from his own accomplishments. The film implies that the desiccated aristocratic tradition that Tony embodies is doomed.

Tony's "conqueror," though, is no messianic hero, cleansing the system of its injustices and its obsolescent rituals. Barrett is a decidedly ignoble victor, if victor he really is. His methods are deceitful—he is a slippery, reptilian, altogether unwholesome adversary, and his gradual dominance over his employer has no higher purpose than simple delight in the downfall of a member of a class that has exploited him. Moreover, Barrett's tenuous victory is threatened by weaknesses in his own character, since the film implies that he is liable to sink to the same depths of lethargy as his erstwhile master. Barrett's claiming control over the house, then, is not to be interpreted as a victory in the Marxist class struggle: *The Servant* is decidedly not an endorsement of proletarian revolt, a vindication of agile left-wing strategy over unthinking right-wing tyranny. The film is anything but a call to action!

The Servant does not really take sides in the class struggle it symbolically reenacts. Master and servant are observed dispassionately, with remarkable political detachment, in fact. Both sides are almost equally culpable, equally deficient and self-serving. That master and servant have reversed roles carries no affirmative social message. "England" is no better off governed by the cunning servant than it was under the rule of the bland and guileless and incompetent master. The film is thus not a polemic about how the British class system should be either abolished or reorganized. Rather, it suggests that the master-servant relationship is more than a social or political one, that it issues from and expresses an elemental psychological need that transcends a specific social framework. Losey said that, for him, the film "is simply about servility—as an attitude of mind."[1] Though it is rooted in the British class system, the film is a universal study of psychological submission and dominance. Tony and Barrett, in this context, are deeply complementary personalities. Tony requires a boss, someone to order and control his life; clearly, before Barrett's appearance, Susan was preparing to do just that: to take over. Barrett, on the other hand, needs someone to control; he requires an emotional invalid who will permit him

to exercise his own lust to dominate. Barrett stage-manages all the action, manipulating Vera and Susan as skillfully as he does Tony. He calls in Vera to pose as his sister when he wants to set a trap for Tony, and he calculatedly edges Susan out of the house, de-sexing her and making her superfluous to Tony's needs. His designation of "servant," clearly, is ironic, since in this household, the servant is master, the master is a willing slave. Barrett and Tony are thus partnered in a perfectly poised sadomasochistic relationship. Tony invites his own destruction. He wants to be relieved of his responsibilities, to be cared for, to be cradled and coddled, and at the same time he wants to be punished for playing the role of the helpless child.

It is, then, as a psychological and sexual allegory that the film is most richly suggestive. The two men satisfy each other's fantasies; they "complete" each other in ways that are mutually self-destructive. We are left at the end with the impression that their menage will continue indefinitely, that in their isolated degradation they have achieved what is for them an inverted state of grace. The homosexual aura of this tangled love-hate relationship is veiled, implicit, though continuously felt as a force that binds the two men and that renders the women at first intrusive or diversionary, and, at last, merely unnecessary. The closest approximation of a love scene in the film is this sly exchange of "vows" between Tony and Barrett:

BARRETT. You know sometimes I get the feeling that we're old pals.
TONY.   That's funny.
BARRETT. Why?
TONY.   I get the same feeling myself. [Pause.]
BARRETT. I've only had that same feeling once before.
TONY.   When was that?
BARRETT. Once in the army.
TONY.   That's funny. I had the same feeling myself there, too. Once.[2]

Pinter and Losey have transformed a heavy-handed novella into a pulsing allegory. While retaining Robin Maugham's basic story line, Pinter has made a series of well-judged cuts and embellishments. Maugham uses a first-person narrator, a friend of Tony's, who reports, often at second hand, on the developing relationship between master and servant. The narrator thus keeps us at a con-

siderable distance from the drama at the same time that he tells us what to think of the characters. Maugham's narrator despises Barrett and is severely critical of Tony's weakness. Barrett is presented in the story as outrageously effeminate while Tony is an abject moral coward, so the characters lack the shading and nuance of the film's treatment of them. Eliminating the stuffed-shirt narrator as both shaping consciousness and participant in the action allows Pinter to dramatize the story in a more straightforward way, without moralistic intrusions.

In addition to reducing the number of characters, Pinter presents the action in fewer settings, and with fewer incidents, than in the novella. Backgrounds, characters, and events are thus confined to an irreducible minimum. Right from the beginning of the film, the house is established as the central (and indeed the only really necessary) setting. As in his plays, Pinter arranges the action as a series of ritualistic psychological combats: from the opening moments it is clear that the film's theme is psychological warfare, with the house serving as the arena. Out of the shapeless novella, Pinter has carved an immaculate structure in which the action is rendered as a progression of psychological games which determine positions of power and subservience.

From the beginning, in subtle ways, Tony and Barrett test each other's masculine strength. When they are reunited after Tony has expelled Barrett, their relationship seems to dwindle to nothing *but* games: they play catch, and an eerie version of hide-and-seek. Vera's seduction of Tony is presented as a charade. Her campaign, under Barrett's strict direction, is waged as a series of quick enticements: she wears a short shirt, she is "caught" taking a bath in Tony's tub, she talks about the heat in the kitchen.

Typical of Pinter's methods, small matters, objects, things, possessions, and isolated words and phrases attain sinister significance. Details in the decor of Tony's house often are the chief weapons in the fight for control. Susan places a vase of flowers in Tony's bedroom when he is ill. Barrett attempts to remove the flowers. Susan orders him to leave them where they are. When Susan announces open warfare, she enters the house to redo Barrett's interior decoration, to liven up the color scheme.

Pinter plans the action in spare, elliptical, fragmented scenes. A good example of his skeletal method occurs near the end, as Tony and Barrett sit amid the clutter and semidarkness that reflect their deterioration.

> Morning. TONY and BARRETT in the dining-room. BARRETT
> is smoking, sitting, doing a crossword puzzle. TONY is looking
> out into the garden. Long silence. Children's voices outside.

TONY. I wouldn't mind going out for a walk. It must be quite nice out.
[He remains still. BARRETT continues his crossword. Silence.]

In language and imagery this brief scene powerfully conveys the
paralysis that has overtaken both master and servant. An equally
striking instance of Pinter's economy is the wordless scene, earlier
in the film, when we see Barrett seated in the kitchen (this is the
first time we have seen him in other than a rigid position of attention), picking his teeth. His mask of decorum dropped, his face
for the first time unfrozen, he looks epicene; in a flash, we know
the vulgarity and evil that lurk beneath the pristine facade.

With clean, sharp, thrifty strokes, Pinter constructs the action to
expose successive layers of the characters: each new contest reveals
further aspects of their moral failure until, in the nightmarish party
scene at the end, they appear utterly hollow.

Although he has frequently retained Maugham's original dialogue, adding to it his own distinctive signature of repetition, pause,
silence, and ellipsis, Pinter invents dialogue for two scenes, one in
a restaurant and one at an aristocratic country home. (Both scenes,
significantly, are among the few that take place outside Tony's
house.) The droll tone of these passages is quintessential Pinter.
The restaurant scene consists of isolated scraps of conversation
among pairs of customers. In addition to Tony and Susan, three
pairs of diners claim our attention: two very austere-looking women;
a curate and a bishop; and a man and woman of society.

> Interior. Soho restaurant. Day. TONY and SU-
> SAN eating main course, with wine. Silence.
> Camera passes them to middle-aged woman and
> young woman sitting at table.

OLDER WOMAN. What did she say to you?

YOUNGER WOMAN. Nothing.

OLDER WOMAN. Oh yes she did. She said something to you.

YOUNGER WOMAN. She didn't. She didn't really.

OLDER WOMAN. She did. I saw her mouth move. She whispered
something to you, didn't she? What was it? What
did she whisper to you?

YOUNGER WOMAN. She didn't whisper anything to me. She didn't
whisper anything!

SUSAN.	Why don't we go away. . .for a few days. . .mm?
TONY.	Where?
SUSAN.	Anywhere.
TONY.	Agatha and Willy Mountset have invited us down actually.
SUSAN.	Well why don't we go there?
TONY.	Yes, we could I suppose. . . .
	. . . . .
BISHOP.	And where are you creeping off to now, my son. . .ah?
CURATE.	Nowhere Your Grace, nowhere. . . . Nowhere at all.
BISHOP.	Is that a fact?
SUSAN.	Why don't you just tell him to go?
TONY.	You must be mad. (Pause.) You just don't care about my. . .and what it amounts to is it's my judgement you're criticizing. It's not only ridiculous it's bloody hurtful.
GIRL.	(at other table) They were gorgeous—absolutely gorgeous.
MAN.	Were they really?
GIRL.	I'm sorry. I'm a fool.
SUSAN.	You are.
TONY.	Well. . .I mean. . . .
GIRL.	Divine, but I simply couldn't get them on.
MAN.	Pity!

The conversations, which punctuate a tête-à-tête between Tony and Susan, are edged with tension; in subtle ways the characters are vying for control and their quiet, pitched battles echo the growing division between Tony and Susan as well as the larger struggle between master and servant. Because we have no background information about the other diners, their exchanges have an air of mystery; because the dialogue has the suggestion of threat and intimidation, it creates an edgy atmosphere; and because the very decision to include these other characters, when the developing tension between Tony and Susan is all that ought to concern us, is itself bizarre, the entire sequence acquires the droll, sly humor, the suggestion of put-on, that is always a part of the texture of Pinter's work. This delicious passage, then, is a miniature summary of Pinter's comic technique, and its presence adds a delightfully idiosyncratic touch to the film.

The scene in Lord and Lady Mountset's drawing room provides another dry grace note. The brief passage of conversation reveals an entire world-view, one of upper-class insularity and vacancy.

LADY MOUNTSET.	Well I'm absolute certain you'll be fascinated by Brazil.
LORD MOUNTSET.	Oh yes.
LADY MOUNTSET.	I was in the Argentine of course, briefly, as a girl. . . . I was certainly fascinated by the Argentine.
TONY.	It should be very interesting.
LADY MOUNTSET.	Fascinating, Tony darling.
LORD MOUNTSET.	How many cities are you going to build?
SUSAN.	Three.
TONY.	Yes, it's—quite a big development.
LORD MOUNTSET.	In the jungle?
TONY.	Not exactly in the jungle, no sir. On the plain.
SUSAN.	Oh but some of the jungle will have to be cleared, won't it?
TONY.	Some of the jungle, yes. A little bit.
LADY MOUNTSET.	That's where the Ponchos are, of course, on the plains.
SUSAN.	Ponchos?
LORD MOUNTSET.	South American cowboys.
SUSAN.	Are they called Ponchos?
LORD MOUNTSET.	They were in my day.
SUSAN.	Aren't they those things they wear? You know, with the slit in the middle for the head to go through?
LORD MOUNTSET.	What do you mean?
SUSAN.	Well, you know. . .hanging down in front and behind. . .the cowboy.
LADY MOUNTSET.	They're called cloaks, dear.

Lord and Lady Mountset are remarkably aloof. Out of politeness, they ask about Tony's plans to carve out a city in the Brazilian wilderness. Their confused geography and their misuse of "poncho" for "gaucho" and "cloak" for "poncho" are droll signs of aristocratic disdain and absent-mindedness. Charged with a dry, nasty humor, this scene indicates the way in which Pinter embellishes the theme with eccentric touches throughout the film.

Losey's direction enhances the tone of Pinter's lean, incisive screenplay. Through decor, camera work, editing, sound, and di-

rection of actors Losey fully realizes Pinter's intentions. Many of Losey's choices—the way he edits or uses the camera, the kinds of compositions he arranges within the frame—are certainly familiar from his earlier work; but he brings to the assignment a maturity and ease, a ripe command of the grammar of film, that far surpass his previous achievements. In almost everything he earlier signed his name to he was clearly an interesting director, one with an unconventional sensibility and a sense of the formal possibilities of film. With *The Servant,* he is no longer merely unusual or eccentric, he is no longer something of an oddity, but a director of the first rank, an absolute master of his craft.

Losey has always been interested in where his characters live. In *The Servant,* decor takes on crucial thematic significance. The house is the central icon in the film, an index of the characters' taste, their place in society, and their relationship to each other. The house assumes different personalities during the course of the film, reflecting the evolution of the master-servant contract. Like places in many Losey films, the house holds an equal status with the people who live in it. At first, as Barrett enters it for his initial interview, the house is bare, its period of disuse indicated by the peeling plaster and the remnants of hideous flowered wallpaper. The place feels gray, uncared-for. Once Barrett and Tony set up house, the worn, faded rooms begin to glow. Barrett's taste in interior design is severe, expensive, neoclassical: a well-placed lamp here, an elegant painting there, a vase of flowers arranged to set off a table or to finish a corner, a mirror to open up a tight space. No clutter, no confusion—"Barrett's" house has an immaculate propriety, and even a kind of warmth: it looks lived in, at any rate. This is indeed the place where a gentleman lives. Susan feels threatened by the house; she misses a feminine touch, and brings in throw pillows to dress up the living room.

The absolute precision of the decor begins to erode as the master-servant relationship unravels. Once the masculine discipline is threatened, the comforting sense of order changes into something else, becomes gradually but irreversibly sinister: the house becomes a place of shadows, hidden corners, secret hideaways. The banisters, and the staircase itself, suggest both separation and imprisonment. Instead of sheltering the characters, the house seems to close in on them; and, like characters in many Losey films, Tony and Barrett are trapped by their environment. The house becomes for both

men a retreat from the outside world. The last action in the film is Barrett's expulsion of Susan and the women at the party. He bolts the door, insuring his and Tony's privacy: there will not be any more intruders. The house belongs to the two of them: and they belong to the house.

Losey's use of the camera reinforces the visual transformation of the house. At first, along with Barrett, we explore the place as outsiders, observers; the camera surveys the house in a neutral, reportorial manner, picking out details but not in any obvious way "interpreting" the environment for us. The camera glides smoothly through the house in the opening sections, tracking and craning with a purposeful but disinterested inquisitiveness. We are encouraged, through this gracefully roving camera, to pay attention to the decor in a more rigorous way than is usually asked of us in movies. The exploring camera invites us to discover meaning in the setting. "There is a great deal of camera movement," Losey said. "There are a lot of sustained shots. . . that run up to five minutes without any intercutting at all. In taking place in one house, one is obviously going up and down stairs and looking at things from different angles . . . the angles have real motivation, as the movements have motivation. . . . I don't think anybody can accuse it of affectation."[3]

Later, as the master-servant hierarchy is undermined from within, the use of the camera changes. It becomes more directly a means of entering into and commenting on the action. Angles are exaggerated. Mirror shots distort the image and suggest both physical and psychological displacement. In Tony and Barrett's game of hide-and-seek, the movement of the camera is noticeably agitated as it travels through the house, up and down stairs: the smoothly flowing rhythm of the opening part of the film has been replaced by nervous, jerky patterns.

The sense of disruption created by both the placement and movement of the camera is intensified by the high-contrast lighting. Toward the climax, the frame is often divided into sharp patterns of light and shadow: the source of light diminishes, and the lighting from below casts elongated and threatening shadows onto the walls. The expressionistic modulations in lighting and composition culminate in the final party scene, which has the surreal, hallucinatory quality of a Fellini revel. For the bizarre finale, Losey offers a controlled view of moral chaos—he presents the characters' deca-

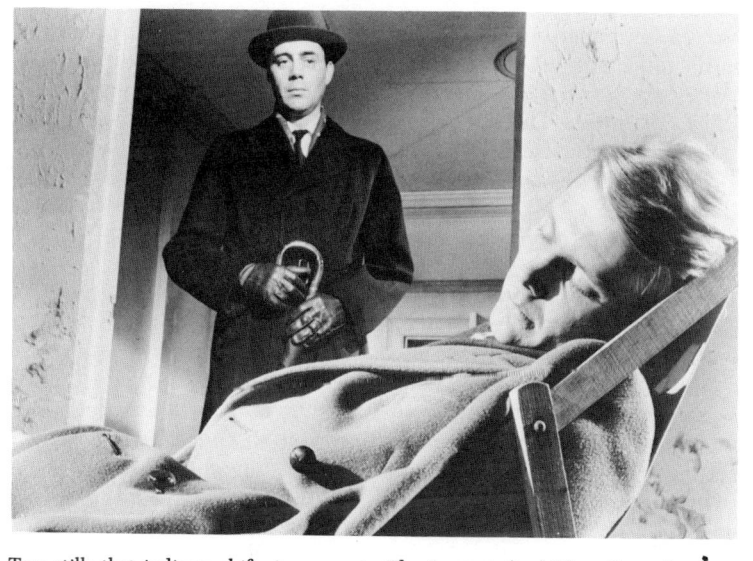

Two stills that indicate shifts in power in *The Servant:* (top) The off-guard master reclines as the erect servant applies for a position; (bottom) the irate master berates his temporarily crestfallen employee.

dence in as calculated a way as he showed their establishment of order. The escalation of visual tension at the end—the theatrical lighting, the extreme angles—creates an atmosphere that is truly unsettling; but it does not suggest that Losey himself joins his characters in their collapse, that he has himself lost control, as some critics suggested who pointed to the climax as evidence of Losey's going haywire on baroque effects. To the contrary, Losey maintains a decided distance from the joyless drugged revelers. The puritan streak that runs throughout his work is perhaps nowhere more blatant than in the harsh way he presents the evidence of his characters' dissolution.

The dark and sinister imagery at the end—the grotesque party scene, followed by Tony's crawling like a helpless child up the shadowed staircase—expresses Losey's condemnation of both his characters. The film's carefully prepared for, surreal conclusion, then, is closely connected to its stern moral judgments.

Losey's placement of characters within the frame is as calculated as his shifts from realism to expressionism. Throughout, the struggle for domination among the characters is underscored by compositional means. The opening encounter between Barrett and Tony indicates Losey's emblematic mise-en-scène. Barrett finds Tony in a back room, stretched out and taking a nap. Tony reclines languidly at the bottom of the frame, as Barrett, rigidly at attention, hovers over him: the placement of the actors provides a visual reversal of their social roles—the master is physically dominated by the servant. The master's laziness and the servant's alertness are thus firmly established through visual means as economical as Pinter's dialogue.

Barrett's threat to the relationship between Tony and Susan is signaled by a recurring triangular composition. Barrett, in the rear of the frame, or entering from the side, disrupts the lovers; he is an intruder who unsettles the tentative balance that Susan is trying to establish with Tony. Vera, the most enigmatic and devious character, is observed less directly, in both visual and aural terms, than the three other characters. We hear her voice over the phone before we see her, and then, when she arrives at the train station, summoned by Barrett as a fellow conspirator, she remains silent, her communication with Barrett held to an exchange of quizzical, knowing glances. Her arrival is intercut with the scene at the restaurant— this is the only occasion in the film in which Losey edits two scenes together. The resulting quality of fragmentation is deliberate: we

are not seeing Vera straight and whole. As she sets about her seduction of Barrett, we glimpse her at the edge or rear of the frame—
an undraped figure behind the frosted glass of the bathroom door,
a leg dangling provocatively from an oversized stuffed chair. When
Tony discovers her in bed with Barrett, we hear her coy, whining
voice while we see only Barrett framed by the doorway of Tony's
room. When Vera returns to the house to ask Tony for money,
claiming that Barrett's story about her running off with another man
is a lie, she seems properly humbled and even pathetic—we tend
to believe her claims of not getting by. Barrett treats her roughly.
He refuses to let Tony give her money, and he brusquely ushers
her out of the house. At the door, however, he pauses, his posture
of authoritarian disapproval relaxing. He rubs one foot against the
other. We don't see Vera, as she is already outside the house. But
Barrett's posture suggests that perhaps the two are still in collusion
against Tony. This moment of calculated visual ambiguity is a brilliant stroke, and it is entirely Losey's idea. In the published screenplay, Barrett orders Tony to throw Vera out, and we aren't given
the possibility that Barrett and Vera may still be leagued against
Tony. That one ambiguous pause, seen from a long shot, with Barrett's back to the camera and Vera hidden by the door, represents
Losey's perfect rapport with Pinter's teasing methods. It is a marvelous moment that exemplifies the atmosphere of uncertainty and
paranoia that enshrouds the house.

Losey breaks the mounting claustrophobia with occasional and
aptly timed shots of the tree-lined square on which the house is set.
(*The Servant* was filmed on Royal Avenue, in Chelsea—the exterior
of the house is one that directly faces Losey's own house on the
other side of the square.) These few shots suggest changing weather
conditions and the passage of seasons, and provide brief glimpses
of a world outside the house. To validate external reality, Losey
also uses the recurrent sound of children's voices. We never see
the source of the voices, but their existence outside the frame deepens the time-space dimension of the image and adds an almost
subliminal tension. Perhaps few viewers will be consciously aware
of the laughing children, and yet the sound subtly modifies the way
we respond to the scene: the children's voices outside are a contrast
to the increasingly slanted reality within the house.

Losey's sound tracks are always immaculate. Realistic sounds, as
in *The Servant*, are used selectively, to heighten mood. The chil-

Symbolic choreography in *The Servant:* (top) The master looks up longingly at the seductive Vera (Sarah Miles); (bottom) in the pointed triangular composition, the servant separates the master from his resentful fiancée (Wendy Craig).

dren's off-screen voices are a subtle sound effect, whereas the use of a dripping faucet during Vera's seduction of Tony is an example of Losey's predilection for blatant symbolic touches. The measured sound of the dripping water is ominously magnified so that the unnatural sound, together with the chiaroscuro lighting, underscores the threatening and joyless quality of the seduction. Sound and image together telegraph Tony's arousal and his downfall.

The cool jazz score that Losey applies generously throughout the film is reminiscent of the music he used for most of his B melodramas in the 1950s. The languorous, sinuous rhythm of the music suggests an aura of casual eroticism; the twists and curves of the music complement the tracking, gliding camera. The same melody changes mood to match the shifts in the story; at first almost gay and frolicsome, it takes on a gloomy aura toward the end. Tony keeps playing the same song, "All Over," again and again. The singer is Cleo Laine, whose rich, purring, deeply sexual voice is also faintly threatening. The lyrics are too patly appropriate, however—Cleo sings of a dissolving romance, of a man who seeks withdrawal and retreat—and the song is overused to the point of monotony; we get the idea long before Losey is willing to let go of it.

Losey's visual and aural enhancement of the material, striking as it is, serves primarily as the frame for four brilliant performances. Of a piece with the writing and the mise-en-scène, the acting is both realistic and subtly stylized. The actors play social types, yet they endow their emblematic characters with the nuance and shading of psychological realism. The flat characters, participants in a moral fable, are given flashes of a complex inner life. We see them from the outside, and we are encouraged to judge them harshly for their weakness, their hypocrisy, their urge to dominate and control or to be subservient, and for their selfishness. Losey observes them coolly, but their decline and degradation are harrowing; the intensity of the performances works against Losey and Pinter's ironic detachment so that *The Servant* is not, finally, another cold Losey film (as the director's critics claimed). We become involved in the characters' deterioration, and watching the film takes a toll on our emotions despite the distancing wit and irony. *The Servant* provides an exhausting and full experience in a way that *Accident*, the following Losey-Pinter collaboration, does not.

The actors portray their characters in a complex double focus,

and we see beneath the social masks, the traditional class posture that the British system has enforced on them. James Fox, as Tony, reveals beneath the aristocratic facade the weakness and dependence, the soft center, that is the character's undoing. Fox has an almost childlike cuteness. He is blond, with immaculate, bland features, and he always looks as if he is about to melt. Fox makes Tony easy and careless—someone just ripe for a fall, while Dirk Bogarde plays Barrett with an angularity that is positively sinister. Dark and brooding, wary, coiled, rapt, his servant is clearly the more secretive and complex character. With his arched eyebrows, his thin, pursed lips, his fussy gestures, erect carriage, and deliberate enunciation, he is almost a parody of an orderly personality. His posture and tone, so slyly subservient, so cunningly mellifluous, inspire discomfort. Bogarde plays the character with a quicksilver combination of intimidating propriety and savage superciliousness. The servant's nastiness, his scorn of the tradition he serves in mock-humility, his thirst for power, all lie palpitating beneath the thin veneer of exaggerated gentility.

Bogarde subtly suggests the character's capacity for evil with a flicker of an eye, a mere suggestion—a whisper—of a sneer, a voice ever so slightly registering disapproval, an ironic twist to the phrasing of a sentence. But he doesn't play Barrett merely as a would-be Machiavelli; he suggests his weakness and his own crippling need to serve. Bogarde plays the scene in the bar, when he meets Tony and begs to be taken back, with seeming sincerity, portraying Barrett as a vulnerable and broken man. When he watches over Tony's decline, Bogarde's interpretation is edged with ambiguity: is Barrett only pretending to share in Tony's deterioration, or has he too collapsed because the master-servant structure has been undermined? Does he, in fact, need the class system as much as Tony does? Bogarde suggests the character's decadence as well as his strength; he reveals that the servant is both tyrant and supplicant. Bogarde does make entirely unambiguous, however, the character's distaste for women. Barrett is an out-and-out misogynist whose supposed sexual attraction to Vera and, at the end, to Susan (when, at the party, he seduces her with wicked indifference) is never convincing.

The menage he governs has decided homosexual overtones. In a markedly unliberated manner, the material implies a link between Tony's weakness and Barrett's decadence and their *possible* hom-

osexuality. This residue of negative associations with homosexuality, whatever reverberations the subject may contain for Losey and Pinter, comes primarily from Maugham's novella, in which Barrett is presented as effeminate, as a prancing, camp caricature. Maugham makes no attempt to conceal his animosity to Barrett, who, in the author's moral scheme, represents abject and irremediable degeneracy. Maugham has written other novels in which a homosexual milieu serves as a backdrop for evil and violence; since Maugham himself is an acknowledged homosexual, these dark stories perhaps contain embittered self-portraits. Homosexuality in Maugham's fiction is almost invariably unsavory and pathological. Pinter and Losey considerably soften Maugham's condemnation of the effeminate or affected homosexual, and Bogarde's subtlety further deepens the character. Unlike the character in the novella, then, the film's servant is not the wicked arch-fiend of a dark homosexual fantasy, but a character whose sexual uncertainty is a part of his generally vulnerable, ambiguous, human presence.

The women are played with a similar double focus. Sarah Miles's Vera is both vulnerable and viperish, a trembling vixen who knows how to use her sexuality. Miles's interpretation is a softer, more balanced version of Maugham's original character, who is a shrill, hard-core nymphomaniac. Miles makes Vera quiveringly sexual, enticing rather than coarse and lascivious, as the character is presented in the novella. Vera is a tart who conspires with Barrett to present herself as a sex object, yet Miles shows us the character's underlying fear and insecurity, her puzzled acquiescence to Barrett, her confusion about why she is being forced to enact a sexual charade. Miles even suggests that Vera may really care for Tony. Droll, ambiguous, sexy, Miles's performance is consistently fresh and surprising.

In the novella, Susan is a more sympathetic character than in the film. She is a friend of the narrator, and we see her through his eyes; we are meant to share his sympathy for her as a woman who has been excluded from her rightful place by an acquisitive and autocratic homosexual. The film holds less sympathy for Susan as a woman ostracized from a male menage and presents her primarily as a representative of a smug and intolerant upper class. Holding to the values of her class, the character regards Barrett as a usurper and a pariah. She cannot respond to Barrett except as a member of the servant class, and therefore as someone who must be made

to keep his place. Because she knows who she is, she is a more skillful antagonist than the wavering and unwary Tony to the social threat posed by Barrett's possessiveness. Susan's arrogant self-assurance inspires Barrett's strategies of revenge.

Losey felt that Wendy Craig, persuasive as she is in the role, did not have the exact manner and accent that would certify her as upper class. But this kind of social discrimination could have meaning only to a British audience. No American spectator is likely to think of Wendy Craig as anything other than a snobbish woman of the British upper crust. Her tight, dry, brittle performance, which avoids any fake sentimental touches, any false attempts to enlist audience sympathy, is superb.

At the time of its release in 1963, *The Servant* seemed to be part of a group of films about varieties of Continental decadence. Iconographically, the film appeared to be a British counterpart to *La Dolce Vita*. Some critics—Pauline Kael was the most vocal—objected to the use of dissipated rich people as representative figures of modern culture. Of what consequence to her, she asked, was the failure of a bunch of rich people to have fun in the big house parties that were the climactic set pieces in films like *La Dolce Vita*, *La Notte*, and *The Servant*? *The Servant* resembles the films of Italian decadence in using rich people as representative social figures and in attaching to their social setting a generalized symbolic significance. But *The Servant* transcends contemporary echoes of early 1960s infatuation with the jaded rich to claim a place for itself as a work of enduring value.

5

Accident

FOR THEIR SECOND collaboration Losey and Pinter chose a story of middle-aged anxiety set in Oxford at summertime. *Accident* is constructed as a series of contests, of games of will and endurance, among its competitive protagonists: Stephen, a forty-year-old philosophy don; William, one of his students; and Charlie, a longtime friend of Stephen's, a popular novelist and sometime don. The rivalry among the three men is sparked by a mysterious and bewitching female student named Anna, whose every glance seems to arouse male lust and uncertainty.

In its dissection of sexual tensions and in the way its characters jockey for positions of superiority, *Accident* clearly recalls *The Servant*. In the earlier film, however, the characters' challenges to each other lead to a progressive moral disintegration, while *Accident* does not have the emotional intensification of *The Servant*, nor does the fate of its characters suggest a general social or political shift. The games in *The Servant* unmask the characters, whereas in *Accident* the characters remain essentially unchanged. *Accident* is a cooler film than *The Servant*. It is an exquisite miniature, a wry cameo portrait of the clash of male egos.

The story begins at the end, with the accident. Stephen, expecting a visit from William and Anna, hears a crash. He runs to the site of the accident to find William's car overturned, with William dead and Anna still alive. He takes Anna back to his house and reports the accident to the police. After they leave, he goes upstairs to see Anna, who is lying on his bed, panting heavily, in deep shock. As he looks at her, the time sequence shifts from the present to the

113

quizzical Dirk Bogarde (Losey's favorite actor) not quite at ease in an Oxford adrangle in Accident.

past. The body of the film dramatizes the events leading up to the accident.

First Stephen (Dirk Bogarde), then William (Michael York), then Charlie (Stanley Baker) becomes infatuated with Anna (Jacqueline Sassard). Designed as variations on a theme, the film consists of jousts, tournaments, and combats both physical and verbal among the three thrusting males. William takes Anna and Stephen rowing. His expert handling of the canoe asserts his youthful vigor and competence; he stands proudly at the rear of the canoe as Stephen and Anna recline languidly, their ease and comfort dependent on his control. To attest to his own bravado, Stephen stands up and attempts to grab on to a low-lying limb of a tree. His timing is off, though, and he falls into the water.

Stephen invites Anna and William to his house to spend a Sunday. Charlie happens to drop by. They play a tense game of tennis in which middle age engages youth as Charlie and Stephen face off against William and Anna. In the background Stephen's pregnant wife, Rosalind, is a passive observer. As they sit in the garden after lunch, Charlie mischievously instructs William in how to write a novel drawn from life. The game he proposes to William is to tell what each of the characters is really thinking: what is going on beneath the placid surface? William's attempts to describe what the characters are feeling is bland. Charlie rebukes him by inventing a spicier interpretation of the garden scene.

CHARLEY. Describe what we're all doing. (WILLIAM looks about the garden.)

WILLIAM. Rosalind's lying down. Stephen's weeding the garden. Anna's making a daisy chain. We're having this conversation.

CHARLEY. Good. But then you could go further. Rosalind is pregnant. Stephen's having an affair with a girl at Oxford. He's reached the age when he can't keep his hands off girls at Oxford.

WILLIAM. What?

CHARLEY. But he feels guilty, of course. So he makes up a story.

WILLIAM. What story?

CHARLEY. This story.

WILLIAM. What are you talking about? (CHARLEY sits up, swats violently at flies.)

CHARLEY. Oh, these flies are terrible.

WILLIAM. What flies? There aren't any flies.

CHARLEY. They're Sicilian horse flies, from Corsica. (CHARLEY shouts across lawn.) Have you heard our conversation? (STEPHEN weeding.)

STEPHEN. Yes!
　　　　ROSALIND lying, eyes closed.
ROSALIND.Yes.
　　　　ANNA carefully places daisy chain around CLARISSA's neck.

　　Charley uses his position as teacher and writer—his adult status—
to belittle William in subtle ways. His absurd, straight-faced description of the flies ("Sicilian horse flies, from Corsica") is a droll
put-down, his tone implying that of course any idiot would know
what kind of flies are buzzing about.
　　William asks Anna to go for a walk. She refuses; she is comfortable
resting. Stephen, testing his manly strength, announces that he is
going for a walk; Anna says she will go with him.
　　William, an aristocrat, invites Stephen to his family's ancestral
home. The chief weekend activity seems to be a game in which all
the male guests participate and which seems like a particularly
vicious version of soccer. Two teams confront each other for possession of a ball. William appoints Stephen goalie and then knocks
into him with his full force. They grapple, as formally dressed ladies
and gentlemen watch the game with polite interest.
　　Charley appears regularly on a television talk show. He is a popular writer and taunts Stephen for being a fusty, cloistered academic.
Stephen says he has arranged an interview with the producer of the
show: he, too, is stepping out into the real world, the *man's*
world, of snappy public relations.
　　On the cricket field, Charley and William block each other's
moves. William catches Charley out as Stephen watches Charley's
defeat with muted satisfaction.
　　Anna, the enigmatic instigator of these exercises in competition
and oneupmanship, observes passively, the princess in her tower
conferring her blessing—or is it her disapproval?—on the knightly
quests. Both Losey and Pinter had been accused before *Accident*
of presenting women in a narrowly emblematic way, as fatal temp-
tresses or destroyers. *Eve* is an extreme instance of the director's
apparent distrust of females, and his tendency to treat women in
symbolic and general ways rather than as individuals. Similarly, in
Pinter's plays, the central focus is almost always on the male characters; like Ruth in *The Homecoming*, women in Pinter are typically
intruders into an all-male enclave, or, like Meg in *The Birthday
Party*, unwitting destroyers of a masculine ego. Several Pinter plays
(The Dumb Waiter, No Man's Land, The Caretaker), like some

Losey films *(Figures in a Landscape, King and Country)*, exclude women altogether. Both Pinter and Losey, then, are primarily concerned with interactions among men, with women often relegated to a distinctly peripheral position. The masculine focus of *Accident* is, therefore, an outgrowth of themes they have each explored on other occasions, and it is perhaps what drew them to the material in the first place.

The four women in the film—Anna; Stephen's wife, Rosalind; Charley's wife, Laura; and Francesca, the provost's daughter and a former girl friend of Stephen's—are seen merely as adjuncts to the men, almost as projections of masculine fantasies. They are observed from a distance, often glimpsed in the rear of the frame (Rosalind watching the tennis game, for instance) or obscured in some way from our view (when Stephen visits Laura, he sees her behind a spraying hose). Significantly, the sequence in which Stephen calls on Francesca, takes her out to a plain restaurant, and then spends the night with her, is done in voiceover, so that the encounter seems to be recalled as in a dream: the counterpoint between sound and image distances the characters, from us as well as from each other, and seems to enclose them in a frame within the frame. In an extreme, though representative way, Francesca is observed, like the other women in the film, more as an object, an accessory to the male ego, than as a person in her own right.

The society the film presents is decidedly sex-coded: the men play according to one set of rules, the women according to another. The men understand each other; the women have their secrets. There are suggestions throughout that the women have a superior perception; they know, without giving their approval to, the kinds of tests of masculine strength in which the men are almost obsessively engaged. Presented from a male point of view, though, the film makes no attempt to reveal the way the women think. Rosalind, standing or sitting in silence most of the time, conveys an aura of inscrutable and Buddha-like omniscience. With the serenity that pregnant women can sometimes have, she sits in mute judgment on the childlike men. Aware of her husband's actual and wished-for infidelities, she nonetheless says nothing, and we are never permitted to see beneath her mask.

In the context of this "man's story," observing Rosalind and Francesca from such a considerable distance is perhaps appropriate; but the ethereal Anna presents a problem. Her characterization, in fact,

is the one real flaw in the three Losey-Pinter collaborations. Anna is meant to be a realistic character, functioning with the other characters in real settings, and yet she is clearly intended to be a symbol of Woman or of aspects of what the creators obviously regard as the Eternal Feminine. She is Eve or Lilith alighting for a time on the Oxford campus. She has been conceived as a presence, not as a person, and Pinter and Losey give her almost nothing to say or do. We are asked to believe that this mere presence is enough to disrupt the lives of a stodgy Oxford don, an earthy popular novelist, and a pampered aristocrat. She is thus a quintessential Pinter intruder— a stranger, mysterious, unknowable, intractable, who has the power to unhinge men whose lives seem firmly rooted.

The invaders in Pinter are typically imagined on the same level as that of the other characters, whereas Anna seems to inhabit some private realm of her own. She not only seems different from the other characters (as Pinter intended), but she has been created in a different style. This generalized, semiabstract presentation of character might be acceptable in a stylized play, but in a film whose action is set in a realistically rendered environment the concept of the character is off balance. Part of the problem with Anna is that the actress Losey selected to play her—Jacqueline Sassard—is neither bewitching (though this, of course, is a subjective matter) nor (this is less a matter of dispute) an actress at all. With uncertain intonations, she delivers her few lines in a flat, singsong voice. Her lack of professional polish is all the more noticeable in contrast to the crisp diction and immaculate phrasing—the ensemble perfection—of the rest of the cast. Sassard doesn't have the presence, the beckoning sexuality, that the role requires; that, indeed, the entire premise of the film rests on. Instead of suggesting the intriguing ambiguity, the attractively mysterious quality that the men are supposedly drawn to, Sassard is simply vague: not there.

The inadequacy of the actress aside, the film's concept of woman as an impassive Eve is disappointingly conventional and naïve. Anna doesn't really do anything except roll her eyes in a vaguely flirtatious way. She registers no identifiable emotions as she simply passes through the scene, a spectral, fleeting presence. After William's death (she was driving, because William was drunk), she hides upstairs when the police come: her instinct for self-preservation at this moment is her one decisive act in the film. At the end, with the help of both Stephen and Charley, she leaves Oxford without

being implicated in the accident. She rides off, scot free, impassive as ever, while one young man is dead, and two middle-aged men have to reestablish the moral order of their private worlds. Yet, is Anna responsible? After all, she hasn't done anything; she is as much the victim of male desire as she is its instigator. Stephen forces her to have sex with him, after the accident, when she is utterly defenseless. The men lead; she follows: or is it the other way around? Victimizer and victim are, in this film, ambiguous designations; since her motives are never examined, since we know virtually nothing about her feelings or her goals, we don't know to what extent she is a temptress, idly courting the favor of one man after another, having an affair with Charley while planning to marry William, or simply the passive plaything of assertive men, doing as she is bid. She seems to be most interested in Stephen, perhaps because he is the least accessible; but, since we never know what she thinks or who she wants, any attempt to describe her feelings is purely conjectural. The victimizer turned victim; the seemingly will-less character having more strength of will than her more assertive antagonists; the fierce and determined aggressiveness of a passive character: these contradictions are of course recurrent motifs in Pinter's work. But here they don't achieve a full richness because the character of Anna has been underwritten and underplayed: she is a cipher at the center of a potentially intriguing Pinter puzzle.

The screenplay nonetheless has many merits. Once again Pinter remodels a distinctly second-rate novel into a taut script. Nicholas Mosley's novel is told from Stephen's point of view, which becomes increasingly private and introspective. Mosley records Stephen's introversion by writing in fragments; the story breaks down, decomposes, into a series of free-form associations which read like a very poor imitation of Joycean stream-of-consciousness. Indirect, cluttered with the metaphorical debris of its protagonist's ruminations, *Accident* is maddeningly pretentious. The scattered images which are meant to indicate the way Stephen's mind works do not further the story or our understanding of the character, so that the style seems more like the author's experimental attempt to render consciousness immediately and directly than an integral way of telling this particular story: the elaborate form of the novel, then, has only the loosest connection to its content. Pinter strips the material of its subjective form, making no attempt to approximate on film the first-person consciousness with which we are trapped in the

novel. "I couldn't find a direct film equivalent to the free-association, stream-of-consciousness style of the novel. It's precious, self-conscious, over-elaborate on film. You should be able to convey the same sort of apprehension not by opening out. . .but by closing in, looking closer and closer, harder and harder at things that are there before you."[1]

No longer is Stephen's consciousness the stage on which the action is set. Stephen appears in every scene of the film, but the events and characters are not filtered through his attitudes as Pinter makes no attempt to translate onto film the novel's Jamesian experiment in limited point of view. Quite the reverse of duplicating or of finding visual equivalents for the interior, increasingly subjective frame of the novel, Pinter presents the story and the characters in a cool, objective manner—we are kept at a distance from all the characters, including Stephen.

As in his work on Maugham's *The Servant*, Pinter "lifts" much of the dialogue from the original source. But in his choice, and his compression, of material, he indicates unerring taste. He turns Mosley's muddy prose into the allusive, rhythmed language that is his trademark. Characters speak in short sentences of mostly monosyllabic words, and they ask a lot of questions that contain hints of threats. The screenplay is constructed of short scenes, some entirely without dialogue, others containing only a word, a phrase, a question and answer thick with implication and innuendo. The ellipses and fragmentation frustrate our emotional commitment to the material while introducing the wry humor that is always a part of Pinter's response to his characters. "Everything in *Accident* is buried," Pinter said. "It is implicit. There is very little dialogue, and that is mostly trivial, meaningless. . .the unforgivable, unforgettable things are never said. . . . One thing happens and then another and eventually an episode closes and something else begins. . . . I do so hate the 'because' of drama. What reason have we to suppose that life is so neat and tidy? In this film, everything happens, nothing is explained. It has been pared down and down."[2]

As in *The Servant*, Pinter's methods of condensation and understatement are often wonderfully suggestive. Stephen announces to Anna: "Philosophy is a process of inquiry only. It does not attempt to find specific answers to specific questions." We hear no more of his lecture than this introductory fragment, yet his formally phrased statement indicates both the character's pomposity (he recalls that

other remote professor of philosophy, the returning son Teddy in *The Homecoming*, written the same year) as well as Pinter's wry disapproval.

A brief scene in a sedate smoking room at Oxford offers a delicious satire of academic insularity. Many of the details of the conversation are borrowed from the novel, but the precision and economy of their arrangement are characteristic of Pinter.

> Interior. Don's Common Room. College. STEPHEN, CHARLEY, the PROVOST and HEDGES, scientist, sit in armchairs, reading. CHARLEY reads a newspaper; the rest, books. Silence.
>
> CHARLEY A statistical analysis of sexual intercourse among students at Colenso University, Milwaukee, showed that 70 per cent did it in the evening, 29.9 per cent between two and four in the afternoon and 0.1 per cent during a lecture on Aristotle.
> Pause.
>
> PROVOST. I'm surprised to hear Aristotle is on the syllabus in the state of Wisconsin.
> Silence.
>
> CHARLEY (still reading from paper) Bus driver found in student's bed.
> Pause.
>
> PROVOST. But was anyone found in the bus driver's bed?
> Pause.
> Did you ever hear the story of my predecessor, Provost Jones, and the step-ladder?
> Pause.
> It's a bizarre story. It'll amuse you. Provost Jones and his good lady decided one day to buy a step-ladder.

The droll exchange reveals Charley's urge to shock and the Provost's devastating detachment. Filled with pregnant pauses and quizzical looks, their conversation is an elegantly deadpan satire of noncommunication.

Pinter's use of implication is so rich that with a single sentence he can summarize the tensions of a complex relationship. "You are not too old for me," Rosalind says to Stephen, after he has spoken to her about his new student Anna. She has sensed his concern about his age, and she wants to reassure him. At the same time, his comments about Anna, though indirect, have inflamed her own insecurity: she too is not so young as she was; she is not the mysterious foreign princess of Stephen's fantasies, but a plain, no-non-

sense British matron, nearing forty herself, who is at the moment very pregnant: "And I am not too old for you,"she says, getting up from her chair to stand over Stephen as she speaks. These two simple, syntactically symmetrical sentences beautifully underscore the characters' teetering relationship.

Pinter has written a sly scene for himself as a preoccupied television executive. The man Stephen has come to see about appearing on a television talk show is in the hospital, and Stephen is referred to an assistant (played by Pinter) who won't stick to the subject, but asks Stephen about Francesca and talks to a fellow employee about their ill colleague. His absentminded patter is a series of diversions: he willfully uses language in order to prevent communication.

As in *The Servant*, Losey's visual style supplies the ideal "frame" for Pinter's verbal style. Losey finds a skillful compromise between the demands of the realistic medium in which he is working and those of the subtly stylized screenplay. His approach to the material is less flamboyant than in *The Servant*—Losey consciously tried to avoid directorial choices that could in any way invite the description of "baroque." Pinter praised "the simplicity and directness" of Losey's treatment of the script: "No elaborations, no odd angles, no darting about. Just a level intense look at people, at things. As though if you look at them hard enough they will give up their secrets."[3] Losey's stylization of physical reality and his techniques of distancing the action are quieter than in *The Servant*, and appropriately so, since *Accident* doesn't have the same symbolic and allegorical thrust as the earlier picture.

Though visually more of a piece than *The Servant*, *Accident* does, in a muted way, contain different textures to enhance narrative development. The opening scenes of the accident and its aftermath look different from the long flashback sequence, most of which takes place during the day, in brilliant sunlight. Through unusually terse cutting, Losey creates in the early scenes an atmosphere of tension and dislocation: the world of objective reality seems altered. The image of William and Anna in the upturned car is especially dreamlike. The landscape, drenched in a strange, moonlike yellow, assumes an almost surreal aspect. Anna emerging from the overturned car in slow motion, her feathered dress blown by the wind, recalls Venus rising from the seashell in Botticelli's painting. Her strangely prolonged movement, the ethereal lighting, the metallic sound effects, the hovering trees that seem to stand like sentinels along the

road, lend Anna an otherworldly aura. This first powerful visual impression of her remains with us throughout the film: rising from the ashes of the accident like a resurrected phoenix, she triumphs over death and chance: she is a survivor.

The natural world, in the body of the film, isn't rendered with the magical overtones of the opening passages. Losey departs from the dominant realism, however, in the interlude between Stephen and Francesca, where the voice over establishes a dissonance between sound and image. The stylistic change sets off this sequence from the rest of the film, giving it a particular emphasis that it doesn't appear to warrant.

Losey frames the film by beginning and ending with a long shot of Stephen's house. The camera is outside the gate that surrounds Stephen's garden: we are placed, right from the start, in the role of outsiders and observers. Losey keeps the camera in a sedentary position for a long take, thereby enforcing on us the importance of the house. Very slowly, the camera moves in toward, but not through, the gate. The length of the shot, as well as its absolutely ordered, symmetrical composition, creates an impression of the solidity of the house and, by extension, of the ordered lives of the people who reside within it. The long-held image of order is counterpointed on the sound track by the screeching sounds of a car accident. Stephen opens the front door, in response to the sounds which threaten the order of the house. The film ends with the same shot of the house, with the camera placed at exactly the same distance outside the gate. Stephen, his children, and his dog go into the house. Again, we hear the sound of the accident, but this time Stephen's door is firmly shut; having been scorched by his experience with Anna, he remains barricaded within his snug compound.

The kind of visual balance and enclosure announced in the shot of the house that opens and closes the film are evident throughout. Characters in exterior as well as interior shots are carefully placed within the frame, and the precise compositions suggest their lack of freedom. Stephen especially is a remote character, and his house, and his office at school, are neat and confining, his environment reflecting his fastidious and limited personality. His house, large and comfortable-looking from the outside, has low-beamed ceilings that seem to weigh down on the characters.

The rigidity of the mise-en-scène provides an ironic contrast to the film's title. In the tight little world that Losey constructs, there

is no room for accident or chance, for improvisation or spontaneity. And there is further ironic clash between Losey's closed frames and the glorious summer setting. The summer world of Oxford, with its streams and fields, is richly though sparingly created; heat and languor envelop the characters. The film has an atmosphere of holiday and relaxation—a perfect background for the release of sexual feeling; but the characters are too tense to be able to enjoy the splendid English summer. In the famous garden scene, the characters (arranged in groups placed at calculated distances from each other) react to the splendor of the day and the setting by mutual baiting. A nasty comedy of manners is played out, in tight-lipped innuendo, against a heroic natural landscape which Losey allows us to see only in small, measured doses. Anna and Stephen go for a walk. Stephen's tension, his inability to reach out to Anna, to express his feelings for her freely and directly, is reflected in the tight framing that offers no sweeping panoramic vistas of the countryside: the character's anxiety seems to shrink the natural landscape.

Like Pinter's screenplay, then, Losey's direction is rigorously ordered and predetermined, calculated down to the most minute pause in the dialogue and the tiniest movement of the camera. Neither the camera nor any of the characters is allowed a single sweeping gesture, a single moment of release or expansion. A recurrent example of Losey's premeditation is his technique of keeping the camera on a scene before and after the characters either enter or depart from it. These scenes, which go on for just a beat or two longer than we would expect, are a visual correlation to Pinter's pauses: in keeping the camera on a landscape or a room for a second or two before a scene begins, or after it is completed, Losey is stylizing his visual syntax the way that Pinter, with his precisely worked out pattern of pauses and silences, stylizes his verbal rhythm. Critics pointed out that this method of visual pause was borrowed from Antonioni and that, like Antonioni, Losey uses it to create a sense of alienation between characters, between character and environment, and between the film and the audience. Losey doesn't overuse the technique to the point where it becomes merely an affectation, or even to the point where the audience is made consciously aware of it, but it does introduce an arhythmic visual beat that further distances the characters.

As in *The Servant*, Losey punctuates the action with visual grace notes. The camera pans the Gothic towers and steeples of Oxford

in the only establishing shot in the film. The pan has no tangible connection to the drama; it doesn't represent what one of the characters sees; it is simply included for its own sake, as yet another stylizing departure from filmic convention. Twice Losey shows a shot of a highway in a pastoral setting which serves as a visual link between Oxford and Stephen's house in the country; the brief shot is an economical means of suggesting the difference between the two places, the passage between which requires a psychic shift for Stephen (one elaborated at tedious length in the novel). There is a charming wordless scene as Rosalind and Anna walk down a country lane. The camera remains stationary as the women walk, in measured pace, into the rear of the frame and then turn left and move out of the top left part of the image. The shot is held far longer than is necessary to convey whatever possible "meaning" the image of the two women may suggest. Its deliberate length, and the static camera, may even indicate a certain ornery relationship to the audience: a defiance of audience expectation. Losey amuses himself with a grace note when, to the rhythm of Oxford bells, he shows a series of close-ups of gargoyles that adorn the Oxford architecture: the sequence is mere visual decoration of the sort that could descend to mannerism if Losey used it more often than he does.

The editing is as poised as the camerawork. The taut angle-reverse-angle cutting is especially appropriate as a way of presenting the various games, all of which depend on the participants' observance of rules. The games—the tennis match, the cricket match, the strange brutal ritual at William's house—are briskly edited. The film's one departure from tight continuity cutting is the slow fade that concludes the "soccer" game—a fitting way of separating this bizarre scene from the rest of the film.

The sound track is elaborate. The progression of sound that accompanies the opening shot—a barking dog, a plane, a car accelerating, braking, and crashing, a medley of barking dogs and crickets—is richly orchestrated. In the garden scene the buzz of flies adds to the feeling of heat and underscores the mounting tension.

Except for the special case of Jacqueline Sassard, the acting is as immaculate as Losey's technique. Unlike *The Servant*, the film almost never becomes more than nuance and implication: repressed tensions never erupt, so there isn't the cathartic satisfaction that

accompanies both *The Servant* and *The Go-Between*. Even more than in *The Servant*, Dirk Bogarde's performance is a matter of inverted eyebrows and small, furtive gestures. Playing a repressed character, whose ordered and fussy life is threatened by his aroused feelings for Anna, Bogarde communicates anxiety with exquisite subtlety. His modulated acting epitomizes the attenuated and rarefied manner in which the film depicts emotion. Deliberately, then, and with great skill, Bogarde designs his performance in a minor key, communicating Stephen's reserve, his unrest, his sexual insecurity, his weariness, his superciliousness, his capacity for cruelty, his wry humor, without recourse to the explosions or any of the big scenes of momentous confrontation or revelation that an actor could count on in almost any other film with the crisis of middle age as its theme.

Stanley Baker as Charley is extroverted, anti-intellectual, vigorous—in presence and delivery, Baker offers a striking contrast to Bogarde. The two actors have given their finest performances under Losey's direction. Losey uses them, not only in this film but in others in which they appear for him separately, as representative male types—the bonhomie, brashness, blatant egotism, and proud virility that Baker always projects is altogether different from Bogarde's more refined and ascetic aura. In *Accident*, the actors' contrasting iconographies become a major thematic focus.

Michael York, who plays William, has a broad face which evokes an image of a peasant more than that of an aristocrat. As a representative of the British upper class, he is less appropriate than James Fox in *The Servant*, but he projects, like Fox, an engaging boyishness that can turn to nastiness. Beneath York's engaging grin and his easy handsomeness there is a surly, sour quality ready to erupt. York plays William as insinuating and supercilious, but also as vulnerable, a spoiled boy not fully equipped to compete on the same level as Stephen and Charley. His aristocratic background gives him an initial edge, perhaps, but the film is a study of sexual rather than class warfare, so his high social place counts for little in the final round. Pummeled by his tutor, by Charley, and by Anna, William is a victim and a patsy: he pays with his life for entering into the sexual competition with the grown-ups; and, beneath the ingenuous smiles and the aristocratic sneers, York manages to suggest the character's doom.

Women are figurines in the man's world that the film sets up.

But through the strength of Vivien Merchant's presence as Rosalind, the character emerges as more of a participant than is indicated in the script. Merchant, married at the time to Pinter (and called by knowing critics Mrs. *Very* Harold Pinter), is, quite simply, the best interpreter of Pinter's work in the world. Her performance as Ruth, the prostitute-wife in *The Homecoming* (on both stage and film), was definitive. Even in the sharply reduced opportunities offered by the role of the wife in *Accident*, there are intimations of Merchant's virtuosity in realizing the full range of her husband's delight in ambiguity and nuance. She delivers her lines with such crisp authority, in a tone of such delicious irony—she seems so wise— that the wife becomes a central focus in the sexual combats in a way that perhaps Losey and Pinter had not originally intended. When Stephen tells her about Charley's affair with Anna, her response ("The bloody bastard!") represents the most forthright expression of feeling in the entire film.

Accident is more closely confined to Pinter's circumscribed depiction of human nature than either of the other films: this is the least charged of the three collaborations, a consummately crafted cameo.

6

The Go-Between

THE THREE Losey-Pinter films share certain formal, tonal, and thematic similarities, but they are not repetitions of a formula. Each of the three films has its own distinct visual personality, its own mood and texture. Of the three, *The Go-Between* is the most generous in its treatment of character, and—up to a point—it allows for a more direct and traditional kind of audience involvement than either of the two earlier works. *The Go-Between* is about an affair, between a lady of station and a farmer, which ends tragically, but, as Losey has said, "It is certainly not a romantic or sentimental piece. It has a surface and coating of romantic melodrama, but it has a bitter core."[1]

Set in the English countryside in 1900, during a summer of record heat, the film recounts a double loss—of a child's innocence, as well as that of the lovers in a doomed affair that crosses class lines. A schoolboy (Leo) is invited to the ancestral home of one of his classmates (Marcus). He develops a crush on Marcus's older sister Marian and, through a series of chance events, he is enlisted as a messenger for both Marian and the farmer (Ted Burgess) with whom she is in love. Proud to carry messages back and forth between the estate to the nearby farm, Leo is unaware at first of the import of his errands. Basking in the attention that Marian and Farmer Burgess bestow on him, he believes that he has been raised to a place of high favor. His adulation of Marian is presexual—he imagines himself as the emissary of a goddess. When he learns the truth about his errands, when he finds out that Marian loves Ted, his childhood fantasy is smashed, and he faces an embittered coming of age.

129

The revelation of the affair has ruinous consequences for the lovers, too. Because of class considerations, Marian must marry a man of her own social level whom she does not love; and Ted, who doesn't have the protections and privileges of class to fall back on, kills himself. The story thus contains a double tragedy: that of the lovers, separated by the rigid and fatal class system, and that of the boy, deeply scarred by the lovers' selfish use of him and by this first disillusioning exposure to the possible results of adult passion.

Like *Accident, The Go-Between* counterpoints two time sequences: the events of the fateful summer of 1900 are seen in retrospect by the adult Leo. "The past is a foreign country: they do things differently there," he announces at the beginning. The older Leo—the Leo of a half century later—is looking back on his young self with a mixture of melancholy and elation. For him, his visit with the Maudsleys had a traumatic and lasting impact. The two discoveries of his visit—the way the lovers used him, and the moment when, held in hand by Marian's distraught mother, he sees Marian and Ted making love—enforced on him an image of himself as an outsider. These early experiences fixed in his mind a picture of love and sexuality as dangerous, criminal, "forbidden"—the adult Leo has never recovered from the boy's perception that passion leads to punishment and perhaps even death. The elder Leo has remained an observer of the world of adult emotion; he is still, fifty years later, a "go-between." A lifelong bachelor, he is dried up inside; but as he looks back on the events of that long-ago summer, he recaptures something of the child Leo's sense of wonder and delight, the child Leo's capacity for romance.

The film's attempt to forge a direct connection between the young go-between and the elderly one is perhaps psychologically facile, and certainly implies a rigidly deterministic view of human nature. The retrospective framework may make the events of the summer of 1900 more central to the development of Leo's character than is psychologically probable; but seeing the action, with Leo, through the distance of time and memory heightens the emotional and symbolic impact of the story. The frame lends to the recollected past something of poetic enchantment and a haunting, lyrical melancholy.

As with his two earlier adaptations, Pinter shifted the subjective point of view of the original to an objective vantage point congenial to films. He retains the novel's time frame, but he does not attempt

to translate into film its limited, interior point of view. The novel is narrated by Leo as he rereads his diary of his visit with the Maudsleys. The elder Leo takes both a kindly and a sad attitude to his younger self, so innocent in the rules of the adult world, so unknowing about the ways that grown-ups devise to create barriers. The novel records, in intimate detail, the process of his moral and psychological development over the course of his fateful visit to his schoolfriend's family, retracing his growing perceptions of the power of the class system. Its focus a private one—the inner workings of a consciousness struggling to come to terms with a strange new world—the novel is clearly in the Jamesian mode. No film can duplicate the novel's fine psychological discriminations, its subtly rendered portrait of the interior process of the boy's dawning rec-ognitions of the rules and the passions of the adult world. In the film, the adult Leo speaks a few lines of narration, but Pinter does not use the character as a shaping consciousness, as a "guide" to our response to the material. He makes no attempt to present the events from Leo's point of view, or to use voiceover narration as an equivalent to the "I" of the novel. The film maintains the es-sentially neutral viewpoint of an outside observer.

The events that take place in the present—Leo's return to the village and to the Maudsleys' house—are filtered, in fragments, throughout the film: the time shifts are disorienting, and meant to be so: an audience seeing the film for the first time will be puzzled at first by the intrusion into the period setting of brief contemporary scenes, with a sleek automobile their chief identifying sign. The scenes in the present, introduced in elliptical fragments, are not "joined" to the period scenes until nearly the end of the film; the juggling of time makes the past and the present commingle in star-tling and unexpected intimacy. The ability of film to "play" with time is here used with particular force, as Losey and Pinter mean to suggest close connections between events separated by a half century.

Pinter's dialogue—characteristically terse, rhythmed, indirect—hasn't in general the same kind of edge as in the two preceding films. The characters don't bait and set traps for each other to the extent that they do in either *The Servant* or *Accident*. Leo is often intimidated by the adults whose behavior he misinterprets: the autocratic Mrs. Maudsley, Marian's mother, is especially a source of discomfort to him, and the remote Mr. Maudsley's repeated

question, "Enjoying yourself?" begins to take on ominous overtones. The atmosphere between Marian and her mother is dense with distrust and accusation. But in general the characters' challenges of each other are concealed beneath a more genteel surface than in the earlier films. Characters at times even address each other in a kindly way. Marian and Ted treat Leo gently, and with genuine warmth, though their interest in him is indirect. The real tension in the story is not between characters but within Leo himself as he begins to adjust his naive childhood vision to the harsh adult reality; and so the language, for the most part, is in a softer and more muted key than is usual for Pinter.

Losey's direction again deepens Pinter's lean, allusive screenplay. Working in ideal harmony with Pinter's tone, Losey "protects" *The Go-Between* from becoming a romantic tearjerker, a popular story about star-crossed lovers. The film's fractured displacements between past and present, and its dry, cryptic dialogue thwart the usual kinds of audience involvement in stories of romantic crisis. Pinter and Losey do not have the patience for a drama of direct or obvious sentimentality, and, significantly, they have selected a story in which the romantic theme is treated indirectly, as an adjunct to the themes of class and of Leo's coming of age. There is no scene in which the lovers meet, or express their feelings to each other: their passion is suggested obliquely, through an excited exchange of letters, through furtive glances, and through Leo's growing understanding. A tearful or impassioned scene between the lovers would be false to the film's essentially dry-eyed tone and to the creators' temperaments: the Losey-Pinter world-view is not that of *Wuthering Heights!*

Still, even if indirect, the love theme is a deeply felt and powerful presence throughout the film. The characters are victims of the class system, destroyed by values outside themselves, by a powerful social tradition which overwhelms them. Because of the enormous pressure they feel as outlaw lovers, Marian and Ted treat Leo with a carelessness that is to have a lasting effect on him. Losey and Pinter regard these three suffering characters with a sympathy that is expressed guardedly, but that nonetheless emerges from their controlled, unemotional style. *The Go-Between* is Losey's warmest film: a genuine romantic tragedy without tears.

To document the power of the class code that dominates the characters, Losey creates two contrasting environments: the or-

dered life at the hall, and the more open world of Ted's farm. Over both hangs the record heat of an English summer; as in *Accident*, the extreme and uncharacteristic heat and the droning buzz of flies create an environment crackling with sexual tension. Running back and forth between the two places, Leo, without realizing it, is tossed between two human possibilities: the tight, closed social world presided over by Mrs. Maudsley, and Ted's open, cavalier life on the farm. Life in the manor house, a microcosm of the British class system, is rendered with a few deft strokes. The formality of this world is suggested by the solemn observance of ritual and the attention to decorum: before breakfast, masters and servants kneel in prayer; at afternoon tea in the garden, the perfect order of the table settings corresponds to the surrounding landscape in which nature has been immaculately clipped and tamed. At breakfast, luncheon, and dinner, Mrs. Maudsley, enthroned at the head of the table, sets agendas for everyone, preplanning their time in neatly ordered segments.

For these scenes of rigid social order, Losey's framing is tight, clean, absolutely symmetrical. His balanced compositions allow no space for the unexpected, no room for spontaneous gestures or displays of open feeling.

The hall has an imposing decor, which we discover along with Leo. The house is dominated by a grand central staircase that implies separation not only between masters and servants, between those who live above stairs and those who reside below, but also between characters of the same class. The rooms are huge and formidable: the breakfast room looks like a chapel; the dining room looks fit only for state occasions. Mr. and Mrs. Maudsley, who barely seem to acknowledge each other's existence, sit on opposite sides of the vast dining hall. Characters have their own rooms, their own place at table, their own section of the lawn: Marian reclines on a hammock which seems to "belong" only to her. Rooms are segregated by sex as well; Leo is admitted at one point, as a special privilege, into the men's smoking room.

The atmosphere at Ted's farm is very different. The small rooms of his cottage are brown and earthy; and his modest dining table is made of rough wood. Throughout the scenes at the farm, the omnipresent sound of animals suggests sexual release and an aura of free and untrammeled natural feeling. First glimpsed as he plunges into the river for a swim, and occupied throughout the film

The go-between conferring with his double-dealing employers: (top) Farmer Burgess (Alan Bates) instructs the boy in the manly art of shooting; (bottom) Marian (Julie Christie) charms him with a dazzling smile.

in working on his land, Ted is an image of natural man, in tune with the sounds and the rhythms of the outdoors. For Leo's encounters with Ted, Losey uses a more open and flowing kind of camera movement than in the formally composed scenes at the hall. His tracking shots, which follow the two characters as they walk through the fields, and his long takes, create a sense of expanding space. We sense Leo's elation in these scenes, his relief at being "released" from the routine at the hall. His first action, when he comes to the farm unexpectedly, on a spontaneous expedition away from the hall on an afternoon "off," is to slide down a haystack—a gesture of freedom that would never be permitted under Mrs. Maudsley's reign. That he slides into a pitchfork at the bottom of the haystack suggests, though, that the farm, too, contains threats and limits to his freedom.

The scenes in which Leo runs through open fields from the hall to the farm are filmed with high-angle long shots that visually underline his exhilaration. These panoramic landscapes in the scenes of Leo's "escape" are more open than anything in the closed worlds of *The Servant* and *Accident*. These scenes are indeed a breath of fresh air, and their expansiveness is enhanced by Michel Legrand's score, which is very different from the cool jazz that Losey used for the two earlier films. Legrand's music is lush and romantic though without the gushing sentimentality that disfigures some of the composer's other movie scores. His main theme has a breathless, staccato rhythm that suggests the movements of a runner and that creates an atmosphere of haste and urgency as well. The music has a melodic fullness, an exuberance, entirely different from the moody jazz that Losey typically favors. Losey uses the music expertly to underscore transitions between the hall and the farm and to highlight climactic moments: the score takes on a particular tension toward the end, as Marian and Ted are about to be discovered. Sometimes Losey withholds the music at expected places: Leo runs into the fields, and the music is delayed for a few beats. Sometimes the music stops abruptly, before his race to the farm is completed. Losey's counterpoint between image and music, his teasing us of the score, adds to the increasing tension.

Since the story centers on a romance that cannot be conducted out in the open, because it violates the rules of the game, none of the characters can express feelings directly or freely. The performances, then, are a matter of varying shades of suppressed emotion,

of constricted passion struggling for release. As the thwarted lovers, Julie Christie and Alan Bates, given no romantic scene together, nonetheless convey the lovers' passion with great force, with such intensity, in fact, that we can believe that Ted would not think life worth living without Marian. Ted's suicide, alluded to cryptically at the end, may seem unconvincing in the light of Alan Bates's vigorous performance: he presents the farmer as such a lusty, natural character, as so free and wholesome, so essentially life-affirming, that the suicide could well seem merely a strained melodramatic device. The "notice" of Ted's death does indeed come as a shock; but Bates has presented the character as so combustible a blend of passion and vulnerability that the tragic outcome is plausible. Without ever seeing the lovers together, except in public scenes where they must pretend to be nodding acquaintances, we are made to believe that their doomed romance has the power to destroy lives.

As representatives of distinct social classes, Bates and Christie are entirely credible. He has an open, appealing, rustic quality, playing here the same kind of natural man that he played opposite Christie in *Far from the Madding Crowd*. Like Bates, Christie has a magnetic sexuality—Losey realized that it was essential to cast the two roles with actors who exude a potent sexual energy. Lounging on the hammock, flirting carelessly with Leo, strolling in the heat on the grounds of the estate, Christie suggests an easy and capacious sensuality, a flowing quality that antagonizes her rigid mother. Though there is something a little too casual in her carriage, her speech, her pouty, sullen, yet beguiling expression, Christie manages traces of a traditional aristocratic bearing—she is clearly playing a character from a different class than that of the "darling" who made her a star.

It is exactly an air of high social breeding that Margaret Leighton captures so fully as Mrs. Maudsley. Her formality suggests a social tradition that cannot condone a romance that crosses class lines. Her severity and archness palpably convey the unbending traditionalism of an entire class. Mrs. Maudsley's way of life is based on the belief that society is divided into masters and servants, and, when she begins to suspect Marian's transgression, she reacts as if her very survival has been challenged. At the end, when Marian doesn't show up for Leo's birthday party, and she is impatient with Leo's evasive answers to her insistent questions, she gets up peremptorily from her chair, throwing it aside as she grabs Leo's hand,

and stalks out into the rain to find Marian. Leighton plays the scene
with such intensity that we feel the character is fighting for her life:
the thought of her daughter's almost unimaginable social lapse
strikes her with horror. Leighton plays an aristocrat not as a social
cariacature, but from the character's own point of view, so that
observance of class distinctions is treated as a matter of the gravest
concern, a matter, quite literally, of life or death. Leighton's im-
mense performance has the consummate grace and style of Comedie
Française; her inspired work has the echo of great classical acting.

It is typical of Losey's sense of proportion that the character of
Marian's fiancé, the Viscount Hugh Trimmingham, is presented
sympathetically. The values he represents and believes in are given
their full weight. As played by Edward Fox, Hugh is a steady,
likable chap, limited but not damaged by the rarefied world into
which his social status has locked him. Fox has a gentle, yielding
quality, and, like Margaret Leighton, he plays an aristocrat from
the character's own point of view rather than that of comedy of
manners caricature.

As Leo, Dominic Guard is extraordinary. Playing a boy from a
humble background thrust into the grandeur of an alien setting,
Guard forcefully suggests Leo's uncertainty among "his betters."
He invests the character with an assortment of tics—a nervous blink,
a stammering, halting manner of speech. Although the film, unlike
the Hartley novel, does not use Leo's consciousness as its narrative
center, we discover the settings—the house and the farm—along
with him, and his reactions to the other characters often trigger our
own response to them. One of the strongest moments of Losey's
modified use of limited point of view is when we discover, at the
same time that Leo does, that Hugh has an enormous scar on the
right side of his face. We are made to share Leo's surprise and
shock.

In the novel, Leo is a magician who gained a certain notoriety
at school by putting the hex on two fellows who had treated him
cruelly. The boy in the novel believes in astrological signs and in
the world of the supernatural; when he sees the belladonna, a wild
poisonous flower growing near an abandoned shed on the Maudsley
estate, he is entranced by it and later concocts a potion from it when
he wants to break the spell that links Marian to Ted. Pinter retains
only the most cryptic references to the novel's detailed supernatural
and mythological motifs; the freely growing belladonna still sits

beside the shed (where, in the finale, Mrs. Maudsley and Leo discover the lovers), a symbol of the doom that awaits the characters; and Leo still attempts to create a spell from its poisonous leaves. Hartley's Leo is a strange little boy, a true loner, teased mercilessly by his school fellows and babied by his kindly mother; Leo's interest in spells and potions is a sign of his oddness. Guard has such a distinctive and unusual presence; he is so thoughtful, so deeply serious and introspective, so private, that he evokes much of the mysterious quality of Hartley's original character without really being given that aspect of the material to play.

He powerfully conveys the character's puzzlement, disillusionment, and essential loneliness, so that there is a connection to the older Leo whom we glimpse in fragments throughout and then see "whole" in the final interview with the aged Marian. Michael Redgrave plays the elder Leo. He has only a few minutes of screen time, and yet he manages to suggest the quality of the character's entire life: this man, with his drooping shoulders, his mournful eyes, his gray and sagging face, is a sad figure. Redgrave uses his face and body and voice to record the character's emotionally impoverished life: we can feel, as Marian says, that he is all dried up inside.

The final interview between Marian, still proud of her passion for Ted (her memories of him have sustained her for a lifetime), and the middle-aged Leo is a moving coda to the film. Marian sends him on one final errand, to deliver a message to her (and Ted's) grandson: "Tell him he can feel proud to be descended from our union, the child of so much happiness and beauty." The film concludes with a sly Pinter touch: "Tell him—" Marian begins to repeat, or to embellish, her final instructions to the go-between, but then halts, abruptly, in mid-sentence, causing the film to end on a droll Pinter pause.

Fifty years later, Marian and Leo are playing the same roles. Marian is the bewitching coquette, proud of her sensuality, Leo is submissive and not quite feeling entitled, in the presence of her radiance and her position, to a life of his own. "You came out of the blue to make us happy," Marian says, still the self-absorbed lover. "And we made you happy, didn't we? We trusted you with our great treasure. You might never have known what it was, you might have gone through life without knowing. Isn't that so?"

The pinnacle of the Losey-Pinter collaboration, and Losey's su-

preme achievement as a director, *The Go-Between* is one of the world's great films.

The Hireling

Two years later, another splendid Hartley novel about the power of the class system to strangle love was adapted into a film. *The Hireling* was not made by Losey and Pinter, though it certainly has the visual and verbal texture of one of their collaborative efforts. Directed by Alan Bridges, and with a screenplay by Wolf Mankowitz, *The Hireling* must be one of the most genteel films ever made. Although it is set in the 1920s, the film suggests the languorous pace of an Edwardian summer. It captures the tone of a time when class counted and when no one questioned the rules of the game as high society played it. Soberly, calmly, the film acknowledges the difference between the rich and the poor, between aristocrat and proletarian. Like Fitzgerald, *The Hireling* is impressed with the fact that the very rich really are different from the rest of us.

The film, though, is not unthinkingly reactionary, as it looks closely and critically at both its well-born heroine and its lowly hero, who are divided by position as well as sensibility. The film regrets their thwarted romance at the same time that it insists on the inevitability of its failure. Both sides are praised and rebuked: the lady has poise and intelligence, but she is diminished by the conventions of class behavior just as the hireling's rugged self-sufficiency is marred by an inveterate "commonness."

The movie takes the odd and unpopular view, then, that the paraphernalia of social position, the code of manners and rank, are stronger than sex. The high-strung aristocrat is attracted to the strong, competent man who drives her from town house to country estate, but she knows the rules, and she will not dishonor or disrespect her place. She cannot allow her feelings to turn serious or to run deep.

The movie denies the Lawrentian myth of romance between a lady and a menial; like *The Go-Between*, it suggests that such a union is destined to be destroyed by the class system. The film's heroine, Lady Franklin, is thus no Lady Chatterley, soothed by sex with a proletarian Dionysus. And though he'd certainly like to, Ledbitter doesn't make it as the questing knight who awakens the

sleeping princess in her tower. Lady Franklin uses Ledbitter for more genteel refreshments—as companion, as entertaining story-teller. Gradually recovering from a nervous breakdown brought on by the death of her husband, Lady Franklin is absorbed by the stories the hireling tells her about his own family; she's unaware that they *are* stories—fabrications—that the cunning driver thinks the pale lady wants to hear. His invented family history offers calming insights into the working class; details of plebeian daily life take Lady Franklin out of herself. These people, whose lives are so removed from her own, provide no threat; they don't really matter, and so, in her precarious emotional state, she can afford to be interested in them. Protected by her own sense of her station, the lady misjudges the driver's attentiveness, thinking that his courtesy and concern simply represent what is due her as the lady of the manor.

Ledbitter knows the rules, too; he's made his way in the world by pretending to be the discreet, deferential servant, a man without opinions, who sees and hears nothing. A cad to women of his own class, he's charmed by his employer's fine ways, but when appreciation turns into adoration, he's broken the law and he is lost. The movie builds up to Ledbitter's two violations of the social code: his confession to Lady Franklin that he loves her; and, after he's been rejected, his drunken harangue of the lady and her fiancé, an oily, effete, but socially acceptable politician, a man of her own class.

It is typical of the film's decorum that the thwarted romance doesn't end in gaudy melodrama; there are no suicides or murders or (unlike the overdone ending of the novel) no catastrophic car accidents. Lives are dented, bruised, and the film wisely doesn't try to underline its theme by involving the characters in a cataclysmic fate. *The Hireling* isn't trying for grand romance or Lawrentian passion—it's as emotionally hidden and indirect as *The Go-Between*. Bridges's direction is as delicate and controlled as Losey's treatment of a similar theme in the earlier film. Bathed in misty grays and browns, the action often framed by or seen through windows and mirrors, the film's images reinforce the theme. Motifs of separation appear throughout. Through the front mirror of his car, Ledbitter covertly glances at Lady Franklin, seated stiffly in the back of the car. The screen that divides front seat from back, the fancy glass windows of Lady Franklin's country house— these are the tokens of "class," the divisions, sanctified by time and custom,

that neither character is able to overcome. Robert Shaw and Sarah Miles act with the subtlety and force and the sly humor familiar from the Losey-Pinter works. Shaw suggests from the beginning strength under control and heaving passion under servile calm. And yet there is a lingering unpleasantness about the character, a menacing, self-satisfied presence that presages catastrophe. Subtly, the actors change places, Shaw moving from manly aloofness to uncontrolled self-pity and anger, Miles taking Lady Franklin from numbness, absolute detachment, to a renewed interest in society. Miles's performance is so detailed, so observant, so carefully modulated, that it has the feel of a real-life case study—we follow her character step by step from deep depression, to tentative gestures of involvement in the life around her, to full participation; we see her move from pale, shrinking hysteria to a blossoming youth and vigor that yet contain reminiscences of sorrows only half forgotten. An infinitely wise performance, it is the perfect centerpiece for this sad, lovely, undemocratic film about class, a film that bears astonishing resemblances to *The Go-Between*.

7

The Losey-Pinter Collaboration: Sequels

SINCE THEIR majestic film of *The Go-Between* in 1971, Losey and Pinter have collaborated on adapting Proust's monumental *roman fleuve, Remembrance of Things Past.* The result of their efforts was published in 1978 as *The Proust Screenplay,* on which Pinter acknowledges his indebtedness both to Losey and to Barbara Bray, a Proust specialist. Although their work was completed in 1974—Pinter spent a year on it, and then he and Losey scouted possible locations—they have still not been able to raise the necessary financing. The screenplay was published in the hope of arousing sufficient interest in the material to hasten its production.

In temperament, culture, use of language, tone, and rhythm, Pinter and Proust are profoundly dissimilar. Proust is the most subjective of novelists, the most private and internalized, and his great book represents his monumental effort to distill, heighten, and shape his own private experience into art. For the last thirteen years of his life, Proust retreated from the world in order to write his book, and his own impassioned, intensely analytical and introspective spirit hovers protectively over it. Proust writes at great length on the most seemingly minor or chance things, events, ideas—the *Remembrance* is filled with fifty-page digressions, with anecdotes, parenthetical asides, with flowing philosophical and aesthetic speculations, and with long discourses on time, memory, art, love, and society.

Pinter's voice could hardly be more radically different. His technique, after all, is one of subtraction rather than, like Proust, of addition. Pinter resolutely keeps himself out of his work, maintaining an almost mocking distance from his characters. His language is spare, elliptical, "simple"—a method the opposite of Proust's

143

brooding and decidedly unromantic Glenda Jackson dominates her lover, a mysterious poet (Helmut Berger), in Losey's Pinteresque The Romantic Englishwoman.

labyrinthine sentences and compulsive volubility. The sheer volume and magnitude of the *Remembrance* offer a stunning contrast to Pinter's trim plays. Proust can't seem to leave anything out; Pinter delights in omitting from his work the kind of description of scene as well as the internal scrutiny of motive, the detailed psychological history, that Proust dwells on at such length.

Pinter's screenplay is eminently though not cripplingly respectful of its source. His work is diligent, occasionally resourceful, remarkably selfless, and (perhaps inevitably) thin. Any adaptation of Proust cannot hope to duplicate the full experience of reading the novel and, realizing this, Pinter does not pretend to offer more than an intelligent and sympathetic gloss on it. The first problem of the adapter is to find a point of view that serves the material and that at the same time is congenial to the film medium. Pinter doesn't try to incorporate into his screenplay the narrative voice whose consciousness orchestrates the novel—that bodiless narrator who is a complex mixture of Proust himself, and of the character Marcel both as a young man and as an older man looking back on his life. The "I" of the book stands both inside and outside the action. The subtle blend of author and persona—the boy Marcel merges into the adult Marcel, who is an extension of the author Marcel—cannot be carried over into films. Pinter settles for an external viewpoint, with characters and scene observed for the most part from the outside, although occasional images are drawn from Marcel's consciousness. To retain the first-person perspective would have involved a heavy narrative voiceover that might have drowned the images and that would, at any rate, have involved the kind of verbal long-windedness that is antithetical to Pinter's style. But discarding the narrative presence means sacrificing much of the novel's texture: its deep introspection, its minute analyses, its entire philosophical and emotional cast of thought. Instead of the novel's close record of the internal growth of an artist, we get a work that concentrates on external drama: Pinter's script is a series of party scenes and quarrels among jealous lovers, with Marcel reduced in large measure to the role of a pale and progressively disillusioned onlooker. The screenplay focuses on sexual power struggles so that much of it is reminiscent of the kind of sexual tension contained in the three Losey-Pinter pieces. The *Remembrance* thus becomes a bitter view of sexual and romantic relationships: lovers taunt, and are taunted by, their beloved ones. No relationship achieves poise and stability.

Each destructive menage mirrors the others, with Marcel's agonizing relationship to the teasing and possibly lesbian Albertine as the centerpiece.

Pinter stresses the homosexual undercurrents in Proust, and in particular gives disproportionate space to the sadomasochistic Baron de Charlus. The screenplay's treatment of homosexuality as primarily decadent and self-destructive may well reflect Proust's ambivalence about his own homosexuality, but it is hardly "modern" or liberated in its tone. There is, in fact, a leering quality here not prominent in Proust; a distrust of and even distaste for all human sexuality pervades Pinter's treatment, and in the grotesque party scene at the end, where most of the characters appear, withered with age, like caricatures out of Daumier or Hogarth, there is a naked horror of the ravages of mortality.

Because it is the aspect of Proust most accessible to films, Pinter thus focuses on the characters' sexual compulsions as well as on their interactions in society. The script amply describes Marcel's deep attraction to the world of high society, represented for him at its apex by the aristocratic Guermantes family. The screenplay contains several long party scenes, where we see the characters in their public social masks. The dominance of the social and sexual themes in Pinter's work reduces to a distinctly minor place the novel's concern with the connections between art and life, and with Marcel's interest in the ways memory shapes and recomposes experience.

Pinter's dialogue is less idiosyncratic than that for any of his other screenplays. He has made a genuinely conscientious attempt to translate Proust rather than to transform Proust into Pinter. The characters are allowed to express themselves at greater length, and with a fuller vocabulary, than in any other Pinter work. Except in a few cases, where they toss intimidating questions at each other, or utter key words and phrases with mocking repetition, the characters do not noticeably sound as if they belong in a Pinter play.

Pinter had decided before he began writing that he would not confine himself to any particular book or group of characters, but that his aim would be to include as wide a portion of the entire novel as possible, and to embrace its vast time scheme. The opening of his script is especially dense, as it moves quickly among a number of different time periods, and introduces a large number of characters, settings, images, and sounds, which then serve as recurrent

motifs throughout: the garden gate at Combray and its jangling bell, a yellow patch from Vermeer's *View of Delft* that serves as a memory screen, Marcel's childhood view of church spires, a row of trees against the sky. For those viewers unfamiliar with Proust's world, this sequence of disparate images is likely to be indecipherable. Once it settles down to a more or less chronological narrative development, the action is easier to follow, although the piece does require prior knowledge to complement the images, to enhance and even, in a sense, to *complete* their meaning. The emblematic characters—Swann and the Guermantes—don't have the symbolic impact of their counterparts in the novel; they need our awareness of the social forces Proust intended them to represent.

The handling of time is accomplished successfully. The fluid shifts between past and present recall the complex, juggled time scheme of *The Go-Between,* in which scenes set in the present periodically interrupt and introduce parallels to the evocation of the past that is the film's principal concern. Isolated repeated images recall key past events, important moments in Marcel's developing aesthetic sense. These images are renderings of subjective experience, and are thus deliberate intrusions into the script's predominantly objective mode. The leitmotifs are visual condensations of complex themes and ideas requiring virtually hundreds of pages of explication in the novel.

Despite its inevitable simplification, its externalizing of Proust's incomparably rich interior methods, does Pinter's screenplay provide the basis for a good (if not great) film? Probably, though it would be a calculated risk. With Losey as director, the textural qualities—the elegance of the social world that Marcel stands in awe of, the grand hotels, the sumptuous apartments, the lavish parties, the poetic countryside associated with Marcel's childhood at Combray—would be sensitively treated. The film would certainly be glorious to look at. And it would certainly, like all of Losey's films, be well acted. The scenes of sexual baiting and tension would have the edge that Losey has perfected in his work with Pinter. The fluid handling of time, the use of leitmotifs, the complex editing patterns—all would have the precision and control born of Losey's long experience, his understanding of the language of film. Because, however, it is based on a novel whose greatness is tied inextricably to its original form, to its specifically literary texture, its reliance on a narrative consciousness not accessible to the primarily external

world of films; because the novel's rich, dense, meandering language cannot be translated into a medium whose impact is primarily visual; because pictures, no matter how skillfully composed, cannot ever achieve as great a complexity as Proust's use of words, it is unlikely that the film would be Losey's masterpiece, an achievement to crown his long career. But Pinter's respectful adaptation, and his proved rapport with Losey, entitle him to realize his work on film: surely Losey and Pinter have earned the right to complete their long-planned project.

Pinter without Losey

To date, Pinter has written three other screenplays that have been turned into films by directors other than Losey: *The Pumpkin Eater*, based on a novel by Penelope Mortimer, directed by Jack Clayton; *The Quiller Memorandum*, based on the novel *The Berlin Memorandum* by Adam Hall, directed by Michael Anderson; and *The Last Tycoon*, based on Fitzgerald's last (and uncompleted) novel, directed by Elia Kazan. The resulting films have been less successful than the Losey-Pinter entries. *The Pumpkin Eater*, the best of them, is in fact only slightly less pointed than *Accident* as a comedy-drama of domestic incompatibility, but *The Quiller Memorandum* and *The Last Tycoon* are measurably weaker.

Like *The Hireling*, *The Pumpkin Eater*, in both tone and subject matter, might well have been a film by Pinter and Losey. It concerns a domestic crisis as a woman with nine children and a new husband whose fidelity she doubts goes through a period of breakdown and recovery. The story of an unstable woman and a shaky marriage is even thinner than the story of *Accident*, and yet Pinter turns it into a droll comedy of modern bad manners. The screenplay is filled with bizarre characters: a self-annointed King of Israel; a woman who goes mad under the hair dryer in a sedate beauty salon; a house guest whose monologues become increasingly menacing. The strange characters reflect the heroine's escalating paranoia and disconnectedness. This modern wife, suffering from modern malaise, feeling herself unused and unappreciated, is locked into a nightmare world that is distinctly Pinteresque. *The Pumpkin Eater* is the most self-indulgent of the playwright's film scripts, the one most marked by his comedy of menace mannerisms. Yet the eccentricities of style

enhance the essentially ordinary story and characters. Working on material much less rich than in his adaptations for Losey, Pinter had to depend to a greater degree on the tics of his own individual style.

As always, Pinter's cryptic, precisely rhythmed dialogue requires skilled actors and a director sensitive to tone and nuance. Jack Clayton (who later directed the elegant and largely unappreciated *The Great Gatsby*) gives the film a trim cutting edge and discovers exactly the right degree of visual and verbal stylization. Appropriately, the world the film creates rotates from the real—the recognizable and the everyday—to the bizarre and nightmarish. Throughout, the point of view shifts, suddenly, from an objective presentation of a mundane reality—the large family seems almost to come from a television situation comedy—to surreal distortions that represent the heroine's fantasies of alienation. Throughout the film, conversations escalate from mundane chit-chat to ominous burlesques of the real and the ordinary. The actors capture Pinter's delicate balance expertly, as Clayton's molding of tone is as sure as Losey's. Anne Bancroft, normally so hard and mannish, so coarse-grained, gives a tight, dry performance poised between American naturalism and British stylization. Peter Finch, as her distracted, straying husband; Maggie Smith, as their jabbering, wacky house guest; and (especially) James Mason, as a murderously jealous husband, are all marvelously menacing and nasty, delivering the droll dialogue in clipped, biting accents.

The Quiller Memorandum is also an ordinary concept that Pinter tries to embellish with his usual style. This is a spy story: an American agent uncovers a group of Nazis in modern-day Germany. The film opens with the death of Quiller's predecessor—a standard opening ploy for films of this kind—and then proceeds with a series of investigations as the clever, intrepid American gets closer to finding and then capturing the enemy. On his investigations he meets the requisite girl. Working in a popular genre, one that is traditionally mysterious and that teasingly withholds information from the audience, Pinter is undercut: his own brand of secrecy is not well matched by the customary withholding patterns of the spy story. And his own menace seems minor compared to that posed by the Nazis. Pinter's humor, at any rate, is inappropriate in the face of the Nazi horror, as is the attempt to borrow the Nazi iconography as the backdrop for a spy thriller that turns cosmic horror

into pulp fiction. The Nazi evil, specific and awesome, casts a dark shadow over Pinter's effort to give some wit and tension to this modest story. Pinter's theatrical manner is inadequate for expressing the enormity of Nazi menace. The writing and the performances have a polished style that, under the circumstances, is irrelevant.

The Last Tycoon is a failure of a different sort. Pinter is far from an ideal choice as an adapter of Fitzgerald, since American romanticism and British irony are not complementary modes. Pinter's treatment of Fitzgerald's romantic satire of a Hollywood mogul seems like a translation from a foreign language: it is glacial and hollow, an external rendering of what, in the original, was an inside view of Hollywood manners. Pinter's cool tone, his cultural distance from a world of American commerce, cut into the energy of the original. He doesn't have Fitzgerald's emotional response to character and setting. Fitzgerald's warmth gives a nostalgic aura to the novel despite his anger at his own mistreatment in Hollywood, his bitterness at his failure to become successful on Hollywood's own terms. To Fitzgerald, money and power were vitally important. There is nothing in Pinter's work to suggest that he shares those values, that he looks with a kind of awe on the inner world of the very rich and the very powerful. In place of Fitzgerald's more complex love-hate relationship to Hollywood, Pinter offers a mordant disapproval.

The damage to Fitzgerald's tone is compounded by the choice of Elia Kazan as director. Returning to films after an absence of several years, Kazan tried consciously to direct in a style that is antithetical to the supercharged emotionalism of his most famous films; he has tried, that is, to direct Pinter's screenplay as if he were Joseph Losey! Kazan deliberately restrains himself, as if accommodating his tone and rhythm to what he perceives are Pinter's. There are no Kazan fireworks here, no Method intensity or neuroticism, no overheated sexuality: the cool blue tones that dominate the color scheme and the detached, almost Brechtian, performances are a far cry from the magnetism of *Baby Doll* or *On the Waterfront* or *A Streetcar Named Desire*. Kazan is working in a constricted emotional register that is altogether alien to him, and the results are forced, tepid. This is the only film by Kazan that contains not a single dynamic or even interesting performance. As the mogul (inspired by Irving Thalberg), Robert De Niro is impossible; he, too, is working against the grain, trying for a complete reversal of

the demonic antihero he so forcefully embodied in *Taxi Driver*. De Niro does not for a moment suggest the intelligence, the ambition, and the cultivation of Fitzgerald's studio boss. This collision of mismatched sensibilities only underlines the strength of the Losey-Pinter collaboration, in which the two artists measurably enhance and give shape to each other's work.

Losey without Pinter: *The Romantic Englishwoman*

All of Losey's work since *The Servant* shows the influence of Pinter. But one of his post-Pinter films, *The Romantic Englishwoman* (1975), is especially close, in theme and tone, to his Pinter collaborations. Like *Accident, The Romantic Englishwoman* is a comedy-drama of middle-aged disaffection; and, like both *Accident* and *The Servant*, it concerns the intrusion of a mysterious and seductive outsider into the lives of the protagonists. Bored with her marriage to a popular novelist, "the romantic Englishwoman" goes on a spree to an elegant German resort where she meets, very casually, a handsome young gigolo with whom she may or may not have a fleeting sexual encounter. The man, who advertises himself as a poet and who has startling erotic promise, invites himself to her house in London and presumes to offer his services as the husband's secretary. The husband welcomes the poet into his house almost as a test of his wife's loyalty. Though at first Elizabeth resists the poet's attentions, she grows somewhat more interested after he succeeds in seducing her servant. Ultimately, she capitulates, becoming obsessed with the intruder. She leaves her husband and son to go off with the poet on a romantic idyll on the Riviera. The husband pursues his wife; the poet, who has mysterious dealings with shady underworld characters, is killed; and husband and wife return to England.

The film never quite takes its lopsided story seriously. Its tone, like its genre, is in a state of almost constant flux: realism collides with fantasy; a domestic melodrama is interrupted by a gangster story from which the exposition has been removed. The film's realistic basic premise—an examination of a shaky marriage—is subjected to a series of stylistic invasions, as if *A Doll's House* had been crossed with the theater of the absurd.

The poet seems more a projection of the fantasies of both the

husband and the wife than a character in his own right. A Pinter-esque foreign intruder, he is a perfect catalyst for the husband's insecurity and he seems almost heaven-sent to satisfy the wife's erotic daydreams. His aggressive intrusion into their house, and his seduction of the servant and the wife, are played for comedy of menace, very much in the Pinter vein. That he has unexplained dealings with underworld characters extends the aura of mystery he brings into the house.

The film is based on a clever novel by Thomas Wiseman which, in its preoccupation with middle-aged sexual neurosis and its sty-listic trickiness, has strong similarities to Nicholas Mosley's *Accident*. Wiseman experiments with apparent shifts in point of view, proceeding from the wife's to the husband's consciousness, though in fact the novel is the husband's projection of Elizabeth's fantasies of rebellion. In art, as in life, the husband attempts to control his wife—he makes her a character in his novel, and so she becomes his fictional creation; through the storytelling process, he becomes the architect of her rebellion. For Lewis, all experience is raw material to be shaped to the demands of his novel; life is useful to him only as a series of potential stories.

Although Wiseman's concept—the husband is writing the novel we are reading—is a familiar modernist strategy, he sustains his material with variations in tone and technique. The husband is a lively, controlling consciousness as he lets his fantasies mount to hallucinatory proportions, writing his story as a way of relieving his animosity toward Elizabeth. Embittered, by turns mad and lyrical, cryptic and effusive, he is good company; his literary game has zest.

In the film, the husband is no longer the shaping consciousness. He is observed on the same level, and from the same distance, as the two other major characters. Losey minimizes the fiction-life contrast that the novel sets up and instead plays the material for its story of a house invaded. Tom Stoppard's screenplay has much of the acerbic wit, the barbed confrontations, and the loaded sexual baiting of *Accident*, but it lacks Pinter's unfaltering control. Stop-pard was called on as a collaborator after Thomas Wiseman had completed a first draft of the script. "Stoppard took Wiseman's original script and treated it with a good deal of irreverence, and made it quite funny," Losey said. "He hardly changed the structure, but he rewrote the dialogue. . . . The story became a pretty bitter comedy of domestic life."[1]

Stoppard's most famous plays—*Rosencrantz and Guildenstern Are Dead, The Real Inspector Hound, Travesties*—concern comic cross-references between life and literature. Stoppard treats literature—*Hamlet* in *Rosencrantz and Guildenstern*, melodrama in *The Real Inspector Hound*, and literary and historical figures like Wilde and Marx in *Travesties*—as fodder for comic jests. The intellectually playful and irreverent spirit of his most characteristic work is well suited to Wiseman's literary sport; but Stoppard doesn't have the same impish fun with Wiseman's characters that he does with his own. The script has darker tones, and a generally heavier quality, than his prankish plays, and the stodgier gait may reflect Wiseman's own more sober temperament as well as that of the director: Losey, after all, is hardly the man to direct the kind of quick-witted, fast-moving verbal comedy that is Stoppard's forte.

Inconsistent in tone, lopsided in its handling of story, *The Romantic Englishwoman* never quite comes into focus. At times seemingly straight, at others a near parody of Pinteresque strategies of invasion and menace, the film is an unblended concoction of motifs Losey had perhaps by this late point—1975—worked with too often. For all its modern acerbic manner, the material seems a little old hat. The film seems more a footnote to Losey's Pinter period than a fully realized project. There is much about it, however, that is worthwhile. It is among Losey's most visually elegant pieces: the opening section in a glamorous German spa and the conclusion in a hilltop Riviera hotel are displays of dazzling Old World decor. Perhaps nowhere else in his work has Losey so freely indulged his taste for rococo embellishment. The two grand hotels that frame the story are meant to reflect Elizabeth's rebellious fantasies: in these exquisite foreign palaces she is living out her daydreams of escape. The scenes in Germany and France have a different texture from the central section set in an English country house that recalls the milieu of *Accident*; there is more sun in the foreign countries than in rainy England, and more open space. But the obvious respect with which Losey presents these glimpses of the haunts of the very rich contradicts their ostensible narrative function: there is no reason why these settings need to be as spectacular as they are, except to be enjoyed for their own sake. The climax—when Lewis comes to reclaim Elizabeth—is played against an awe-inspiring view of the blue Mediterranean on a perfect late afternoon. The slanting quality of the light, the moving camera and deep-focus

composition, the view of the interior of the hotel, with a matron seated at an elegantly appointed window table which commands a sweeping view of the ocean, attain a magical richness against which the story and the characters haven't a fair chance at our attention. Losey's images, bathed in a preternaturally soft light, achieve a heady intoxication that transcends the story requirements. Although form does not exactly follow function in these lush scenes, it would be a most ungrateful viewer indeed who could not revel in the world of material wealth which saturates the film.

Losey's delight in decor and composition may reach dizzying proportions, but his direction of his actors reveals his characteristic control. Michael Caine and Glenda Jackson perform in an astringent style that cuts through any possible residue of sentimentality in the material. Jackson's dry, tight-lipped delivery, her biting, embittered rhetorical manner, make the title an obvious irony: this hard-edged, tough-minded, singularly unhandsome actress is anything but romantic or sentimental. "The woman comes off worst," Losey feels. "And I'm sorry in a way that it works out like this because I'm not—in spite of my reputation—anti-woman. . . . In both the film and the novel, the character of Elizabeth is voracious—she wanted everything; her idea of romance was total bourgeois consumption of man. . . . If ever there was an unromantic woman, it's this one."[2] Jackson, however, makes the character stronger and more independent than the heroine in the novel. The knowing, cynical Jackson seems equally disenchanted by both men, she is "on" to their masquerades, and her decision to have an affair with the poet and then to run away with him is more an act of will than the impulsive choice of the character in the novel. In bearing and temperament Jackson is clearly unsuited to play the variation on Ibsen's Nora that is part of the scheme of the novel. Like Losey she stands as chorus to the action, commenting with wry disapproval on the foolishness of her autocratic husband and the exaggerated sexuality of the intruding poet. In the novel, Elizabeth is "created" by her husband, while in the film the strong actress lends the character her own authority: this Elizabeth is responsible to no one but herself. Jackson is more forceful than Michael Caine, though he gives her a good fight, in his best snarling manner, and she is certainly superior in intellect and self-control to Helmut Berger's poet. Berger is a pretty boy—more feminine than Jackson and far less insinuating than his counterpart in the novel.

Jackson's cool tone works with Losey's to overturn generic convention and audience expectation. Losey did not want to make an ordinary romantic triangle that audiences could respond to with customary emotional identification. Working against its formulaic story of domestic crisis, and borrowing its ironic tone and its atmosphere of charged and indirect confrontation from Pinter, *The Romantic Englishwoman* is a summary of two recurrent aspects of Losey's style. The film hasn't the impeccable finish of the Pinter collaborations—it is irregular, oddly bemused in both shape and tone. As a footnote to Pinter's influence on Losey, though, it has a genuine appeal.

8

Dramas of Enclosure: Two with Elizabeth Taylor

THE FORM OF *The Servant*—a clash of wills between two characters in a confined setting—becomes a recurring pattern in most of Losey's major films in the 1960s and 1970s. His methods in these enclosed dramas are sternly symbolic: the embattled characters represent forces larger than themselves: their struggles reveal political, social, or psychological tensions of general significance; and the severe concentration of place, time, and number of characters gives the stories a microcosmic thrust. Losey's realistic, concretely rendered closed worlds have allegorical force.

Whereas the psychological and sexual war of wills in *Boom* and *Secret Ceremony* is private in focus, the collision of characters in *King and Country, Figures in a Landscape, The Assassination of Trotsky,* and *Mr. Klein* is played out against a political context. Because their characters and settings do not have the social dimension of the other confined dramas, *Boom* and *Secret Ceremony* reveal the attraction to the baroque that has been another of Losey's lingering signatures. The grand houses of these two films are among the most elegant of any of Losey's interiors.

All six films about doomed characters, however, are directed in a detached style. The clinical technique matches the fatalistic themes as the films proceed, in an inexorable rhythm, toward the characters' dissolution. Losey's rigorously closed form corresponds to the grimly deterministic world-view of the films and enforces the sense of inevitability that tracks the ill-fated characters.

Boom

Although Losey has not directed a film in America since the early 1950s, he was hired by two major American studios after the in-

esplendent Elizabeth Taylor as Sissy Goforth in Boom, *Losey's visually stunning sion of an odd sexual allegory by Tennessee Williams.*

ternational success of *The Servant* gave his career a temporary commercial gloss. In 1966, 20th Century–Fox signed him to direct
Modesty Blaise, and in 1968 he worked for Universal on *Boom* and
Secret Ceremony. All three films had high budgets, and all three,
at least in prospect, had popular potential—*Modesty Blaise,* because
of its apparent connections to the James Bond thrillers of the 1960s,
and *Boom* and *Secret Ceremony,* because they both starred Elizabeth Taylor. At the time of her appearance in *Boom,* Taylor was
still the top-ranking movie star in the world, fresh from her excellent
performances in *Who's Afraid of Virginia Woolf?,* *The Taming of
the Shrew,* and *Reflections in a Golden Eye. Boom* had additional
box-office insurance since it was based on a play by Tennessee
Williams—almost all of the Williams plays adapted into films had
proved both financially and artistically successful.

But none of these films pleased either popular audiences or (most
of) the critics. *Modesty Blaise* was a formally self-conscious burlesque of spy thrillers rather than the genuine article, and the two
Taylor films turned out to be exceedingly odd star vehicles. (After
this fling with Hollywood big money, Losey returned to working
with Harold Pinter!) For major studio Hollywood films, starring the
most high-priced actress in the world (at the time), *Boom* and *Secret
Ceremony* are decidedly quirky—exotic both in setting and theme.
That Taylor did agree to appear in both was a measure of her trust
in Losey and her openness to experimentation. Before these two
films Taylor was Hollywood's most bankable star; after her work
with Losey, her name above the title could no longer guarantee
producers a sure profit. *Boom* is commonly regarded as the beginning of Taylor's slide from preeminence. Her performances for Losey, as well as in a series of other offbeat vehicles in the last decade,
are mannered and shrill; and though she is always interesting (and
always likable), her range becomes narrower. The great natural
beauty of *A Place in the Sun* and *Giant,* the skillful character actress
of *Cat on a Hot Tin Roof* and *Suddenly Last Summer* and *Who's
Afraid of Virginia Woolf?,* became the self-conscious bawd, the
sharp-tongued shrew, of *XY and Zee* and *Hammersmith Is Out,*
cutting up for her fans in spectacular displays of good-natured self-
parody.

If *Boom* marks the beginning of Taylor's fall from Hollywood
favor, it also signaled the start of Tennessee Williams's decline from
popularity. The play on which the film is based—*The Milk Train*

Doesn't Stop Here Any More—was the first of a series of failed efforts; this was the first play in which Williams was unable to convert private neurotic fantasy, the source of all his work, into popular art. A star no longer secure in her powers, a playwright no longer able to relate to a vast public: the ingredients were precisely the kind to attract Losey's interest!

For most of Williams's work, Losey would be an especially inappropriate interpreter. His ironic distancing would be altogether the wrong quality for coiled, sexually charged plays like *A Streetcar Named Desire* or *Cat on a Hot Tin Roof* or *Suddenly Last Summer*. Losey's aloofness would undercut Williams's impassioned lyricism. The ideal Williams director is of course Elia Kazan, just as Losey is the perfect collaborator for Pinter; significantly, though hardly surprisingly, when Kazan and Pinter worked together, on *The Last Tycoon*, the results were dismal. Losey's collaboration with Williams on *Milk Train*, however, is not so colossal a misalliance as Kazan and Pinter on Fitzgerald (or as Losey and Williams on one of Williams's great plays would have been) because in this play Williams treats his characters with the emotional and aesthetic distance that is comfortably within Losey's temperamental range.

Designed as an allegory of death, *Milk Train* was not intended to have the overheated aura of any of the playwright's more typical, and more successful, dramas. Williams planned *Milk Train* as a highly stylized version of a sexual conflict that figures importantly throughout his writing. His two protagonists, Chris Flanders and Flora Goforth, reenact in a self-consciously symbolic mode the same kind of sexual battle as Blanche Du Bois and Stanley Kowalski in *A Streetcar Named Desire*. Chris is one of a long line of Williams's sexual heroes who save and becalm a desperate female. For Williams, as for many of his characters, the sexual promise of the beautiful male contains a kind of holiness; most of Williams's ravenous women lust after sexy men to fulfill them as well as, in a curious and usually unexamined way, to absolve them. But since Williams is at heart something of a puritan—at the least, a reluctant Dionysian, a guilty reveler—he usually links sexual fulfillment with some form of punishment. His spectacularly sexual heroes are often maimed, derided, exposed, or annihilated, before they are elevated to sexual sainthood. Sex in Williams, then, is dangerous as well as potentially healing. In several of the plays, the release that sex offers is associated with death. The character of Chris Flanders combines

Williams's tangled, intensely contradictory notions about sex, mortality, and transcendence.

A mystic poet seeking union with a realm beyond that of mere sensual gratification, Chris wants to be "excused" from sex. He has found his vocation as an angel of mercy who superintends the deaths of rich, dying old women and men. He "saves" them by refusing to give them his body, by making them aware—through the beauty of his physical presence—that there is a world beyond, one higher than that of the flesh. Williams had an enormous battle with this character. Although he rewrote the role many times, he never succeeded in making Chris believable as a realistic character, perhaps because he is himself uncertain about the ability of the flesh to transcend itself. The path that the character traces—a life of the body yielding to a life of the spirit—is one that Williams would like to believe in, but can't, quite; and his efforts to unite the duality of flesh and spirit in the figure of the saintly, otherworldly hustler are understandably confused. Williams could not resolve the contradictions inherent in his concept of the hustler as spiritual savior.

In creating Mrs. Goforth, he had a much easier time. The character is one of his great bawds, a loud, coarse strumpet, once a Follies girl and now the dying widow of a millionaire. Shrieking her memoirs into a tape recorder, she is a woman obsessed by bodies—her own, as well as those of the men she has slept with. In the play's blatant symbolic scheme, she is Flesh to Chris (Chris=Christ) Flanders's Spirit. Chris intrudes into her villa by climbing up her steep mountain, and she courts him in the aggressive and manipulative way she has treated all the men she has desired. Williams mocks the character, as he almost always derides his women who are desperate for a man. Goforth's self-proclaimed sexual prowess is not entirely convincing, and is at any rate more a memory than a fact: she is now a shriveled remnant of her fleshy self, a gruesome reminder of the impermanence of a life devoted to sensual pleasure. Williams has said that he based the characterization on his friend Tallulah Bankhead; if this is the case, Tallulah didn't need any enemies. But, gamely, she played the part—her final role—in the second ill-fated Broadway production; Tab Hunter, an excellent choice, played Chris. By this time, she was simply putting on campy self-parodies for her coterie following, and the similarities between Tallulah, a legendary personality ravaged by drugs and alcohol, and the wasted character she was playing, were gruesome.

For Williams, the male and female antagonists of *Milk Train* transcend realism to become archetypal sexual forces: Chris Flanders is Williams's ultimate stud as savior, Flora Goforth his ultimate ravenous female. They are presented in an extreme way that borders on caricature and self-parody. These two Williams archetypes are no longer earthly creatures; Williams has made these figures drawn from his private mythology distinctly larger than life: semidivine. And the fact that their battle is conducted so far from Williams's steamy, benighted South, on a spectacular mountain overlooking the Mediterranean, adds to the play's remoteness from a recognizable reality. These mythic characters, placed in a cosmic setting, engage in the strangest and most baroque of Williams's sexual contests: a dance of death between a world-famous whore and an otherworldly stud in which the man refuses to enter the woman's bedroom. Chris, a self-declared angel of mercy, has come to Mrs. Goforth's hilltop villa in order to ease her transition into the next world. Around this "death of a clown," as Williams calls it, he has woven one of his oddest and least convincing dramas.

Williams never quite found an appropriate diction for the play. Flora speaks in a hyped-up style, all camp pose and vaudevillian bluster, while Chris intones his speeches in a mystical pseudopoetry. Their clashing styles—necessary, to a point, for thematic emphasis—rarely seem, however, to belong to the same play. Veering from the earthy to the saintly, from sloppy colloquialism to operatic recitative, the language is a patchwork of differing and disconnected voices.

An equally serious problem is that the characters are not strong enough to support Williams's allegorical framework. Flora is too bizarre a character for her death to have the universal reverberations that Williams is aiming for. He gives the audience no means of either identifying with or caring about his boisterous dragon lady, whom he treats with an unresolved mixture of contempt and complicity: she seems like something of a private joke to Williams, a high camp buffoon, a woman conceived through a particular kind of ironic, mordant, gay sensibility. This gaudy drag queen doesn't have the humanity of Beckett's clowns in *Waiting for Godot* or of the King in Ionesco's *Exit the King*, yet Williams is trying for the same kind of allegorical generalization. Unlike Beckett's waiting clowns or Ionesco's expiring King, Flora doesn't deserve the great symbolic role in which Williams has cast her.

To reinforce his allegorical intentions, Williams, in the process of numerous revisions, gave the material an increasingly stylized and theatrical framework. In the published version, he introduces elements of Kabuki Theater; the Oriental influence in the staging is meant both to lift the drama from a daily reality to a timeless realm and to underscore the Eastern mysticism and serenity—the cosmic poise—that Chris is supposed to embody.

For this stylized and solemnly symbolic Williams play, Losey is an appropriate director. Story and setting recall many other Losey films. *Boom* is about a complex, layered power struggle between master and servant, between flesh and spirit, between life and death, that is enacted in a confined setting whose decor underscores the mood and the meaning of the dramatic conflict. The film is Losey's most visually striking treatment of his favorite theme of a house invaded.

Losey's studied visual texture, his schematic use of color, and his orchestrated placement of characters within the settings—his symbolic use of decor—enhance both Williams's mannered dialogue and the symbolic surge of the material: *Boom* looks unmistakably like an allegory! As Andrew Sarris wrote, "*Boom* is a prime example of the power of mise-en-scène to translate a relatively trivial enterprise into a beautiful entertainment."[1]

Color and settings enclose the characters in a stylized frame. Colors are bright and primary. Goforth's two villas, one gleaming white, the other hot pink, are framed by the deep blue of the Mediterranean. The main villa, within and without, is dominated by stark white walls. The rooms, which have a variety of strangely shaped windows, are large, sparely and severely furnished, with black, squat chairs and couches. The terrace on which much of the action takes place is also a large neutral area, with never more than a table and a chair or two. Objects—a birdcage, a large, sculpted figure in a flowing golden robe (the angel of death?), a black sculpture and mobiles in the style of Calder—stand out boldly against the sharp and omnipresent whiteness. The walls, both inside and outside the villa, are relieved by gargoyles that provide a mute chorus to the human drama. Mrs. Goforth's insignia, a golden griffin, half-horse, half-beast, is a repeated motif throughout the house, appearing in the flag on the roof, emblazoned in gold in wall friezes or etched directly onto the walls. On the harsh landscape beyond the terrace there are figures, carved out of rock, that continue the

Elegant Losey mise-en-scène with Elizabeth Taylor in ceremonial costume in *Boom*.

mythological conceit: these Druidic stone sculptures, reminiscent of Stonehenge, resemble primitive death's heads. The villa contains two paintings—one of a chess set, in Renaissance style, in the living room; and one, in the pink villa, of a flying angel in the style of Chagall. Losey, of course, selected the paintings for their thematic associations as well as their ornamental value: the Chagall angel is a visual echo of Chris's self-designated role as angel of mercy; the chess set is an oblique echo of the metaphoric game of chess between Death and the questing knight in Bergman's *The Seventh Seal*— chess was a medieval and Renaissance symbol of Fate and Death, a recurrent image in prints and woodcuts. Losey includes a floor mosaic in Goforth's living room that is another mythological image of death: a central sunburst around which there are four black fig- ures, half-men, half-beast, carrying swords in both hands as another sword is thrust down their throats. Enclosed by glaring whiteness and surrounded by inanimate objects heralding death, Flora is thus rendered in visual terms as a doomed figure, a sitting duck.

(Top) Chris Flanders, the Angel of Death (Richard Burton), and his wealthy victim (Elizabeth Taylor) in symbolic dress; and (bottom) placed pointedly against primitive stone faces.

The stark costumes are equally symbolic. Chris is dressed in a black samurai robe, with a sword around his waist that recalls the ominous floor design. Mrs. Goforth dresses either in basic white or black; for "relief," she wears in one scene a white hood fringed with deep purple. After he has made many requests for food, Flora serves Chris black coffee, announcing fiercely that the milk train doesn't stop here anymore. Her dry, disapproving secretary, Blackie, is distinctly exempt from the austere chiaroscuro: she lives in a blue bedroom, and wears a purple dress. White and black, then, are the film's dominant, symbolically contrasted colors, with a scattering of purples, golds, and blues to offset the visual repetition. As Flora nears her end, the lighting takes on a rich golden hue— natural light is transformed into the stylized quality of light, the virtuoso chiaroscuro, of a de la Tour painting.

Losey's superb use of the wide screen complements the elegance of his decor. Compositions are unfailingly formal. Typical of Losey's precise mise-en-scène is a long take in Flora's living room in which, in the left rear of the frame, Chris is talking on the phone, his figure framed by an arch, while Mrs. Goforth is seated in the right foreground, set against a straight wall. The room is divided by a chair and by huge purple leaves resting in a white vase. The image thus has three separate centers of interest, and the decor has an importance equal to that of the characters: Chris and Flora occupy their own separate space within the frame, placed against backgrounds of differing textures that provide further visual distance between them. The characters' physical distance from each other, emphasized by the whiteness as well as by the horizontality of the wide screen image, is used throughout, in similar compositions, to enforce their temperamental and symbolic opposition.

The camera remains in place for long takes. Movement is reserved for key moments, as when the camera glides through the house in an elegantly sustained tracking shot as, in voiceover, Chris recites the opening of "Kubla Khan" to his temporarily becalmed hostess, or when, near the beginning, the camera follows Flora as she walks through her house, her servants ceremoniously closing sliding doors in rhythmical accompaniment to her processional. For the climactic seduction, as Flora lies in bed while Chris tells her about how he discovered his vocation (he helped an old man to drown himself), the camera circles the characters slowly, its deliberate movement enfolding them in an aura of ritual.

Losey opens the film with a splash of virtuoso editing and camera movement before settling down to a sedate rhythm. The first image (like the last) is of crashing waves, the boom! of the ocean's ceaseless roar. The camera pulls back through a narrow slit in a turret, the expanse of the ocean confined to a mere speck of blue glimpsed through the strangely shaped barricade (looking like something that might have sprung from the hallucinatory imagination of Gaudi). Long shots of Mrs. Goforth's villa and of the surrounding rocky landscape are followed by a close-up of a diamond on her hand, followed by a match cut to the brilliant sun. Chris in the next shot emerges from the sunlit sea, calling out Mrs. Goforth's name as the image switches abruptly to a close-up of Mrs. Goforth being injected with a needle. With a few carefully selected details, this stunning opening contrasts Flora's vulgar materialism and mortality with Chris's ethereal otherworldliness. Framing both characters is the ocean, from which life evolves and to which it returns: Chris rises out of the sea in the opening, harbinger of death, as Flora, on her deathbed at the end, dissolves into it, literally overcome, in Losey's beautiful imagery, by a force greater than herself. The sound of the sea, the "boom" that we hear in the background throughout the film and that figures as a leitmotif in the poet's set speeches, is a token of the ocean's eternal power and cosmic indifference. (As the title for the film, though, "boom" is unfortunate—an easy invitation to critical barbs about *Boom* being a bomb.)

Losey's exquisite film enriches Williams's interesting, belabored play, giving full value to its mystical and allegorical tendencies. Critics at the time praised Losey's visual elegance but were harsh about the Burtons, who certainly seem miscast. Burton is too old for the play's strapping youthful poet, Taylor too young and far too luscious for the dying, withering courtesan. Iconographically, neither is correct for the parts as Williams originally conceived them. Liz simply doesn't look like a woman on death's doorstep, and Burton is frankly too dissipated to look convincing as an ethereal "messenger." Yet temperamentally—and vocally—they bring exactly the right qualities to their roles. Burton's mellifluous voice lends a rich, sonorous tonality to Williams's poetry: the character's conquest of the woman by his voice is expertly rendered. And Liz has just the good-natured vulgarity, the wit and sarcasm, to offset the poet's airiness. She plays Flora as a brassy dame, and though she sometimes lapses into her slack, post-*Virginia Woolf* manner-

isms, her raffish, bitchy tone is perfectly in character. She is especially witty in a long scene with Noel Coward as a gossipy jet setter, the Witch of Capri—in the play, a part for a female. The Burtons play well together, her earthiness and shrillness complementing his melodious baritone, her vulnerability underlining his strength. Chris, after all, wins in this dance of death, and Burton's presence makes the victory convincing: we believe that he has the power to subdue this haughty, resistant, yet basically uncertain woman. Burton's performance is sly and quiet, while Liz cuts up outrageously, putting on a whale of a show for her fans. She is undisciplined, but wickedly amusing, anchoring Williams's and Losey's abstract allegorizing in an earthy realism. She endows the remote pageant with a lively and poignant humanity.

Critically and financially unsuccessful, *Boom* is one of the many Losey films that have acquired a "posthumous" cult reputation. Losey himself is especially fond of it, sometimes citing it as his personal favorite among his works. He knew that it would not be well received, however: "In New York, there was a personal attack on the Burtons and Tennessee Williams. I predicted in advance that the Burtons would be criticized for going arty by working with me and that I would be criticized for going commercial by working with them. Well, I liked *Boom* for what it was, and so did the Burtons, who were very pleased with their performances and with the look of the film, as well they might have been."[2]

Secret Ceremony

Secret Ceremony is one of Losey's most intensely claustrophobic films. Two women, isolated in a baroque London mansion, enact a "secret ceremony" in which fantasy overtakes reality. A strange young girl, Cenci, brings home a prostitute, Leonora, whom she meets on a bus and who resembles her dead mother. She dresses Leonora in her mother's clothes and installs her in her mother's bedroom. Leonora, whose own daughter died by drowning, and who lives in a bare, almost conventlike flat, is dazzled by her new surroundings and decides to adapt to the girl's fantasy. Their secret masquerade is interrupted by the appearance of Cenci's stepfather, Albert, whose lust for Cenci breaks the bond the two women have tentatively established. Pretending to be pregnant, after claiming

to have slept with Albert, Cenci turns against Leonora, ordering her to take off her mother's clothes. The "ceremony" ends with Cenci's suicide and with Leonora stabbing Albert, the fatal intruder, over Cenci's coffin. Only Leonora survives, confined in the grim, bare room in which we see her at the beginning. Lying prone on her bed, she recites a parable which has obvious symbolic reference to her life with Cenci: "Two mice fell into a bucket of milk. One cried for help and drowned. The other kept paddling until he found himself standing on butter."[3]

Losey's other dramas of entrapment (with the exception of *Boom*) are anchored in a realistic premise, while in *Secret Ceremony* we are plunged from the start into a private world that has scarcely any reference to an external or objective reality. The film begins where *The Servant* ends, with its contrasted characters having already reached a psychotic level, and with the expressionistic exaggerations at the end of *The Servant* serving as the dominant mode throughout the later film. As dramatic characters, Cenci and Leonora lack the symbolic resonances of the master-servant figures in *The Servant*; and the characters' conflict is even less sharply pointed, less thematically accessible than the struggle between Mrs. Goforth and the angel of death in *Boom*. *Secret Ceremony* doesn't have the social or political dimension of most of Losey's stories of confined power struggles, yet it is made as if the events that take place in the isolated house are pregnant with meaning. In its Pirandellian oppositions between appearance and reality, the story palpitates with fashionable modernist themes; but the parade of intellectual motifs has less substance than show: the film's weighty manner promises more than it delivers.

Secret Ceremony, then, is Losey at his most pretentious. It is a dark, sour film in which the incest motif, whether actual or fanciful, is nonetheless gratuitously unpleasant; and the grim conclusion, in which Leonora kills Albert, does not flow organically from story or characterizations; Leonora seems too sane to yield to such an impulsive act. If Albert broke up her fantasy menage, she seems like the kind of resilient, no-nonsense woman (especially as Elizabeth Taylor plays her) who would simply move on, surviving as best she could.

For all its thematic deficiencies, the film is in many ways remarkable. Losey's mise-en-scène is characteristically brilliant, his control of mood and atmosphere unwavering in its visual power,

and (within the limits of the script) both Elizabeth Taylor and Mia Farrow are equally splendid. The house in which the story transpires is the single most elaborate setting in Losey's work. It is presented in extraordinary detail, with a visual richness and suggestiveness that give it an equal status with the characters. "The house was built by several architects from 1896 to 1904," Losey said. "It was never completely finished. It is in a pseudo-modern style, but not quite. I've known it for years, since I've lived in London. It is occupied now by a foundation for the convalescence of the mentally ill. It's an enclave outside time and totally outside contemporary London. . . . It's like a cloister in a pre-Raphaelite style."⁴ A riot of Renaissance, Byzantine, and art nouveau architecture and objets d'art, it is an extension of the characters' fantasies, the perfect setting for the characters' manic obsessions, their lunatic role-playing.

Because the story concerns dreamlike wish-fulfillment, Losey gives the film a stylized ambiance right from the beginning. From the opening shot, as Leonora in blond wig looks at herself in a mirror, the events are subtly distanced from reality. Sounds—of closing doors, of traffic, of planes, of children at play, of a music box with a haunting melody repeated throughout the film—are metallic and exaggerated. The house is introduced through a variety of distorting high and low angles; it is presented to us as a sinister, hovering presence. As she moves through the halls and up and down the stairs of this bejeweled palace, exploring this strange new world for the first time, Leonora gasps in wonderment: so do we, and so, for that matter, does Losey. As Philip Strick commented, "Losey places himself with his audience. An intense curiosity is prominent. . . , as though he too were seeing the characters and their settings for the first time and felt slightly in awe of them. . . . The film has an atmosphere of expectancy."⁵

The halls are lined with blue and green tiles, and in an array of polished light and dark woods. Mosaics depict heroic scenes from classical mythology. The living room, with its stone balcony and stained glass, looks like a Byzantine church. Leonora's yellow bedroom is predominantly art nouveau—the dressing table and the bedposts have graceful, flowing curves; the room has an ornate mirrored dresser and a three-part mirror over the dressing table. A cross is placed over the bed. The large circular bathtub looks like a leftover from *Cleopatra*. As the camera moves calmly through the house, it seems to endow all the objects—the paintings, murals,

busts, the Tiffany lamps, the grandiose furnishings—with a trembling inner life. In a superb discussion of the film, Roger Greenspun suggested that its "special quality" is in "the transformations that take place in the miraculous space between the camera and whatever it is photographing. That quality, insubstantial but very real, is continually felt as presence rather than premonition. Its essence is mystery, but not mysteriousness."

Losey's exploring, tracking camera makes the house appear wonderfully, quiveringly alive. This house, steeped in a dark past that is palpably felt, is filled with secrets. It is a maze to be penetrated and deciphered. It is, as Roger Greenspun continues, "a place to live in, a place that has been lived in, a shelter rather than either a museum or a work of art. It isn't haunted. It epitomizes the luxury of being indoors. Long days to be alone in many comfortable rooms, pleasing things to touch, places to sit, the feel of morning sunlight, an afternoon in bed, lamplight, firelight, the calm surfaces of many mirrors."[6]

Soon after she arrives, Leonora hears a siren and peers through the heavy drapery of a downstairs window. The furtive gesture signals the beginning of her retreat from the outside world. The siren belongs to a reality that she is no longer a part of. She becomes suspicious of people and sounds that are connected to the world beyond the front gate. When she hears Albert's whistle, and glimpses him through a window, she cowers behind the drapery, recognizing him at once as a threat to her special relationship with Cenci. The house has taken its hold on her, and it isn't until the end, when Cenci dismisses her, and we hear the resounding echo of a closing door as she leaves for the last time, that she escapes its spell. The house thus enfolds the characters, protecting them from a hostile external reality. With its mixture of architectural and decorative styles, the house is outside time, belonging to no identifiable era, and thereby suspending the characters in a twilight zone. And the awesome formality of the decor underlines the sense of ritual—of "ceremony"—that pervades the story.

Part of the almost supernatural aura of the house is the bluegreen color that seems to wash over it. At the end, Leonora's parable of drowning mice is a verbal echo of the underwater imagery suggested throughout by the controlled color scheme. The bluegreen seems to increase on the lower levels of the house, with the dark watery color, the thick green of the ground-floor kitchen, forming a contrast

Cenci (Mia Farrow) lost among the heavy furnishings in *Secret Ceremony* (top); (bottom) Leonora (Elizabeth Taylor) pleads with Cenci to continue their mother-daughter charade.

to the reigning yellow of Leonora's upstairs bedroom. The most bizarre scene—Cenci's erotic fantasy of losing her virginity with her stepfather, and her cutting of Albert's beard near a chopping board—takes place in the kitchen, the bluegreen of its tiles, walls, and floors providing a kind of dreamlike screen for the action. When Cenci falls off the balcony, after having taken sleeping pills, she seems to be going underwater; a disorienting high angle zoom shot, along with the symbolic color, creates a sense of her dissolution, her death a visual echo of Leonora's drowned daughter.

Like the characters, the house, too, undergoes an actual as well as a ritualistic death. Cenci, stopping the "play," puts the house up for sale, and, at the end, stripped of most of its furnishings, the house looks like a mausoleum. The last interview between Cenci and Leonora takes place in a bare yellow bedroom, with Cenci seated in a plain chair, in a ghostly white light, as Leonora, in a whore's short white skirt (a far cry from the rich greens and purples that she wore as she played Margaret), circles her, begging to be taken back. The house looks devitalized, drained, responding in a kind of sympathetic vibration to the characters.

There are two other significant sets besides the house: an antique shop run by Cenci's two crazed, dead-faced lesbian aunts (Pamela Brown and Peggy Ashcroft, in what is surely the worst moment of their careers), filled with objects that the women have pilfered from Cenci. Their cramped shop, overrun with odd objects, is like a nightmare version of the house. At one point, as Leonora struggles with one of the mad sisters over a stuffed doll, its arm comes off, in an obvious prefiguring of Cenci's annihilation.

The other setting outside the house is an elegant seaside hotel (filmed in Holland, because Losey couldn't find any English resorts that had exactly the qualities he wanted) to which Leonora and Cenci go for a holiday. The scenes at the hotel have a different color and rhythm from those set in the mansion. The framing in these passages is more open and the lighting is brighter. A festive mood predominates as the two women explore this new and rapturously beautiful environment. A burst of lively organ music accompanies their entrance into the hotel, and a golden sunset bathes them in a preternatural glow near the end of their holiday. But the initial celebratory spirit darkens when Albert appears on the beach. He confronts Leonora for the first time: "You look more like a cow than my wife. You have to let her go," he tells Leonora, as there follows

a haunting shot of Cenci riding a horse along the beach, with an eerie variation on the recurrent music-box theme to heighten the power of the image. The scenes at the resort then imitate the descent into darkness described by the main action set within the mansion.

Mia Farrow plays Cenci as a demented child, wide-eyed and dangerous, an unsettling combination of innocence and evil. Cenci is clearly mad, while Leonora is only pretending to be, and so Elizabeth Taylor has the more difficult role. More divided than Cenci, and a stranger to the girl's private fantasy world, Leonora has to be seen in a kind of double focus, as a character playing a part: she is an embittered prostitute imperfectly attempting the role of a grand dame (sometimes, with a crude inflection, or a raffish laugh, she gives herself away). Drawn to Cenci as a reminder of her own drowned daughter, but also shocked by her, she moves in and out of the girl's controlling fantasy. It is a complex part; we are never sure exactly to what degree she is submerged in her disguise, to what level she has lost herself in her adopted daughter's imagination. Taylor's work in this role within a role is continually layered and interesting, but she projects an essential sanity and directness, and so Leonora's seeming capitulation at the end, first when she begs Cenci to stay on as "Margaret," and when she kills Albert, are not entirely convincing: no-nonsense Liz as crazed murderer is a violation of the Taylor iconography.

She and Farrow act together responsively; but Taylor is remarkably awkward in her scenes with the grotesque lesbians and with Robert Mitchum, almost as if, since these characters know she is not Margaret, she is left with no character to play and so falls back on Taylor mannerisms, *Virginia Woolf* bitchiness, stammers, erratic phrasing. Mitchum's droll, macabre performance echoes the classic Mitchum monster, the preacher in *The Night of the Hunter*. He is marvelously wicked in the seduction scene with Cenci: "You've never understood the extraordinary purity of my longings," he whispers insinuatingly. Often glimpsed in the background, seen in long shot through windows as he wanders the gardens of the mansion, Mitchum is a hulking figure of doom.

Secret Ceremony provides the ultimate showcase for Losey's "caressing camera and his love of depths and surfaces," as Roger Greenspun wrote. The difference between "what the project offers and what the director gets" makes *Secret Ceremony* a work of "unexpected grace."[7]

9

Dramas of Enclosure: Four Political Films

THOUGH SCATTERED through Losey's later career (*King and Country* was released in 1964, while the others are products of the 1970s), all four political films are moral tales, although only *King and Country* has the overtly didactic tone of Losey's early work in Hollywood. The situations in the later films are more abstract, the political backgrounds kept deliberately vague. *Figures in a Landscape* and *Mr. Klein*, especially, suppress realistic details in order to suspend the action in a generalized allegorical framework. Losey does not organize his stories in the straightforward journalistic manner of *The Lawless;* the strain of social consciousness that has been part of the fabric of his work since his stint as a director for the Living Newspaper is, in these later pieces, muted and qualified by an interest in ambiguity. An air of the mysterious hangs over these stark dramas, as the influence of Kafka and Pinter has overtaken Brecht's in Losey's handling of political themes.

King and Country (1966)

It is no small distinction to claim *King and Country* as Losey's most claustrophobic film. After a prologue which offers brief glimpses of an outside world, the film is confined to a makeshift army camp where a corporal is tried and executed for desertion. As Brendan Gill vividly writes, "Losey pitches us headlong into the very center of a filthy, sodden, vermin-infested landscape and forces us to observe there the scourging of a poor young dolt."[1] The severe constriction of story and setting heightens the moral indignation of Losey's attack on the kind of false patriotic sentiment evoked by the title. The military establishment that tries and convicts Corporal

ursued by a hovering helicopter in Figures in a Landscape. *Even wide-open spaces re arenas of entrapment.*

Hamp is indicted for its inhuman bureaucracy, its rigidity, its moral and political hypocrisy. The film's targets go beyond the military to include a general condemnation of the senselessness and waste of war.

Losey's theme, then, is honorable, but routine: there is nothing surprising about the film's antimilitary, antiwar position; but, within the framework of its traditional liberal sympathies, it achieves real power. Losey's rendering of mood and atmosphere, and his handling of the actors, transform a standard liberal tract into a powerful drama of personal conflict.

The film focuses on the interaction between two vastly different characters, the innocent, inarticulate Hamp, and the officer charged with defending him. The defense counsel has prejudged his client and agrees to go through the motions of representing him because that is his duty. Hargreaves is a cool character, initially very sure of the correctness of his views. For him, duty to "king and country" supersedes all other considerations. Hargreaves is as eloquent in speech as Hamp is mute. Hamp cannot explain why he deserted— he simply wanted to go home to England because the war was more than he could bear. He can't defend himself and doesn't even try to. Hargreaves's self-righteous belief in patriotic abstractions begins to erode as he gets to know the accused, and as he comes to recognize Hamp's true innocence. His attitude toward the prisoner changes from authoritarian disapproval to fatherly solicitude. At the end, after the firing squad cannot bring themselves to shoot directly at Hamp, and he lies wounded, Hargreaves completes the execution by pointing his gun in Hamp's mouth. It is an act of love; and that we "read" it as such is a tribute to the actors.

The evolving relationship between the two men reverses the pattern of *The Servant*. In *King and Country* two men who differ in station and in character prove to be good for each other; instead of the dissolution of personality that results from confinement in *The Servant*, here prolonged and enforced contact leads to a kind of transcendence. Hamp modifies Hargreaves's initial rigidity, while Hargreaves offers to the condemned man an ideal of personal honor and of social responsibility.

Tom Courtenay and Dirk Bogarde play beautifully opposite each other, discovering complexity in characters that could be interpreted merely as types. In directing them Losey as always is careful to avoid sentimentality. Both characters are presented as flawed,

struggling, contradictory: both are limited in their views of "right" and "wrong," and both need the other in order to become whole. Courtenay plays Hamp as a frightened child, a holy simpleton wide-eyed with terror and lack of comprehension, his face a mask of bewilderment. He makes Hamp too dim to be a hero and clearly unequal to the role of martyr that his trial and execution enforces on him. Courtenay's speech is halting, his Cockney accent gruff and ugly. To Courtenay's rustic simplicity, Bogarde as Hargreaves opposes a worldly self-assurance. His face set, at first, in a perpetual sneer, his eyebrows arched in supercilious disdain, his voice the epitome of urbane cultivation, Bogarde creates a persuasive and maddening figure of self-designated moral virtue. The character is a prig, and yet, like Courtenay's simpleton, he grows and changes as the drama unfolds, his carriage becoming noticeably less erect, his pose of superiority gradually, though never entirely, eroded. Bogarde and Losey are too honest to present a complete character transformation, so that Hargreaves's halting defense of Hamp at the trial indicates internal conflict: the character is divided between his duty to "king and country" and his human obligation to Hamp.

King and Country contains less visual embroidery than any other Losey film. The camera, for the most part, remains stationary, a neutral observer of the action. The images are often taut and still. The entire film takes place in a setting virtually no larger than that of a proscenium stage, but Losey's use of space, with his deep focus compositions which often show several groups of characters within the same frame, and his preservation of natural time by means of long takes, create a palpably realistic environment, one entirely devoid of the cramped, stilted look of filmed theater.

The reality of the image is strengthened by Losey's sound track, which is wonderfully alive with the continuous noise of rain, dripping water, riveting, and the background buzz of excited voices. The sounds suggest an ongoing reality outside the closed frame of the action while establishing a steady undercurrent of tension. Hamp plays the harmonica (he communicates more easily through music than through words), and, suitably, his simple haunting melodies provide the film's sole musical accompaniment.

Typically Losey introduces a "frame" for his confined setting. The film opens with a shot of the Royal Artillery war monument. To the swelling sounds of traffic, the camera circles the monument with ironic intent, as if questioning its idealized image of military glory.

Hamp (Tom Courtenay) is trapped between two of his superior officers (Dirk Bogarde, left) in *King and Country*, Losey's most claustrophobic film.

Losey cuts to stock footage of violent war scenes and then fades into an establishing shot of the dreary makeshift camp that serves as the drama's setting. In a brief expository passage, then, Losey takes us from an idealized view of war to an image of its stark, grim reality, the rain-soaked, rat-infested camp standing in eloquent contrast to the gleaming white marble of the monument. Throughout the story, as a reminder of an external reality, Losey intercuts still photographs that depict romantic views of military heroism, of officers dressed proudly in their traditional regalia.

Losey's fondness for metaphor and ironic contrast is less successful in his use of rats as a reflection of Hamp's imprisonment and, beyond that, as an image of men in war. The young soldiers' mock-trial of a rat is an attempt at a kind of Shakespearean comic subplot or thematic doubling that doesn't work. Losey's freeze frame of a boot at the end, with Bogarde's voice reading a letter of conventional condolence to Hamp's family, is also heavy-handed.

Aside from some too insistent symbolism, Losey's direction is as

utterly controlled and precise as in his films with Pinter. His deliberate pacing, his use of stasis, his supervision of a steadily rising tension, have the bare, inexorable quality of classical tragedy. Like *Oedipus,* the story proceeds in unbroken rhythm to its ghastly foregone conclusion. We watch helplessly and in mounting anger as an insensitive and misguided military establishment is determined to crucify the guileless, sweet-natured, childlike antihero.

Two Allegories: *Figures in a Landscape* and *Mr. Klein*

King and Country is the most closely confined of Losey's films; *Figures in a Landscape,* which ranges over vast deserts, valleys, and mountains, is the most open-ended. And yet both films are equally concerned with entrapment; the doomed protagonists of *Figures in a Landscape* are as imprisoned by the panoramic landscapes as Hamp is by the claustrophobic army camp.

The crisis of *King and Country* is examined in realistic detail. Hamp is given a full psychological history; we know something about his life in the outside world, about his wife, about why he volunteered. Yet the setting in which his story is enacted is realistic only to a limited extent: the microcosmic world the film sets up is parallel to rather than identical with the world of objective reality. The "reality" of *King and Country* is studio-created, whereas *Figures in a Landscape,* a spectacular location film, is set in the real world. Yet the story and the characterizations are kept deliberately vague—are "unreal"—in order to enforce an allegorical reading. *Figures in a Landscape* has the most threadbare script of any Losey film.

Two men, escaped prisoners, are on the run from an army of faceless pursuers and an ominous, persistent helicopter. We are told nothing about these men: we don't know why they were imprisoned or from whom they are fleeing; we know neither the place nor the time of the action. The entire film is concerned with the details of their flight. And yet, paradoxically, for all the reality of the landscape and the precisely recorded moment-by-moment account of the men's attempted escape, this is Losey's most abstract film. The deliberate sketchiness is meant to transform an action drama in the vein of *The Guns of Navarone* or *The Pride and the Passion* into a universal statement of flight and entrapment. But the

characters and the story, more suited to high adventure than to allegory, aren't suggestive enough to support the cosmic reading that Losey intends. The skeletal narrative evokes memories of but cannot really sustain serious comparisons to the parables of Kafka.

As an allegory of modern man in a hostile environment, then, and as a statement of cosmic fatality, the film strains beyond its natural limits; but as a tense adventure drama containing a simple moral about man's will to survive, it is, like the novel on which it is based, genuinely exciting. Robert Shaw's screenplay, and Losey's direction, retain the matter-of-fact, objective tone of Barry England's novel. England writes in a vivid, hard-hitting style of the characters' battles with man and nature. The novel gives us a sense of participation in the characters' epic ordeal. The two men are contrasting types—"complementary halves of a kind of contemporary Everyman," as Vincent Canby wrote.[2] The leader, MacConnachie, is a gruff, burly sort with keen instincts; he is a natural man who knows how to take the measure of nature, treating it as both ally and adversary. His companion, Ansell, is a man of the city, ill equipped to confront the dangers posed by the natural world but more balanced and rational, more wary, than MacConnachie. Like Hamp and Hargreaves in *King and Country*, and like Tony and Barrett in *The Servant*, the two men initially are natural enemies, separated by intellect, age, and character. Yet, in the course of their ordeal, they begin to develop a respect for each other, and they grow to a state of mutual dependence as well. When Ansell cracks, MacConnachie cradles him protectively. MacConnachie the pragmatist, the hard-headed realist, responds only to matters of the moment, whereas the younger man can construct longer-range plans. The older man is clearly more brutal than his partner, yet he has a sense of personal honor, and he is proud of his ability to cope with and to subdue the forces of nature. Because both men are so absorbed in the present, having constantly to be wary of the land, the weather, and their pursuers, we get to know very little about them. We are told that Ansell in the "outside world" likes to pick up girls. We know that MacConnachie has a wife and daughter. Toward the end, he begins to talk about his wife compulsively, musing almost to himself about how he courted her, and about how she waited for him while he was in the army.

The two roles are well cast. Robert Shaw, as MacConnachie, has the ruggedness, the strutting masculinity, and the gruff edge the

part requires, while Malcolm MacDowell, with his slim build, seems suitably ill at ease in the vast and menacing landscapes. Yet Shaw's surliness contains an underlying warmth, and MacDowell's more refined manner only partially conceals a fundamental hardness. Skillful as they are in suggesting a coiled inner life for their characters, they are prevented from realizing full-fledged characterizations because of the film's abstract concept and the sub-Pinter dialogue. The clipped, monosyllabic exchanges echo the rhythm of Pinter's contests of wills, and in his screenplay Shaw tries to set up a tension between what is left unsaid and the often banal or inappropriate quality of what the characters do say. But the language misses the sly humor, the silky allusiveness of Pinter and for the most part seems merely attenuated rather than evocative or interestingly mysterious.

Visually, though, if not intellectually, the film is a tour de force. Depending on images that are often literal recreations of the title, with the fleeing characters glimpsed in only a fragment of the frame, Losey's use of the wide screen is exhilarating, pointing up throughout an ironic contrast between the panoramic vistas and the characters' increasing sense of entrapment. Observed from extreme high angle long shots that reduce them to specks on the land, the men are overwhelmed by an indifferent natural world as pregnant with doom as the eerie, claustrophobic interiors that are the director's usual milieu. The recurrent bird's-eye view from the avenging helicopter—a black skeleton—becomes an image of a grim and inexorable fate.

The threatening, impersonal natural world that the film depicts is one of extreme contrasts, from bare deserts to dense, rain-soaked mountain forests, from overwhelming heat to paralyzing cold. To convey the full range and immensity of the settings, Losey uses a more varied visual style than usual. With its tracking shots, its aerial shots, its circular pans, its gliding crane shots, the film has a vigorous, athletic, thrusting forward movement. In a virtuoso display of technique, Losey makes use of striking visual contrasts between long shot and close-up; between movement and stasis; between long takes and Eisensteinian fragmentation. To heighten the sense of terror, he will often show both the victims and their oppressors within the same frame, the two men huddled in the bottom foreground of the image as their pursuers can be glimpsed in the distance or the helicopter circles wrathfully overhead.

Natural sounds—driving rain, a raging fire, the drone of the hovering helicopter, the buzz of flies, the whir of bullets—are as varied and as kinetic as the camera movement, adding realism and tension to the image. Sometimes, sounds are used for shock effect, as when a woman, surprised by the two men, emits a piercing scream, and when a sudden blare of music on loudspeakers precedes a volley of bullets. And there are startling contrasts between sound and an utter, piercing silence. The dissonant, sparingly used score (by Richard Rodney Bennett) further underlines the film's fatalistic worldview.

The action sequences have more energy than we might reasonably have expected from Losey. The men's recurrent fights with the swooping, buzzing helicopter, which plays a teasing game with them, achieve a macabre poetry.

In the final images, the landscape erases the figures entirely. The two men encounter a cadre of soldiers ranged tensely along a steeply sloping, snow-covered hill: Have they found freedom or captivity? Ansell walks up to the soldiers as a sweeping helicopter shot removes us from the scene. The aerial shot pulls back to an extreme high angle, with Ansell and the soldiers mere specks against the snowy white immensity. The figures become a blot on the landscape before the camera loses sight of them altogether— the figures in a landscape disappear into an infinite whiteness. This final image, seemingly the most "open" in Losey's work, is as chillingly enclosed as the close-up on the imprisoning banister that concludes *The Servant*.

The film, for the most part, was poorly received. "It intermittently reveals Losey at his worst," wrote Jay Cocks in *Time*. "It is all very pompous, the kind of vague allegory that is open to any number of interpretations and able to sustain none."[3] Quickly withdrawn from circulation, the film numbers among Losey's extreme financial failures. But since its sporadic release in 1971, however, it has become a staple in repertory cinemas and has acquired a cult reputation as a Losey tour de force, a film of extraordinary visual and aural virtuosity.

In *Mr. Klein*, as in *Figures in a Landscape*, a story that has the shape of a conventional thriller is transformed into an abstract statement about the human condition. In both films the protagonists are victims of powerful, anonymous forces, of faceless oppressors who conduct relentless witch hunts. In these two late works Losey crosses Brechtian social consciousness with Kafkaesque mystery to

produce abstract political thrillers that strain for metaphysical impact.

The premise of *Mr. Klein* has echoes of Dostoyevsky's *Double* and Conrad's *Secret Sharer*. An art dealer in World War II Paris is mistaken for another man who bears his name. This other Mr. Klein (the "K" of Klein has echoes of Kafka's beleaguered K in *The Trial*, who is also accused of a "crime" he knows nothing about) is a Jewish activist engaged in a plot to bomb the headquarters of the Gestapo. Accused of being a Jew, the Gentile art dealer (Alain Delon) tries to clear himself both by attempting to prove his "racial purity" and by trying to locate the "guilty" Mr. Klein.

As he searches for his elusive namesake, the art dealer becomes a haunted man. His search for the other Mr. K. changes his life as, one by one, he loses his possessions, his mistress, his prominent social status. His hunt forces him to become involved in the hideous and pervasive repercussions of the spreading Nazi power; stripped of his material possessions, the objets d'art that had defined his life, he becomes a more sympathetic character than the indifferent dealer we first see: the Mr. Klein whom we see at the beginning is indeed a "small" character ("klein" means "small" in German). He becomes so divorced from the person he was before his life was invaded that he cares less about his freedom than about finding the other Mr. Klein. When his lawyer comes to him with papers of release, as he is about to be herded into a railroad car with other Jews, he is more concerned with following a man who answered to the name of Klein during the roll call: Has he at last cornered his quarry? He is willing to risk his life—to become Jewish—in order to confront his mysterious and powerful adversary. Our final glimpse of Mr. Klein is of his eyes staring out at us from between the slats of a railroad car as he is being carried to a concentration camp with a trainload of other victims.

Though there is sufficient evidence that another Mr. Klein does exist—he has an apartment and a girl friend, and the art dealer manages to trace a married woman with whom he had an affair— this is less important than the moral and psychological consequences of the search on the non-Jewish Mr. Klein. The film is about the protagonist's confrontation of the "other" both outside and within himself. In imagery and narrative details, the theme of doubleness is insisted upon. Literally, as well as symbolically, there are two Mr. Kleins, and they are linked through a number of factual par-

Images of enclosure in *Mr. Klein:* (top) Mr. Klein (Alain Delon) accused by authorities of being a Jew; (bottom) Mr. Klein lost among other victims in the film's chilling finale.

allels. Both have mistresses; both have had affairs with older married women. Mr. Klein lives in a house filled with paintings and with elegant furniture. The other Mr. Klein lives in a dingy, practically bare apartment. Mr. Klein lives among paintings, while the other Klein is a musician, a flutist. In a long scene early in the film, Robert Klein's mistress reads him a passage from *Moby Dick*, and calls herself Ishmael. Is she, in fact, Ishmael—chorus—to his Ahab? Robert Klein, like Melville's possessed hero, is in pursuit of an elusive and ultimately all-consuming catch. The Melvillean parallel is reinforced when Mr. Klein discovers a copy of *Moby Dick* in the other man's apartment.

Robert Klein has had an affair with his lawyer's wife. The other K. has had an affair with a married aristocrat. When Mr. Klein goes to question this woman in her chateau, she runs out during the night to keep a rendezvous with a lover. As Robert Klein looks on through an upper-story window, his reflection in the glass merges his image with that of the mysterious lover—the other Mr. K.? Our first view of Mr. Klein is in his mirrored bathroom, where his image is reflected in triplicate. After the first "invasion" when he receives a copy of a Jewish newspaper, he looks at himself in a mirror, as if to check his identity. His gaze is troubled, self-questioning, apprehensive: is he really who he says he is, or who he thinks he is? When the other Mr. Klein is paged in a busy restaurant, the protagonist is seen in a mirror as he tries to locate his adversary: there are indeed two Mr. Kleins.

The mirror shots are so recurrent a feature of Losey's mise-en-scène that they are part of his directorial signature, cited by critics as an example of his overelaborate decor; the mirror shots in *Mr. Klein*, though, have particular thematic relevance: the mirror images indicate the character's growing alienation from himself, and the gradual disintegration of his former way of life. Ironically, as he splits into two, as he is progressively dissociated from his former self, he is more whole than the glacially self-contained dealer to whom we are first introduced. In losing himself, he finds himself: the film offers an intriguing variation on this familiar psychological paradox. Although there are no magical transformations of character—the man remains an alienated figure by the force of his obsession—he has yet been made to confront himself at a level that shatters his formerly insulated world-view. Bizarre circumstances have knocked him off his pedestal of privilege; chance has compelled

him into becoming personally involved with the holocaust nightmare erupting all around him. Being a victim has pushed him out
of his isolation, has challenged his social detachment and irrespon-
sibility. Whether or not he is himself Jewish, a grim fate has forced
him to see his connection to the persecuted Jews. At the end, being
carried away to his death, he has merged with the group; he has
become, in symbol if not in fact, a "Jew": a victim.

Placed in an absurd situation, accused of a "crime" of which he
is technically "innocent," Robert Klein does what anyone else would
do: he tries to clear his name. He is not a Jew: why should he share
the fate of the Jews? Yet, as he searches into Mr. Klein's life, as
well as burrowing into his own roots, the dividing line between
himself and the other K., between Jew and non-Jew, becomes, for
him, a dangerously thin one. There may in fact be a trace of Jewish
blood among his ancestors, but that matters less than the fact that,
in an environment where people for the mere accident of belonging
to a particular race are herded like cattle into trains that carry them
to their death, no one is safe, and questions of "guilt" and "innocence" are impossibly blurred if not altogether irrelevant. Under
the Nazi insanity, everyone is a potential victim, a figurative if not
actual "Jew," as the film's beleaguered protagonist learns. This alienated and cold-hearted man, this uninvolved Gentile, confronts
the fact of his human connection to all the "other" Mr. Ks.

Utterly controlled, the film has a consistently glacial quality that
reflects the character of its protagonist. "The theme is indifference,"
Losey said, "the inhumanity of man against man. It is filled with
motifs of indifference."[4] The images are rendered, for the most part,
in cool blues and greens, as if the action is taking place under water.
Paris looks leaden: this is not the city of love, gay and sophisticated,
but a tense, besieged metropolis, "painted" in funereal colors. The
color scheme changes abruptly when Robert Klein goes to visit an
uncle in Strasbourg, which is presented in bright whites and yellows, in the colors of a daytime world sharply differentiated from
the glum nighttime Paris that is the setting for the rest of the film.

Losey's pacing is solemn, heavy. There isn't a single light moment
in the film. Everything is carefully prearranged—objects, paintings,
and tapestries are there for symbolic intent. A tapestry depicting
a vulture pierced through its heart appears under the titles, and
then reappears as it is up for auction at an art gallery that Mr. Klein
patronizes. The wounded vulture is obviously a symbol for the

character of the art dealer as well as for the larger political milieu against which his urgent quest is set. K is a vulture, feeding off the misery of others as he buys paintings from fleeing Jews; but he too is pierced by the Nazi menace, vulnerable to its predatory attacks. At the beginning, he buys a painting—*The Gentleman from Holland*, by A. Van Ostade—from a Jew who needs the money to escape.⁵ K's tone is indifferent—he is remote from the man's predicament. At the end, we see the man among the group at the round-up, as their opening conversation, of buying and selling, is repeated on the sound track, to convict the protagonist once again for his coldness. The film is filled with similar echoes and repetitions, with pieces made to fit precisely into an intricate grand design. Losey's decor is so calculated that, in a minor moment, K's mistress, reclining on a bed, repeats the image of a reclining woman in a painting that hangs over the bed: Losey demands our absolute vigilance at every point. We are never allowed to relax, as the accumulation and repetition of motifs fill in the pieces of the mystery. All of this precision results, ironically, in the final ambiguity of whether or not Mr. Klein has finally found his adversary.

This puzzlelike format, in which we are urged to piece together the various visual clues, as in a mystery, tarnishes the film's powerful moral statement. The elaborate network of correspondences among characters, objects, and places gives the film an inappropriate veneer of "cleverness." One example of the "planted" details occurs when Mr. Klein visits the chateau of the other Klein's mistress. A chamber-music concert is in progress. One member of the ensemble is missing, and a flute rests on the chair of the absent musician. The alert viewer will recall that the other Mr. Klein plays the flute. The presence of the flute, like many details throughout the film, is an oblique, sly reference to the reality of the hunted man. But all these allusions, correspondences, echoes, merely tease us with information that is incidental to the film's moral concerns, its examination of the themes of guilt and responsibility; the tricky Pirandellian coating dilutes the potentially profound subject.

The film's dispassionate tone is announced in the prologue, a chilling medical examination of a woman to determine whether or not she is Jewish. "The anonymous face with which the film opens," Losey said, "is a visage of anguish, of tragedy, and of humiliated feminine dignity. She is a human incarnation of the history that the film recounts."⁶ The doctor treats the woman like a laboratory spec-

imen. The film's sober tone is a defense against the inherently emotional subject and a means, as well, of underlining the grim moral lesson. We are never allowed to identify with the harried protagonist to the extent that we lose sight of the larger psychological, moral, and social issues which his search signifies. Losey thus remains a dedicated Brechtian. "I didn't want the film to be too specific," Losey said. "I didn't want the audience to become involved exclusively in Klein's destiny—after all, he was only one of thirty million people deported that day."[7]

The Nazi menace is conveyed elliptically. Intercut throughout the action is a long shot of a group of anonymous men seated at a table, a map of Paris placed prominently on the wall behind them. Is this the Gestapo, planning its control over the city? The most ominous shot of the meeting room is when, for a moment, we see the table, from a low angle, without anyone seated around it: the empty room makes the Nazi power seem devastating and absolute. The escalating Nazi threat is further evoked in a brief sequence of a number of black cars driving through the city, in what we learn only at a later point is a practice test for the round-up of Jews that ends the film. The sleek black cars snaking through the leaden streets look like harbingers of death; like the helicopter in *Figures in a Landscape*, they are an image of a ghastly and incontrovertible fate. In a few scattered images Losey suggests the presence in the city of a sinister external force that enfolds Mr. Klein's private drama.

A scene in a crowded restaurant, and one at a music-hall performance, further convey the mounting tension that throttles the besieged city. The restaurant, where a Mr. Klein is paged but never seems to appear, is a hubbub of noise—the boisterous diners are overexcited, the room feels ready to explode. This tense background mirrors the questing Mr. Klein's own private anxiety. At another point in his search, Mr. Klein goes to a vaudeville entertainment where the audience looks like caricatures from a Georg Grosz cartoon. The lighting from below in this scene makes the faces look grotesque, reptilian: the rich, decadent audience, which carries to surreal dimensions the film's motif of indifference, laughs lasciviously at a burlesque of Jewish persecution. In a ghoulish premonition of holocaust, this well-fed audience screeches like a pack of vultures at the mock antics of the onstage racial comedy.

In the final sequence, the hints sprinkled throughout the film of

approaching doom are dramatized with stunning impact. To depict the pogrom, in which the Jews are herded into a stadium and arranged in alphabetical groupings, Losey drains the image of color—the action is shot in a deadly, neutral gray. The frames become increasingly crowded, and Losey uses jerky hand-held cameras to give the sequence a sense of documentary immediacy. Visually, these gray, densely populated, movement-filled scenes are set off from the rest of the film. *Mr. Klein* ends with a chilling descent into darkness, as the protagonist's eyes stare out at us from among the huddled, shadowy figures that surround and engulf him in the packed car. Like *Figures in a Landscape*, *Mr. Klein* ends with its protagonist caged by the faceless and omnipotent enemy.

The Assassination of Trotsky

The Assassination of Trotsky is surprisingly modest. With goals far less lofty than the allegorical intentions of *Figures in a Landscape* and *Mr. Klein*, the film emerges as a good political thriller in which a specific historical event serves as the basis for another Losey story about a house invaded. The film offers only a sketchy account of Trotsky as a political figure. Losey's character seems curiously disconnected from his past—his legendary association with Lenin, his sustained and prophetic criticism of Stalin, his importance as a political thinker and orator are alluded to only briefly. In exile in a barricaded villa in Mexico, Trotsky lives in a severely circumscribed world, his eminent role in world-shaking events only a faint echo. Losey is more interested in the psychological effects of Trotsky's confinement than in the character's seminal place in political history. "He was a very sad man," Losey said, "a hounded man who had beome a neurasthenic. . . . If you can imagine yourself cofounder of the revolution, head of the Red Army, closed up in that crummy little garden in the middle of 1940 Mexico, what could life be like?"[8]

When he first began planning the film, Losey assumed that audiences would be familiar with the political background and that he could therefore concentrate on what Trotsky had become in his exile rather than on what he had been, in the past, in his prime, as a chief architect of the Russian Revolution. "I assumed that everyone knew who Trotsky was. And I quickly found out that most

people didn't know. I tried to cram a lot of ideological material into the tapes [that Trotsky records, as part of his political autobiography] to give some idea of the background. And I started out with a technical idea, that I could project images of the Russian Revolution on to the walls of the garden. . . have all kinds of floating images of the past working within that confined story. It simply, mechanically, didn't work."[9]

In a reversal of his usual methods, then, Losey doesn't give his material symbolic amplification but treats the death of Trotsky as the focus of a taut thriller. On this level, the film is skillfully constructed, establishing, through a continual and increasingly tense pattern of cross-cutting, the worlds of both Trotsky and his assassin. Both characters live in equally enclosed environments, Trotsky by necessity sequestered in a heavily-guarded villa, and the assassin, Frank Jackson, seen most often in a squalid, bare hotel room. Both men are presented as equally mysterious, private, unreachable. The sullen assassin, given to sudden explosions of temper, often sits in a catatonic stupor, his eyes shielded behind dark glasses. He is often placed in the rear or at the side of the frame, to underscore his outsider status. His evolving physical relationship to the villa, and to Trotsky, is carefully traced. He is seen first outside the walls of the villa, from a high angle long shot that diminishes his height and that makes the villa seem like a fortress that he must penetrate and conquer. His first entrance into the villa is photographed in long shot, from the street outside, as he walks tentatively into its dark recesses. He has been invited to a luncheon party, yet he remains physically aloof from the host and the other guests.

The contact between the two men—the invader and his quarry—remains distant. Frank gains access to Trotsky because his girl friend is one of Trotsky's most trusted assistants, and Frank poses as a student of the Revolution. With each visit, he becomes more integrated into Trotsky's world. From lurking at the edges of the frame, he begins to occupy a more central place in the group of characters surrounding Trotsky until, in the stunningly staged assassination, the two men are seen alone in the frame, together for the first time. "I shall die believing in the Communist future," Trotsky says into one of his tapes. As he speaks, a circular pan takes us from his desk to the garden outside his study window; his wife, Natasha, opens the window into the garden, and leaves the room. Losey holds the camera in place for a daringly long take on the empty, sun-filled garden. Then, in dark glasses, the messenger of

death given easy access to the master's study, no longer an outsider, Frank Jackson enters the frame: it is a chilling moment, its impact strengthened by Losey's careful visual transformation of the assassin from remote outsider to a trusted member of Trotsky's inner circle.

Handsome, sneering, diabolical, Frank Jackson (brilliantly played by Alain Delon) looks like a gangster from a 1930s melodrama. And like the archetypal gangster figures played by Cagney and Robinson, he is presented as psychologically damaged, as sexually maladjusted in some unexplained way. Sinister, filled with rage, he is a dangerous, dark stranger, a psychotic recluse in the pay of an anonymous boss: a hit man. Frank treats his girl friend, Gita, with uncontrollable flashes of contempt. Obsessed with him, sensing his distance, his essential indifference to her, Gita threatens to kill herself if he leaves her. "I can't take these mood of yours. . . . If you go, I'll kill myself. I don't know who I am, I don't know who you are." Early in the film, the two go to a bullfight. As the bull is gored, Frank sits there coolly, immobile behind the ominous dark glasses, while Gita is sickened by the violence. At a later point, we see Frank fondling a knife, his image reflected in the mirrors of the huge, ugly dresser in his rundown hotel room. He clearly relishes violence, and his tensed, hunched posture suggests imminent eruption.

We are told nothing of his political motives. He seems, in fact, to be simply a hired killer acting from base mercenary motives rather than political conviction. When he and his "contact" meet to discuss strategy, they look and act like underworld figures. When Frank is arrested, after the assassination, he shouts deliriously for his mother. "Who are you?" a police inspector asks him. "I killed Trotsky," he answers, chillingly, as his hardened, defiant, mad face is held in a freeze frame. More than that bare fact we are never told. The character remains a mask, sinister and impenetrable. "I find characters like that very interesting," Losey said. "The mysterious poet in *The Romantic Englishwoman* is the same kind of remote figure."[10]

As the assassin, Alain Delon (who was a powerful, brooding presence as Mr. Klein as well) gives what is probably his finest performance, cold-eyed, wary, a figure of insinuating nervous energy. And yet, as he ingratiates himself with Trotsky, he becomes, in fleeting moments, an appealing character; we can understand Trotsky's attraction to him.

Frank Jackson is presented, then, as a mythic nemesis, an un-

knowable, shadowy figure, and it is one of Losey's typical reversals that his Trotsky is as dark and as unexamined a character as the fateful intruder. Far from being set up as a transcendent, pursued hero, Trotsky is remote, glacial, inaccessible to the other characters or to us. Politically, the film's Trotsky is little more than a collection of topic sentences: "I am a proletarian revolutionary, a Marxist, a dialectical materialist, an irreconcilable atheist." "Art is one of the ways man finds his bearings in the world." "Art under Stalin marks the decline of the proletarian revolution." At the beginning of the film, after the titles, Trotsky states, in a voiceover, "A revolution takes place only when there is no other way out." His fabled brilliance as an orator, his ability as an organizer, his disaffection from Lenin and Stalin, his miscalculations about intraparty strategy—all these stages of his career as a political activist at the very center of revolutionary activity were well in the past, a world removed from the Mexican garden in which he is now confined. In the final period of his life that the film covers, Trotsky was absorbed entirely by his writing; his world was an interior one, as he struggled against failing health (and perhaps a premonition of doom, a foreboding that someone would be able to break through the cordon of guards standing watch on the ramparts of his villa) to finish the record of his political and intellectual autobiography. The inner drama of a writer is not very promising material for a filmmaker, and so Losey is left with an essentially static, sedentary figure who recites political generalizations: Trotsky as a writer is no more compelling or usable a dramatic character than Picasso as a painter or Wagner as a composer. In the film, then, Trotsky is less visually or emotionally striking than his assassin; he is a basically ornamental figure, important to the drama for, in a sense, his "name" value only. Losey's refusal to treat the Communist exile as a great man, or even as a tortured one, is enforced by Richard Burton's austere performance. Consciously subduing his usual oratorical flourish, Burton plays the historical character as a sober intellectual, a man who lives almost entirely within his mind. To erase any suggestion that Trotsky is a larger-than-life hero, Burton speaks in a mellow monotone, erasing the inflections of his usual declamatory style. Drained of primary vocal and emotional coloring, his interpretation is indeed Brechtian. Burton makes no attempt to sound like anyone other than himself, in self-conscious low gear: there is no effort at vocal imitation, there is no trace of a Russian accent, although Burton is made up, in

beard and pince-nez, to at least suggest visual echoes of the real-life Trotsky.

Any actor playing a legendary historical character must decide how far he should attempt to imitate the mannerisms and the appearance of the original. Any world-famous actor, like Burton, with an individual sound and style of his own, is at an even greater disadvantage in such an assignment, unless he has the mimetic virtuosity of Laurence Olivier, which Burton decidedly has not. We are then conscious of the fact that Richard Burton is playing Trotsky in a detached and minimalist way, in a cool style designed to frustrate audience sympathy. Losey wanted Burton for the role because he felt that "Trotsky needed to be an 'actor' because Trotsky himself was an actor, and also a man with a voice."[11] In casting Burton, he got a "voice," but not much else—which was, apparently, exactly his intent.

With neither Trotsky nor his assassin allowed heroic gestures, political idealism is reserved, briefly, for a group of anti-Trotsky Mexican Communists who attempt an unsuccessful invasion of Trotsky's compound. Their leader is a handsome, vigorous figure, iconographically a vision out of an Orozco mural. A high-powered worker, he calls Trotsky "an idealist, an enemy to the proletarian revolution, a counterrevolutionary." Since he is so dynamic, are we meant to take his assertions seriously? The political position of the Mexican Communists is examined no more closely than any of the other political stances, and, after their failed invasion and their arrest, they disappear from the film, as characters and as a political force. That their leader has been presented as a hero, even if only briefly, introduces a political ambiguity that is never resolved.

Losey's treatment of politics is thus disappointingly thin—the film is something of a high-class *Day of the Jackal*—but his handling of atmosphere, and his mixture of realist and formative techniques, are characteristically striking. For the May Day parade that begins the film and for the scene of reporters converging on the police station where the assassin has been taken, Losey experiments with a cinema verité effect, using a jerky hand-held camera to impart a sense of historical immediacy. These documentary touches deliberately clash with the often stylized sound track and the director's characteristic use of works of art as symbolic commentary. The film risks strong shifts in style as it blends nature and artifice in effective counterpoint.

The sound track rearranges connections between time and place. Burton's voiceover is often used to link scenes or is heard over the action; frequently we hear Trotsky before we see him. As he was in real life, Trotsky *is* his voice. In the bullfight scene, natural sound is suppressed as indecipherable whisperings and chants accompany the violent imagery. Whenever Frank calls at the villa, the bell sounds with a terrible doom-ridden clanging. After Frank announces, "I killed Trotsky," the screen is "filled" with a deathly and prolonged silence, as all natural sound is erased. As the police question Frank, the metallic recording of sound corresponds to the distortions of space created by the use of a wide-angle lens: these expressionist techniques suggest the challenge to the moral order which the assassination of Trotsky has provoked.

Murals by Orozco and Rivera of revolutionary scenes and of proletarian life are recurrent visual motifs. The semiabstract, muscular figures in the murals suggest a political force that emanates from neither Trotsky nor his assassin. Losey is clearly fascinated by the kinetic energy, the vigor and muscularity, of the emblematic figures in the murals; he returns to them throughout the film, almost in ironic counterpoint to the political limpness of his characters.

The film's color does not echo the grim browns and blacks of the murals. Instead, Losey's images are often bathed in a shimmering yellow; as in *Accident* and *The Go-Between,* Losey powerfully creates the effect of steamy weather on a group of tense characters. Trotsky's wife says, "It's so hot in here—it's like being drowned." Trotsky and Frank Jackson hide out in cramped, prisonlike rooms with walls that drip from the awful humidity of the Mexican climate. The heat enervates and paralyzes the characters, making them moody, irritable, prone to violent rages. Trotsky's garden is bathed in a hot yellow light, luminous and suffocating. It is in its textural qualities—its closed rooms and heavy atmosphere of terrific heat, its use of murals, its transformations of natural sounds, its rendering of Trotsky's villa as a hermetic and yet vulnerable environment— rather than in its political discourse, its presentations of ideological debate, that the film achieves real distinction. *The Assassination of Trotsky* is less an account of the last days of the Communist leader than a texturally stunning variation on the recurrent Losey theme of a house invaded by a menacing outsider.

10

Two Plays on Film:
A Doll's House and *Galileo*

TWO OF LOSEY'S most interesting recent films, *A Doll's House* (1973) and *Galileo* (1975), are adaptations of seminal modern plays. Losey approaches the two works in entirely different styles; for *A Doll's House* his method is one of scrupulous cinematic realism; for *Galileo*, one of theatrical stylization. His version of Ibsen's drama has the look and feel of a movie, while his treatment of Brecht deliberately has the aura of filmed theater. Shot on location in a small Norwegian town, *A Doll's House* is "authentic," while *Galileo* is set against a distinctly studio-created background. The visual "frame" in each case is appropriate, since the physical reality of Losey's *Doll's House* heightens Ibsens's psychological realism, while the more remote and abstract settings for *Galileo* preserve Brecht's alienation from historical reality.

Although their methods are radically different, both plays have a didactic intent. Ibsen's moral lessons are filtered through complex characterizations and a story that encourages audience identification; Brecht, on the other hand, places his ideology at the center of his drama: the ideas themselves are more prominent than the characters who express them. *Galileo* is one of the few Brecht plays which at least partially realizes the stated goal of the alienation technique to promote an idea, a lesson, an ideology, rather than to arouse audience sympathy for specific characters in a specific situation. Frequently as in *The Good Woman of Setzuan* or *The Caucasian Chalk Circle* or *Mother Courage*, Brecht created such dramatically engaging characters that audiences couldn't help responding warmly to them, as they would to any well-drawn and fully rounded figures. Brecht's own impassioned responses to his

197

characters often made them more heroic and complex than he intended; but Galileo is a difficult character to warm to, and there is little chance for audiences to become emotionally involved with him at the expense of considering the larger philosophical and political questions which his conflict of conscience addresses.

In his choice of visual styles for the two adaptations, then, Losey honors the essential spirit of the originals. Both adaptations, which employ different techniques to make plays look comfortable within the film frame, are further evidence of Losey's remarkable sensitivity as a collaborator.

Losey's film of *A Doll's House* (with Jane Fonda) was made in the same year as another version directed by Patrick Garland and starring Claire Bloom. This latter film was released theatrically in the United States, while Losey's was shown on television (and has only recently begun to be shown in repertory cinemas). The decision was ironic, for the theatrical Garland adaptation would be more at home on television, while Losey's version belongs on movie screens. Garland's film is a straightforward rendering of the play, uninflected in visual style or in performance; it is intelligent, but thoroughly uninspired. Attempting no changes in the play's handling of time and place, the film inadvertently exposes Ibsen's old-fashioned, well-made-play dramaturgy. Ibsen's characterizations (the play was written in 1879) were strikingly modern, and his ideas about marriage are still pertinent, "timely," but his narrative construction is rooted firmly in an outmoded nineteenth-century theatrical tradition. The play has a complicated plot in which past events exert an enormous pressure on the present. To save her husband's life, Nora borrowed money from Krogstad, forging her dying father's signature on the promissory note. Now Krogstad, who works for Nora's husband in a bank, is faced with the loss of his job, and he threatens to expose Nora's crime if she doesn't convince her husband not to fire him. Krogstad writes a letter to Torvald which accuses Nora: that letter becomes the primary dramatic catalyst. When Torvald reads it, he explodes, charging Nora with having wrecked his career. His response is shockingly different from the "miracle" Nora had imagined would take place, in which Torvald would heroically accept the burden of her crime, although she would not let him. When Krogstad writes another letter, withdrawing his charge, Torvald relents; but his earlier explosion has disabused Nora of her romantic schoolgirl notions and she sees the hollowness of her mar-

riage and the self-denying role she has been playing in it. Events, neatly timed, thus precipitate crisis and control character development; in technique, though not in character drawing, the play is a well-made melodrama, its plotting airless and artificial, meticulously preplanned.

Stories in well-made plays like *A Doll's House* are divided into a tidy five-act structure in which tension builds steadily from exposition to complication to a final unraveling. Ibsen's plotting is thus frankly contrived, as a series of events occur within a limited time span and a single setting. The play's compression of time and place, and its dependence on coincidence and on props like letters to move the action forward, belong to a set of theatrical conventions no longer in use (and no longer usable, unless parodied or concealed with unusual dexterity). Dramatists building their plays according to the well-made formula often exhibited great ingenuity in their ability to contain the complicated action and what was usually a large cast of characters within a single setting. Characters referred to past events (the retrospective method) to inform the audience of material that could not be shown within the severely limited time/space framework. Characters exited and entered the drawing rooms of well-made plays on cue, whenever the plot demanded their appearance; and events transpired in a crescendo of climax and catastrophe. The world of the well-made play, then, is a rigorously closed one, and therefore alien to the inherent open-endedness as well as the affinity for objective reality, of films. What passes for reality in the well-made play is too mechanical and circumscribed, too immaculate, to be convincing within the film frame.

In Garland's adaptation, which does nothing to accommodate Ibsen to a new medium, the story feels patently untrue. The film never achieves a natural, flowing rhythm. The house in which the action is set looks perfectly realistic, as opposed to being a stage set; but the director's treatment of the available space is essentially theatrical—the actors look as if they are on a stage, under a spotlight, rather than occupying a space that is both real and deep.

Losey and his scenarist, the playwright David Mercer, recognized the hazard of transporting Ibsen's narrative structure intact, and therefore opened up the material, extending its dimensions in both time and space. Events that precede the action of the play, and that strongly influence it—the death of Nora's father, Torvald's illness, the family's departure from cold Norway to temperate Italy for

Torvald's health, the friendship of Nora and Kristine, the relationship between Kristine and Krogstad—are shown in the film's suc-
cinct opening section. This prologue thus dramatizes material that
the characters refer to in the play's entangled Act I exposition, and
connects the central action—the events leading up to Nora's departure from her husband and her children—to a tangible past, one
that we have seen. The entire movement of the story is now less
mechanical than in Ibsen's tightly compressed drama. In the theater, the events leading to Nora's moment of revelation happen so
quickly that her decision to leave her home can seem abrupt and
mechanical, something that happens on cue, according to the playwright's master plan. In Losey's film, with the action taking place
over a much greater range of time, we can see Nora's victimization
in a way that is both more gradual and more direct, and hence one
that takes advantage of the syntax of film rather than theater.

Once the film reaches the point at which the play begins, Losey
does not simply settle in by limiting the action to the Helmers'
house. This kind of confinement would contradict the openness of
the introductory scenes, making them seem like a halfhearted effort
to "open up" proscenium-bound material. Losey wants to preserve
the movielike pace and texture of his opening, and so throughout
the film he breaks up the theatrical time/space continuum by setting
the action in a variety of locations and by cross-cutting among them
for dramatic emphasis and tension. Most of the settings are interiors—Dr. Rank's apartment, Krogstad's house, Helmer's bank office, Mrs. Linde's rooms, and two restaurants, in addition to the
Helmers' rooms. Some transitional scenes take place in the snow-
covered streets of the town; the charged confrontation between
Nora and Krogstad, who is threatening to blackmail her, is set on
a wooden bridge that spans a frozen stream; as Krogstad threatens
to expose Nora for forging her father's signature, she looks trapped
by the overhead beams of the bridge, her physical confinement a
striking reflection of her mounting sense of doom.

Losey's extension of the action in time and place was greeted
with the expected critical objections. The complainers argued that
Nora is a prisoner in her husband's house, entrapped in the role
of his pretty, dimwitted doll, and that, in taking so much of the
action outside this doll's house, into the real world, and a beautiful,
almost fairyland environment of quaint architecture and immaculate
snow-covered streets at that, Losey diluted and fatally "sweetened"

Krogstad (Edward Fox) "trapped" beneath the beams of a bridge in *A Doll's House*.

the context in which Nora's struggle occurs. But Nora's "imprisonment" is psychological, not physical. She is free to come and go as she pleases, but she is never free of her mask as a flirtatious, childlike wife. Helmer's tyranny does not extend to keeping Nora at home; quite the opposite, he is proud to take her out, to show her off. Nora doesn't have much to do at home; her responsibilities are taken care of by maids, so she has the time and the freedom to go out. In the first scene of the play, after all, she is returning home from a shopping spree with her children. Showing Nora in the "outside" world is merely a way of taking advantage of what a film can do more fully and with more conviction than a play can—it in no way violates the truth of Ibsen's psychological portrait.

The multiple settings are not then simply an arbitrary way of relieving visual monotony. They are chosen purposefully, for their aptness in revealing character (as in the tensely framed exterior shots between Nora and Krogstad, and the charming scene of Nora grabbing cakes in a frilly tea room). Losey's avoidance of theatrical

confinement achieves real distinction in the sequence of cross-cutting between the Stenborgs' party, where Nora dances the tarantella, and a conversation between Kristine and Krogstad in which Kristine tries to persuade Krogstad to retrieve his letter. Nora's dance and the conversation are closely connected, since, after the party, Helmer will open the letter unless Kristine can convince Krogstad to retract it. Nora dances with frenzy, as if her life depended on it (which, in her view, it does). In the play, we don't see the party, and the interview between Krogstad and Kristine takes place, improbably, in the Helmers' apartment, as sounds from the party upstairs are heard as offstage noises. In the film the two events transpire in separate places: Kristine, quite logically, has gone to Krogstad's house to speak to him, but, through cross-cutting from one place to the other, Losey suggests simultaneity and creates a sense of urgency, of escalating tension rising to a climax. The passage is a striking instance of the ability of film to create spatial and temporal connections through parallel editing.

Losey's deep focus compositions protect the material from seeming stagy. Many interior scenes contain windows through which can be glimpsed an ongoing reality: Nora's drama is part of the flow of life of the town rather than being isolated from it. There is the sense throughout of a world beyond the frame. The Helmer's large apartment is a series of rooms that open into one another, so that there is a sense of deep and receding space; behind the living room can be seen the dining room; on the other side of the stairs from Nora's bedroom is the children's room—the physical separation between Nora and her children, the children glimpsed in the rear of the frame with their nurse, makes a telling point about Nora's distance from them. Losey's filmic use of space is announced in the first scene as Nora and Kristine sip hot chocolate in a restaurant. The two women, meeting for a last time before Nora is married, are seated next to a large window through which can be seen skaters moving in graceful circles and pirouettes. The counterpoint between the seated women and the revolving skaters, and the deep focus which presents two fields of action within the same frame, immediately announce the kind of visual generosity and complexity that Losey will use throughout.

Spatial depth is reinforced by Losey's use of natural sounds: the jangling bells of horses' harnesses and of sleighs traveling through the snow, tolling church bells, the music of Christmas revelers

surround the action. These realistically rendered off-screen sounds of the town deepen the reality of the image. The ticking clocks that are heard as aural accompaniment in many interior shots also validate objective reality, and in their insistent, measured beat they introduce an underlying tension as well.

The settings, as always in Losey's work, are carefully chosen to reflect character. The Helmers' apartment is particularly subtle. Its personality reflects Helmer rather than Nora. The rooms are sedate, heavy, utterly ordered and dignified: nothing is out of place in these rich and elegant rooms; every painting and ornament, every piece of furniture, is perfectly placed, perfectly coordinated in size and color to the overall design of the room. The apartment, in short, looks nothing like a doll's house, being clearly the residence of very sober and well-off adults. There is no sign of Nora in these stiff and beautifully appointed rooms, no expression of her lightheartedness and charm. The mise-en-scène makes her seem like a stranger in her own house: she seems far more in her element in the bright tea shop where she munches happily on rich pastries.

The extreme order of this household—do people really live here?—is underscored by the steadily ticking clocks and by the vases of flowers placed on tables. The studied, formal, elegant floral arrangements become something of a sly comment on the perfection of the interior design.

Losey's color scheme bathes much of the action in a cool blue light that conveys an immediate sense of the cold northern climate. Indoor warmth and outside cold, the misted windows suggesting the difference in temperature, are rendered with a directness that we can almost feel. The Helmers' apartment is dominated by rich shades of brown which evoke an image of Torvald's masculine control, while Nora's white bedroom offers a relief from the prevailing heaviness and maleness of the decor. Dr. Rank's dark apartment is emblematic of his own impending death, while Krogstad's barely furnished house has a different color altogether, a cold blue green that has none of the solidity of Helmer's rooms and that suggests his outsider status, his growing desperation to find a secure place for himself: his house has the look of impermanence, a residence that has not yet been settled into.

The surrounding white landscape is a contrast to these dark, heavy interiors. Another color contrast is in the way that Nora dresses—except for when she is in red, masquerading as a gypsy for her

dance at the party, Nora appears throughout in black, as if she were
in mourning. The sober colors are an ironic counterpoint to her
lively personality, her childlike manner, and subvert audience expectation as well.

The film's array of textures—the rich, subdued color, the furnishings, the velvet draperies, the flowers, the delicate china, the
silver coffee service, the ceramic pot-bellied stove—is complemented by Michel Legand's elegant score, which, like his music for
The Go-Between, suggests hurried movement. Its pace is particularly appropriate as a transitional device in the opening passages,
where time and action are telescoped. The quick, darting rhythms
imitate the graceful motion of the ice skaters in the first scene. The
melodically full score, highlighted by the purity of the recurrent
solo French horn, assumes a variety of tones, from festive to lyric
to melancholic.

The world that the film creates, both within the Helmers' house
and outside, in the magically beautiful town, is thus an idealized
one. This quaint and immaculate Norwegian village, untouched by
the modern world, is enchanting, and the snow that covers the earth
and the buildings in pristine whiteness lends the setting a fairy-tale
charm. Is the film too elegant, its surface textures too beguiling,
for Ibsen's portrait of an unhealthy marriage? Perhaps here, as in
some other films (notably the conclusion to *The Romantic Englishwoman* and the lush scenes at the hotel in *Secret Ceremony*), Losey
permitted himself to get a little carried away by his own delight in
interior design. But Nora's world is one of physical comfort; and
Losey's impeccable taste in mise-en-scène is never indulged at the
expense of interpretation or psychological insight.

As Nora, Jane Fonda is tracing a parallel evolution in her own
life and career, from the star of Broadway fluff like *Barefoot in the
Park* and the pin-up doll of *Barbarella* to the political activist and
serious actress who blossomed in the late 1960s. But Fonda, thank
goodness, has the integrity not to turn Nora into a humorless modern feminist. There is in her work no strident or self-conscious
pointing to contemporary parallels. Nora is presented as a woman
of a particular time and place and class, and her decision at the end
to strike out on her own is not a victory for 1970s feminism but
instead an appropriate and daring choice for a woman of an earlier
age. Fonda also sounds convincing as a nineteenth-century woman,
which is surprsing since her voice often has a harsh and distinctly

contemporary middle American twang. Her pronunciation is softer here than usual, her speech more mellow and fluent, although, in an attempt to downplay her American quality, she sometimes affects a strained British accent. Like her director, Fonda demonstrates respect for the past: there is no condescension in her work to a character who lives in a world with values different from her own.

Any actress who plays Nora faces the problem of how to make the character's final departure from her husband and children seem convincing. If she plays Nora as a simpering fool who becomes bitterly disillusioned when Helmer reveals himself, in his rage over Krogstad's letter, the character's new-found strength and resolve are not likely to be believable. But if, like Fonda, she plays Nora as clever and strong right from the beginning (as the part is written), then her final action does not seem either sudden or shocking, but springs from her character in an integral way. Fonda indicates Nora's intelligence and determination; when she is being silly or childlike, when she acts the "squirel" or the "skylark," it is clear that she is only playing a part: she is pretending to be what her society expects of a pretty young wife. Fonda lets us see how Nora uses her sex appeal to manipulate not only her husband—who is no match for her—but everyone else as well. She makes Nora a conniving woman who uses her womanliness as a weapon; it is the only kind of self-defense that her society has allowed her. But Fonda's interpretation, while giving full value to Nora's innate shrewdness, does not make her humorless or coldly calculating. Her Nora is a tease who likes to enjoy herself, who plays like a child with her children, who stages childlike and petulant rebellions against her husband's rules by sneakily eating macaroons, who flirts mindlessly with Dr. Rank and gossips giddily with Kristine. Her Nora is clearly a child-woman much in need of development. Her performance builds in intensity, as Nora feels her situation growing more desperate; her tarantella, at the emotional high point just before the confrontation with Torvald, has real passion.

Fonda and her director did not get along—one of the few times that Losey and one of his stars clashed. Fonda wanted to play the role in a warmer, more emotional way than Losey allowed. Her natural animation collided with Losey's more restrained temperament. As she worked for arousing audience identification, Losey was edging toward an almost Brechtian detachment. The "hot" star and her "cool" director finally worked out a compromise, one that

in fact beautifully serves Ibsen: Fonda's work is nicely shaded so that the character's initial liveliness is balanced by her sobriety at the end. Fonda's may well be the most open and giving performance in any Losey film, despite the director's controlling influence, and yet, especially in the final scene, we can feel the director's restraints on her: her great energy is held in check, her power curbed by Losey's decorum. As a result, Fonda's energy is partly internalized, giving the performance a tension that works for the material. Losey clamps down on the final encounter between Nora and Helmer, where she announces her intention to leave. Determined not to give the scene a big, heroic reading, Losey cuts the dialogue to a minimum and directs Fonda in a severe style: no melodrama here, no histrionics. Fonda is not pronouncing radical doctrine, she is talking to her husband, unmasked, for the first time. The smiles, the flounces, the flighty gestures, are erased. She speaks her mind in a simple, straightforward manner. Working against theatrical stereotype, Losey directs the famous scene in an understated style. Nora, after all, feels immensely saddened rather than triumphant about the uncertain fate that awaits her, and the quiet delivery is therefore more appropriate than the bravura set piece that egocentric actresses typically offer for the climax. Nora is one of Fonda's most subtle and intelligent performances, and it deserves far more recognition than it has received.

Losey surrounds Fonda with an excellent company whose performances balance hers. Like Fonda, the other actors avoid melodramatic simplification, presenting their characters as rounded and complex figures. David Warner thus does not interpret Torvald as the monochromatic villain of the piece: he is a stiff, pompous man, thoroughly conventional, thoroughly self-seeking, and as much a victim of his society's sexist attitudes as Nora is. Warner suggests that Torvald cares for Nora, and he makes very convincing the husband's sexual attraction to his wife. His Torvald is not the stick figure of theatrical tradition, but a proud, quick-tempered, weak man of flesh and blood. Trevor Howard makes of the dying Dr. Rank (whom we first see dressed in customary black, framed in a mirror in his dark house) an ironic figure of doom. Howard invests Rank with a sardonic humor, lacing the character's mournful valedictory speeches with a grim and mordant wit.

As the secondary couple, Krogstad and Kristine, whose developing relationship and growing trust of each other point a sharp

contrast to Nora and Helmer, Edward Fox and Delphine Seyrig are truly distinguished. Fox plays Krogstad as a desperate character, fighting to hold onto his job and his respectability, rather than merely as Nora's nemesis. Losey permits Fox to scale his performance very high, at a feverish pitch; his threats to Nora are hurled forth with terrific force. But as he comes under the influence of Mrs. Linde, his explosions are softened. As Ibsen intended, the character moves in a contrary direction to Nora—his anxiety lessens as hers increases; at the end, he has begun to establish a place for himself in society, just as Nora is about to abandon hers. As Mrs. Linde, Delphine Seyrig, the most charming of actresses, is the calm at the center of the storm. Seyrig's own womanliness and wisdom counterpoint Nora's childlike ways, and her stability corrects Krogstad's volatile temperament. Yet, like Werle in the *The Wild Duck,* Mrs. Linde is one of Ibsen's meddlers; after all, it is she who decides that Nora and Helmer must face "the truth." She first convinces Krogstad to retract his letter, then takes it upon herself to push the Helmers to a reckoning, thereby hastening Nora's epiphany. Kristine is the self-appointed moral arbiter, the kind of idealist that Ibsen always regarded with some distrust. Seyrig's own serenity and worldliness make the character stronger than perhaps Ibsen intended; but this interpretation of Kristine enhances the play. Seyrig provides sturdy support to the other actors.

A model of transference from theater to film, Losey's *Doll's House* ought to be readily available to students of modern drama and to film students interested in problems of adaptation. Losey and his collaborators have transformed Ibsen's play into a fluent and elegant film.

Galileo

Brecht's alienation theory removes his work even further from the film frame than Ibsen's adherence to the narrative conventions of the well-made play. Brecht's theory stresses the artifice of the theatrical occasion: he wanted his audiences to be aware at all times that they were watching a performance. Brecht wanted house lights kept on during the show so audiences would not "lose" themselves. To insure that his ideas and his moral instruction remained the focus of the performance, Brecht wanted his actors to perform in a cool,

objective style. To enforce distance between audience and performance, Brecht's theater is strongly presentational: placards announce the theme of each scene; songs comment on characters and
situations, actors step out of character, or at least are encouraged
to think of their characters in the third person. The action is episodic, fragmentary, disjointed, the story arranged as variations on
the motivating idea the play is written to promote.

Brecht, however, was too interesting a writer, too close a student
of the contradictions of human nature, and too much of an ironist
to end up with the kind of dry and programmatic theater that his
alienation theory would seem to point toward. Although he did not
want to stress psychology, to explore motivation and the inner workings of his heroes and antiheroes, he nonetheless created complex
characters who "escaped" from their preassigned place in the ideological kind of play that he always started out to write. Brecht's
drama is filled with a darting wit, a love of paradox, a delight in
debate and dialectic and ambiguity that lifts it far above the level
of propaganda or a merely forensic presentation of ideas. For Brecht,
as for Shaw (with whom, among major modern playwrights, he has
most in common), the discussion of ideas is itself highly emotional;
for both writers, plays about the clash of ideas generate tension and
create charged, intriguing dramatic characters as well.

Brecht's messages were not, then, as "cool" and direct as he may
originally have intended, just as his characters often aroused audience empathy more than a strict observance of the alienation
theory would allow. "From my personal experience of working with
Brecht," Losey said, "I can say that he didn't follow his theories in
a rigid way. . .he suspected them at least as much as he respected
them. Concerning the actor, he used what worked: if the Stanislavski
method was convenient, fine, but if he thought to use an exterior
approach for the actor, then that was the method he used. . . .
Theory is useful for critics, but not for writers or directors."[1]

But Brecht's methods, regardless of the emotional temperature
of the plays, are staunchly antiillusionist. Brecht has no use for
imitating reality, and the rigorously stylized quality of his work is
antagonistic to film's inherent naturalism. Brecht's plays require a
kind of distancing and a visual abstraction that will always seem
uncomfortable on film.

In adapting *Galileo* Losey follows Brecht's text almost to the
letter, making a stylized film out of a stylized play. For *A Doll's*

House he converted the closed form of the play into a model of filmic openness. For *Galileo* he retains Brecht's alienation from physical reality. Brecht often places his dramas in historical settings which he then treats with a blithe disregard for historical accuracy. The seventeenth-century world recreated for *Galileo* is thus not authentic. The frame of a "historical" play like *Galileo* is doubly removed from a mimetic mode: the seventeenth-century setting is used to highlight a twentieth-century problem (Brecht always looks at the past from a distinctly modern perspective; he is interested in the past only to the degree that it throws light on the present) while his historical characters speak in colloquial, contemporary, unheroic diction. Anachronistic in language and setting, a "historical" play like *Galileo* alienates us from both a historical as well as a contemporary reality.

"The play must not be done in a realistic manner," Losey said, "with real exteriors in Rome and Florence; reality must be carefully chosen and reconstructed."[2] Losey's opening shot is an overview

Theatrical set for group shot from *Galileo*, representative of the film's stylized decor. Losey maintains a "filmed theater" look, unlike his approach to *A Doll's House*.

of a studio set: what we are going to see is not the real world, but a made-up one, a fake one, enclosed within the makebelieve of movie artifice. The film's immaculate sets are distinctly remote from reality; spare, white, simplified, they provide a semiabstract frame for the action. "I wanted texture," Losey said, "suggestions rather than literal or naturalistic reproductions. So we did architectural suggestions, using wood and metal and stone."[3] "I wanted to treat reality by use of light and a limiting of objects in a way that would seem abstract. . . . Brecht had a clean eye—he hated cluttered rooms, cluttered sets, superfluous movements, and these are things I've guarded against."[4] Yet the austere, pristine sets, which deliberately look like sets, have depth, and Losey's use of them is cinematic rather than theatrical. His direction depends on the realist film techniques of deep focus and the long take; and, as always, Losey's sound track is scrupulously real, as sounds of horses' hooves, church bells, and children at play surround the interior settings. For a scene in a stylized garden, Losey uses the natural sounds of birds to accompany the dialogue. Losey thus slyly counterpoints the real and the artificial, the cinematic and the theatrical, as in an exterior shot in a studio-created Venice in which there is a glimpse, in the rear of the frame, of real ships on real water. Losey's balance of physical reality and theatrical fakery creates its own "alienation" effect.

Like the sets, Losey's direction is simple, clear, precise, although throughout the film there are subtle shifts in the use of the camera, in visual stylization, in editing rhythms, and in color schemes. Losey creates visual contrasts between the scenes with Galileo and his pupils and those of Galileo's confrontations with the church. The scenes of Galileo as a teacher are especially uncluttered, with the camera in a fixed position as the character speaks directly to us: Losey wants us to concentrate on what Galileo says rather than to be distracted by mise-en-scène. For the scenes at the Vatican the compositions are denser, the choice of colors more vivid. The colored marble walls and floors of the Vatican, while retaining the setlike quality of Galileo's house, offer a relief from the prevailing austerity. Losey carefully choreographs the action within this set, contrasting the cardinals' red and black robes with the peasant browns of Galileo and his students, and arranging the movements of clusters of characters in different planes within the frame.

For scenes of church ceremony, Losey's approach is rigidly sym-

metrical: in a scene in which the pope dresses in ceremonial robes, the camera remains firmly in place as, in the depth of the frame, there is a steady procession of churchmen carrying flags and filing off screen in opposite directions. For the musical interludes Losey adopts a lighter and more flowing style. A boys' choir, which sings the introductions to each scene, appear in front of the sets and the action, as if on a forestage, or before a curtain. Our first view of them is from a high angle, and Losey continues throughout to present them in a different time/space framework from the rest of the action. The film's liveliest sequence is a musical number (set in a marketplace) which offers a tart, satiric comment on the consequences of the independent spirit that Galileo's inquiries represent: what would happen, the song asks ironically, if everyone did exactly as he pleased? Losey films the song with more momentum, and a greater amount and variety of intercutting, than he provides for any other episode. In editing style, camera work, and color scheme (browns and blacks, like a Brueghel fair come to life), the sequence is properly set off from the rest of the film.

Toward the climax, in the events leading up to and following Galileo's recantation, there is a noticeable shift in style. As Galileo's followers wait to hear if the scientist has yielded to church pressure, the space becomes more open, as if the action is taking place on a bare stage, and elongated shadows are thrown against a wide scrim at the back of the image. The exaggerated and theatrical lighting in the scene gives the action special emphasis.

Within the prevailing austerity and simplicity of his approach, then, Losey has managed to introduce some visual variety; but he has been careful not to turn the play into a showcase for his own directorial ingenuity. This is one of Losey's quietest performances. Honoring Brecht's intentions, Losey sees to it that the material does not become a popular, easy, predictable story of a hero. *Galileo* is an antiplay about an antihero, and Losey preserves Brecht's "unpopular" approach.

Brecht wrote two versions of *Galileo*, in both of which his major problem was how to handle the fact of his protagonist's recantation. In his first treatment of the story, in 1938, he gives a heroic dimension to the recantation: Galileo told the clergy what they wanted to hear—that the earth does not rotate about the sun, and that therefore man is still the center of the universe—only in order to be able to continue his research in secret. Brecht presents the

character's refusal to become a martyr as more truly heroic and more socially useful than noble self-sacrifice. Galileo is thus one of the playwright's cunning protagonists, a sly antihero. At the time, Brecht saw in Galileo's plight a reflection of his own experience in Hitler's Germany, where, as in seventeenth-century Italy, no scholar or scientist or artist was free to speak his mind or to conduct independent research. Galileo's victory over tyranny represented for Brecht an image of his own escape from Nazism. In 1945 and 1946, after he had fled Germany and was living in Los Angeles, Brecht began to rethink the play, no longer regarding Galileo's recantation as the act of a clever hero but as a gesture of cowardice and betrayal. Brecht worked on the revisions with Charles Laughton, who was eager to play Galileo and who persuaded the playwright to turn the originally thin, puritanical character into a man who indulged his appetites. The well-ordered protagonist of the 1938 version was thus transformed into the sloppy, heavyset antihero—a more complex and interesting character—of the 1947 production. This second Galileo, more than the first, is a compromiser and a scalawag; he passes off a Dutch telescope as the product of his own research; in a ploy to gain court patronage, he names stars after the ruling Medici family. Although he too recants in order to be able to pursue his research and although, in the end, as in the first version, he has one of his students smuggle his book out of Italy, Brecht wants to present Galileo's recantation as a betrayal of his responsibilities to science and society:

As a scientist I had an almost unique opportunity. In my day astronomy emerged into the market place. At that particular time, had one man put up a fight, it could have had wide repercussions. I have come to believe that I was never in real danger; for some years I was as strong as the authorities, and I surrendered my knowledge to the powers that be, to use it, no, not *use* it, *abuse* it, as it suits their ends. I have betrayed my profession. Any man who does what I have done must not be tolerated in the ranks of science.[5]

In addition to the self-castigation, Brecht introduces another element in Galileo's final speech, a theme he added after the atomic bomb had been used in Hiroshima: the possibly cataclysmic consequences of scientific research that is not impeded by either external or internal controls: "I take it the intent of science is to ease

human existence. If you give way to coercion, science can be crippled, and your new machines may simply suggest new drudgeries. Should you, then, in time, discover all there is to be discovered, your progress must become a progress away from the bulk of humanity. The gulf might even grow so wide that the sound of your cheering at some new achievement would be echoed by a universal howl of horror." This motif of the scientist plagued by the results of his investigations is irrelevant to the play's framework and even contradicts Brecht's emphasis on the importance of the scientist's freedom to pursue knowledge.

In the play's penultimate scene, then, Brecht in his revised version presents his character in a state of agitated self-criticism, insisting that his actions were those of a coward, and that the Church has been the victor despite the fact that he has been able to trick his inquisitors by working in secret on his research. The guilt and the breast-beating do not quite ring true; typically, Brecht has created a heroic character who resists the playwright's attempts to reverse or to undermine his heroism, and most audiences are likely to think of Galileo as a cunning hero despite the last-minute self-accusations that Brecht imposes. The embittered self-incrimination at the end has not grown organically from the play, but seems like an idea that Brecht has intruded in order to force a point. Galileo is certainly not a pure hero—he loves paradox and ambiguity as much as Brecht does—and he adopts unscrupulous means to reach noble ends. But this struggling, imperfect, contradictory character does not seem to merit the label of coward and betrayer with which Brecht seems intent on branding him at the conclusion.

In the original version Laughton played Galileo as morally weak and as sensually self-indulgent, though he also made him more ingratiating than Brecht intended. In this respect, Losey's casting of Topol was closer to Brecht's concept for his 1947 Galileo—Topol does not have the star aura that always emanated from Laughton, and Losey was careful to tone down the audience-pleasing folksiness that Topol had adopted for his likable performance as Tevye in the film of *Fiddler on the Roof*. "I am astonished that a number of people seem to be put off by Topol's performance, which they find too warm," Losey said. "I think the word used is 'benign,' which Galileo certainly wasn't; and I don't think Topol was, either. . .while Laughton was perhaps more malicious, more sly, and certainly never benign, he was weak—Galileo was weak, and so is Topol weak,

but Laughton was weak in weaker ways."[6] (In his attitude to the character, Losey in this statement is clearly reflecting Brecht's efforts to make Galileo antiheroic.)

Topol plays in a distanced and at times severe vein, giving a dry performance; when he demonstrates his theories to his students, he seems like a crusty professor lecturing in a classroom rather than a star actor courting the approval of an audience. Cunning, lazy, self-indulgent, distracted from human contact by his preoccupation with his work, Topol's Galileo has no tragedy or exaltation. The performance, following Brecht's dictum, stresses the character's love of thought, his faith in the life of the mind, rather than his capacity for emotion or for heroism.

In its distance from the conventional depiction of tragic heroes, Topol's interpretation is of a piece with Brecht's dramaturgy: here is a play built around a spectacular trial leading to an epochal recantation in which both the trial and the recantation are omitted! Brecht deliberately downplays the dramatic conflict inherent in the situation, preferring to stress Galileo's ideas about man's place in the cosmos and about the eternal conflict between reason and faith which those ideas engender rather than the details of his clash with an authoritarian church. Brecht's avoidance of theatrical cliché and climax is also evident in the final scene in which Galileo's student tries to prove to a little boy that the shadow he sees is not a witch but a woman making porridge. After he shows reality to the boy— proves to him that the woman is not, in fact, a witch—the boy continues to believe what he wants to believe, accepting the shadow as his truth. This ironic coda suggests that the possession of knowledge does not necessarily lead to a belief in truth, and that the battle to overcome superstition and blind faith is a long and difficult one. The last scene, with its mocking disbelief in the common man, corrects any notions we may hold of Galileo's triumph, or the victory of reason over faith: the world, it is clear, is still run by willful ignorance.

Losey's adaption is scrupulously Brechtian. To showcase Brecht's dialectic, his love of inversions, of ideological clash, of moral instruction, Losey chooses an appropriately stark visual frame. The film's exiguous decor gives central importance to Brecht's debate between church and science, faith and doubt, heroic martyrdom and cowardly recantation. Losey blends cinematic realism with theatrical stylization to create an environment as removed from his-

torical authenticity as the play's language and characterization. In his every choice, Losey serves Brecht intelligently. Losey had been thinking about the play since he had directed the American premiere in 1947; in the 1950s and 1960s he planned a stage production in London and a film version, but neither project materialized. When he finally had the opportunity to make a film of *Galileo*, under the auspices of the American Film Theater, he turned out what is probably his most self-effacing work, an interpretation of the play that is one of the purest examples on record of Brecht's famed alienation theory. This austere, deliberate, semiabstract film is a tribute to the playwright who has remained one of the major sources of Losey's inspiration.

11

Losey's Achievement

MOVING FROM THE Federal Theater of the 1930s to Hollywood in the late 1940s, and to Italy, England, and France since the early 1950s, Losey has had a peripatetic career. Wherever he has been, and whatever artistic or political movement his work has been a part of, Losey has absorbed his surroundings, so that his direction reveals a variety of textures and styles. His earliest work, as a stage director, was antirealist and explicitly political. His first films contained the social consciousness of his Living Newspaper productions of the 1930s, although his originally radical politics were muted, in Hollywood, to a safer liberalism. In the first decade after he left America, because of the blacklist, his films ranged in style from the neorealism of *Stranger on the Prowl* to the Continental sophistication of *Eve*. After his first great international success, in 1963, with *The Servant*, his work became noticeably more stylized and baroque—the interest in mise-en-scène that had always been evident in his films was escalated to occasionally excessive proportions. The atmosphere of his films became increasingly European; surely it would be impossible to tell that the recent *Mr. Klein* was directed by an American. And yet, despite the changes in locale, despite the overall progression from a cinema addressed to broad public themes to one of more private focus, despite the bravura departures from and transformations of physical reality, Losey's entire canon bears the stamp of his particular personality: he is a true auteur.

"A director should have a 'signature,' " Losey has said, "an immediately recognizable style."[1] "Any film which doesn't have the personal imprint of its director is not a good film. The director's

217

Margaret Leighton as the dowager in The Go-Between: *the crowning touch to Losey's finest film.*

personality must be seen at every moment."[2] Although he has always maintained that "style is something that should be recognizable in any first grade director," he has cautioned that "if it's simply repetitive, then it's nothing. Personal style is accumulative."[3] True to his theories, Losey's own style is powerful, immediately identifiable, and yet traces a steady process of change and evolution over a thirty-year period.

Regardless, then, of the circumstances in which he worked—the modest budgets, the routine scripts early in his career, the rushed shooting schedules—Losey's oeuvre reveals a surprising consistency both in themes and directorial methods. Losey's films, typically, create closed worlds which entrap his characters. Both the claustrophobic settings and the haunted, pursued characters are emblematic of a larger social or political reality: the manhunts that are a recurrent pattern in his novice Hollywood films reflect contemporary political paranoia triggered by the House Un-American Activities Committee; the enclosed power struggles of many of his English films have symbolic links to the rigid British class system. Retaining the social thrust of the material he directed for the Living Newspapers, the closed frames of Losey's films are to varying degrees stylized and symbolic images of large-scale social realities. His films can often be read as fables, metaphors, and parables.

As he attained stature and recognition, and as he won greater control over his projects, Losey's methods became more mandarin and inflected as his response to his characters grew more detached. His early films, both in Hollywood and in England, contain a more direct expression of his feelings; he presents his crumbling and often violent protagonists, and their often violent milieu, in a more heated and emotional way than in his later, more distanced work, with its tendency toward allegorical abstraction and generalization. Losey is a stern moralist who uses his stories, his settings, and his characters to provide lessons and examples. As Gilles Jacob has written, "For Losey to say something means to explain, translate, explain again, and offer analogies; and it also means a rigorous exclusion of non-essentials. A film becomes a series of equals signs. . . a closed circuit collection of signposts. Losey's world is not so much a world as a setting for an allegory."[4]

In both his marked distance from his characters, and his interest in moral education, Losey is a true Brechtian. His experience, in 1947, working with Brecht on *Galileo*, was a seminal influence on

his own methods, for no matter how much, in his later pieces, he may have diverged from Brecht in terms of pictorial style, he held on to an abiding primary belief in the effectiveness of the alienation technique. Almost of all Losey's work, even the films with a purely domestic focus, have a didactic underpinning and are more concerned with making a point than with seeking the emotional involvement of the audience.

Regardless, then, of the degree of stylization of any individual film, Losey's direction is taut, controlled, distanced. The world within his frames is one that he has skillfully manipulated in order to conform to a predetermined design. Reality in his work is thus reconstructed, to varying degrees, in order to enforce the theme. There is no room for spontaneity in Losey's cinema, no place for chance or improvisation, for the purely (or merely) objective rendering of the flow of life. Losey's reformations of reality become increasingly more rigorous and abstract; at heart, Losey is a symbolist who uses settings, objects, and characters for their emblematic value.

Mirrors and paintings are the most repeated symbolic motifs in his films, and his almost obsessive reliance on them indicates the way in which decor comments on and even shapes his articulation of character and theme. Mirrors and paintings are real objects, a realistic part of decor, after all, yet Losey uses them not so much as realistic background detail, but as part of a calculated strategy of symbolic intensification: mirrors in his work are images of paranoia, duplicity, schizophrenia, chaos—they are always more than simply a neutral or uninflected reflection of reality. The paintings that line the walls of most of his interiors are likewise shrewdly placed for thematic reinforcement, offering more or less stylized comments on the foreground action—they "indicate" meaning. Losey's frames are filled with many such indicators; the characteristic Losey tracking shot, in which his camera moves through an environment that is often new to his characters as well as to us, reveals decor as symbol. Losey's decor becomes more elaborate and exotic in his later pieces, but his own response to the ornate environments of films like *Boom* and *Secret Ceremony* remains detached, objective, investigatory. With the purposefulness of an avid journalist, his camera probes the settings for "clues." The Losey frame is a minefield of signs and portents.

Losey's deterministic methods reflect the typical fate of his

doomed characters. There is very little chance for free will in the closed and fatalistic environments he creates. His films almost always end in defeat, their world-view essentially negative, their sense of the possibilities of human nature and society deeply pessimistic. Certainly little joy of life emanates from his work—Losey's own dour, somber, ungracious temperament dominates the tone of his films. Only in his collaborations with Harold Pinter is there more than a passing suggestion of humor. Losey is a sober, nononsense moralist, with a consistently dark vision of human nature: happy endings are virtually nonexistent in the Losey canon, and the few that there are seem forced upon their stories (perhaps by a front office worried about protecting its investment).

Losey's teacherly inclinations, his penchant for symbolic abstraction, his cool tone toward his characters, his extreme control and calculation, his preoccupation with entrapment and doom—all these recurrent elements of his work have insured that he would never become a popular director. Until *The Servant*, he rarely had a choice of material, but he was never a compliant house director, dutifully churning out commodity products to please his bosses or to fulfill a contract. He is stubborn, temperamental, difficult with crass producers, though not with actors, who often return to work for him a second or third or fourth time. Even after he had been driven from Hollywood, Losey managed to maintain his integrity and his essential independence. He is the antithesis of the company man, and his films always have his own stylistic signature rather than that of a studio.

Losey, then, has never worked to formula, even when he was handed routine crime melodramas. He has never made a film that was "easy" or designed merely to please in superficial ways: no one simply drops in to catch a Losey movie. Losey evidently has a horror of the ordinary and the glib—and his work is stamped with the signs of his own ornery intelligence, his knotty, embattled individuality.

Losey's work is thus neither popular nor immediately accessible, and it certainly isn't affirmative. He has never aspired to be, and he has indeed never become, a slick, big-time commercial director. On the contrary, he has been accused of being "arty" and "baroque," of making movies that are stylistically self-conscious, and both visually and thematically claustrophobic. He has been both praised (in France) and condemned (in America) for being a cult director turning out symbolic doomsday melodramas. In America Losey has

never achieved widespread popularity or even recognition. His work perhaps is too specialized, too formally self-conscious, to satisfy the demands of popular American taste. American critics have often charged him with making decadent films and with being unduly influenced by European trends and styles: with being, in this sense, "un-American." The Communist taint, which led him to exile in England, hovers over his reputation still; he remains an outsider to the American film establishment, a man with suspect political leanings and an "unwholesome" attraction both to Germanic pessimism and to Continental "sophistication." Starting with his early studies with Eisenstein, his influences and models have indeed been almost entirely foreign: Brecht, Pinter, Kafka, Italian neorealism, German expressionism. There is very little of a native American strain in his work; like Jules Dassin and Richard Lester, he is an expatriate who absorbed the tone and inflections of a foreign culture. He is surely the most European of American directors.

Pauline Kael distrusts him, accusing him of "weighty emptiness": all promise and no delivery. She suggests that his excessive concern with mise-en-scène at the expense of theme has placed him "next to God" in the French critics' pantheon. Andrew Sarris is more generous toward Losey, ranking him in "the far side of paradise" category (one rung below that of the "pantheon directors") among such directors as Robert Aldrich, Samuel Fuller, Anthony Mann, Nicholas Ray, Otto Preminger, and Raoul Walsh. "Joseph Losey may not actually thrive on controversy," Sarris writes, "but he seems to arouse it on every level, from the most vulgar to the most esoteric. . . . He seemed by all indications to belong to the committed Left. In quick succession, he was embraced by a rightist faction in *Cahiers du Cinema*, enthroned by *Movie*, and repudiated by *Sight and Sound*. Realist critics have always resisted the intensity and sweep of his style, the steady hysteria of his actors, the violence of his plots. By any standards, Losey's is a technique that calls attention to itself or, more properly, to the personal feelings of Joseph Losey."[5]

In England Losey's reputation has teetered between sharp criticism and adulation. *Sight and Sound* accused him, in the 1950s and early 1960s, of being a socially irresponsible genre director. In the 1970s his reputation has escalated, and he has been claimed, finally, as one of England's own, a leader in the rejuvenation of the British film industry in the 1960s, when films like *The Servant* helped to

acquire a new international stature for the native film industry and launched a cycle of films that satirized the British establishment.

Losey's most consistently impassioned following has been in France, where he has long been considered an auteur of the first rank: a pantheon director par excellence. In *Cahiers du cinema* and *Positif*, Losey's work—especially his novice American films—has been unabashedly overpraised, with the usual enthusiasm of the French for what they take to be "American" authenticity. In these high-toned French film journals, Losey's early work has been subjected to absurd overinterpretation and greeted with a kind of ecstatic praise that is really quite mindless. "In Losey's films," writes Michel Mourlet in *Cahiers du cinema*, "it is not a question of *a* universe, but of *the* universe, not a possible or impossible world, but a real world. We expect in his films the vivid, fresh sensation of the truth; never before has one been as close to human beings, their flesh, their nerve, the pulse of their blood."[6] Typically, Losey has taken the veneration of French cineastes in a spirit of ironic detachment. In 1970 he was awarded (and accepted, despite his skepticism) France's Knight of the Order of Arts and Letters.

Losey is still very much an active director. At this writing, a new film (like *Mr. Klein*, made in France in French), a political story with Yves Montand called *Southern Routes*, awaits American distribution; and he is presently editing a film of Mozart's opera *Don Giovanni*. He is anything but past his prime; his most recent film released in America, *Mr. Klein*, is perhaps his most utterly controlled piece of direction. Losey feels that, if he is able to raise the money for it, his long-contemplated film of Proust will be the culmination of his career; but even if he is unable to proceed with the project, it is not unlikely that he will direct other distinguished films. He continues to be a serious and able craftsman and an artist capable of inspiration. The bulk of his career, though, is behind him, and it is not premature to assess the size and scope of his achievement.

Gilles Jacob, an astute critic of Losey's work, wrote (in 1966) that the director's career is "a mutilated body of work—a sort of dress rehearsal for an ideal film which never materializes."[7] Other critics as well have regarded the canon as a series of continuously interesting failures, of brave experiments that, for one reason or another, never entirely succeeded. Certainly this pattern applies to Losey's career in Hollywood from 1948 to 1951 and in England from 1953

to 1963; but it does not apply to his career as a whole. Over the long period stretching from the late 1940s to the early 1960s, which spanned parts of three decades spent on two continents, Losey was prevented by external pressures from turning out a fully finished piece, a film in which form fully served content in an entirely integral way. But, with *The Servant*, Losey found a subject to match his particular interest in film form, and the tone and rhythm that he had been developing over his unduly protracted apprenticeship result in a powerful allegory that *is* a fully realized achievement, one of the great films, in fact, of the modern repertory.

Losey's partnership with Harold Pinter was the most fortunate of his career. The two men helped to shape and enhance each other's work; theirs is a model of artistic collaboration. Their work together has so far produced two films of the very first rank—the exquisite *The Go-Between*, in addition to *The Servant*—as well as *Accident*, a film of "secondary" brilliance.

His three collaborative efforts with Pinter, and his elegant adaptations of two plays by preeminent modern dramatists, Ibsen's *A Doll's House* and Tennessee Williams's *Boom*, are his strongest pieces. A social and psychological portrait of rare insight, *The Go-Between* is a work of true grandeur. *Accident* and *The Servant* are shrewd analyses of complex power struggles. His striking *A Doll's House* is an inspired expansion of a closed-form play to the larger and more open dimensions of the film frame, while *Boom* is a work of visual virtuosity, a rapturous employment of color, wide screen, music, and decor, resulting in the most richly textured film in a canon remarkable for its textural qualities.

Is Losey a great director? His record is certainly uneven, wavering more or less in sympathetic response to the quality of his material. When he has a taut, cunning script by Pinter, his performance is impeccable, his use of his medium unerring in its control. When he has a routine script, or one that is in some way unfinished, his work can then be strained, overreaching, inorganic: the form can become a means of concealing, of covering over, rather than enhancing the content. It is on weak or radically flawed scripts like *Eve* or *These Are The Damned* that Losey's work can seem merely exotic or ornamental: baroque.

Losey's influence has not been widespread. He is not a trendsetter; he has not been a seminal force in any particular style or movement in film history. But he has carved out a place for himself

as a director of genuine skill and integrity, a true artist of film; and the Losey-Pinter collaboration is a landmark in contemporary films. Not a single Losey film is without visual interest; his understanding and use of film technique—his composition, editing, use of color and sound and wide screen, his camera movement and placement demonstrate a continuing maturity. A visual stylist of uncommon gifts, Losey is also an expert director of actors: Dirk Bogarde, the quintessential Losey performer, developed his subtle, shaded, deliciously nuanced style through his many performances for Losey; in *A Doll's House* Jane Fonda gives one of her most intelligent performances; in *The Servant* Bogarde, James Fox, Sarah Miles, and Wendy Craig are a marvelous ensemble, skillfully waging challenges and laying traps for each other; Alain Delon gives the performances of a career in *The Assassination of Trotsky* and *Mr. Klein*; and, in *The Go-Between*, Margaret Leighton, as the imperious dowager, and Dominic Guard, as the disillusioned messenger, achieve true radiance.

Losey's achievement—uneven, occasionally arty and forced—is on balance a distinguished one. His visually striking renderings of a predominantly dark and claustrophobic world-view demand the attention of anyone seriously interested in the art of film.

Notes and References

Preface

1. *New York Times,* November 17, 1968.
2. Interview with Judy Stone, *Saturday Review,* October 7, 1972.

Chapter One

1. Losey's life and career have striking parallels to those of Nicholas Ray. Ray, like Losey, was born in La Crosse, Wisconsin, and started in films at RKO, under the supervision of Dore Schary, after initial experience in theater and radio. Ray acted in one of Losey's Living Newspaper productions. Both are now cult directors, admired (though not always by the same critical factions) for their idiosyncratic approach to genre material and their emphatic visual style.
2. Michel Ciment, Interview with Losey, *Positif* 186 (October 1976). Translations from the French are by the author.
3. Eugene Archer, *New York Times* March 15, 1964.
4. Ciment, *Positif,* No. 186.
5. Ibid.
6. Losey, who favors long takes and camera movement as opposed to montage, has said about Eisenstein: "Perhaps this is heresy, but I've never been able to take seriously the laborious work of Eisenstein. I attended classes of his in Moscow—I found his theories dull and really without interest. I don't deny that Eisenstein brought something to films, but his films seem now to be heavy and academic." (In *Cahiers du Cinema,* No. 111.)
7. Losey, Interview in *Cahiers du Cinema* 114(1961): 30.
8. Bosley Crowther, *New York Times,* March 16, 1936.

Chapter Two

1. Quoted in *Losey on Losey,* edited and introduced by Tom Milne (New York, 1968), p. 73.
2. Ibid., p. 69.

3. Ibid., p. 70.
4. Interview in *Cahiers du Cinema*, No. 111, p. 10.
5. Milne, pp. 77–78.
6. Howard Barnes, *New York Herald Tribune*, June 23, 1950.
7. Bosley Crowther, *New York Times*, June 23, 1950.
8. Marc Bernard, *Cahiers du Cinema*, No. 111, p. 33.
9. Pierre Rissient, *Cahiers du Cinema*, No. 111, p. 27.
10. Quoted in *Sight and Sound*, August 1961, p. 186.
11. *Cahiers du Cinema*, No. 111, p. 12.
12. Paul Mayersberg, *Movie* 9(1963): 34.

Chapter Three

1. *Films and Filming*, October 1963, p. 54.
2. "Puritan Maids," *Films and Filming*, April 1966, p. 32.
3. The most complete extant version of the film—the one closest to the film Losey shot and edited—is in the British Film Institute.
4. Durgnat, *Films and Filming*, p. 28.
5. Pierre Rissient, *Cahiers du Cinema*, No. 111, p. 31.
6. Paul Beckley, *New York Herald Tribune*, November 23, 1957.
7. *Films and Filming*, October 1963, p. 55.
8. "Joseph Losey; or, The Camera Calls," *Sight and Sound*, Spring 1966, p. 65.
9. *Cahiers du Cinema*, No. 111, p. 10.
10. *New York Times*, September 27, 1960.
11. Interview with Gordon Gow, *Films and Filming*, October 1971, p. 34.
12. Ibid.
13. Interview with Guy Hennebelle, *Cinema International* 17 (January-February 1968): 762.
14. Paul Mayersberg, "The Damned," *Movie* 9 (May 1963): 31.
15. Ibid.
16. Losey, *Films and Filming*, October 1963, p. 54.
17. "Losey's Paper Handkerchief," *Sight and Sound*, Summer 1966, p. 142.
18. Ibid., p. 143.

Chapter Four

1. Quoted in Durgnat, "Puritan Maids," *Films and Filming*, May 1966, p. 30.
2. Harold Pinter, *The Servant*, in *Five Screenplays* (New York, 1973), p. 52. All further quotations from Pinter's screenplays are from this edition.

3. "The Monkey on My Back," *Films and Filming,* October 1963, p. 55.

Chapter Five

1. Losey, Interview with John Russell Taylor, *Sight and Sound,* Autumn 1966, p. 184.
2. Ibid.
3. Ibid.

Chapter Six

1. Interview with Mel Gussow, *New York Times,* August 11, 1971,

Chapter Seven

1. Losey, Interview with Richard Combs, *Sight and Sound,* Summer 1975, p. 141.
2. Ibid., p. 142.

Chapter Eight

1. *Village Voice,* June 6, 1968.
2. Interview with Joseph Gelmis, *Newsday,* September 16, 1968, p.
3. In the version of the film "adapted" for television—one that Losey and Elizabeth Taylor took legal action to prevent being shown—the story is given a preposterous frame in which two psychiatrists explain and interpret the action. The characters are thus treated as studies of bizarre psychological "cases." The absurdly literal examination of their behavior, reminiscent of the "explanation" of Norman Bates's split personality at the end of *Psycho,* robs the story of its aura of mystery and intrigue.
4. Interview with Michel Ciment, *L'Avant-scene* 93 (June 1969):10.
5. "The Mice in the Milk," *Sight and Sound,* Spring 1969, p. 78.
6. *New York Times,* November 17, 1968.
7. Ibid.

Chapter Nine

1. *New Yorker,* February 5, 1966, p. 71.
2. *New York Times,* July 19, 1971.
3. *Time,* August 7, 1971, p. 63.
4. *Positif* 186 (October 1976): p. 3.
5. I am indebted to Denise Jemmott Wejchert for identifying the painting.

6. *Positif,* No. 186, p. 4.
7. Ibid., p. 24.
8. Leslie Rayner, "Losey on Trotsky," *Film* (April 1973): 12.
9. Combs, *Sight and Sound,* Summer 1975, p. 141.
10. Ibid.
11. Rayner, p. 13.

Chapter Ten

1. *Cahiers du cinema,* No. 111, p. 3.
2. Ibid., No. 114, p. 31.
3. Combs, *Sight and Sound,* Summer 1975, p. 139.
4. Howard Kissel, *Womens Wear Daily,* January 22, 1975.
5. Brecht, *Galileo,* tr. by Charles Laughton (New York, 1966), p. 124.
6. Combs, p. 140.

Chapter Eleven

1. Interview with *Sight and Sound,* August 1961, p. 187.
2. *Cahiers du cinema,* No. 111, p. 7.
3. *Films and Filming,* October 1963, p. 54.
4. *Sight and Sound,* Spring 1966, p. 67.
5. *The American Cinema* (New York, 1968), p. 96.
6. *Cahiers du cinema,* No. 111, p. 38.
7. *Sight and Sound,* Spring 1966, p. 62.

Selected Bibliography

1. Books

LEAHY, JAMES. *The Cinema of Joseph Losey.* New York: A. S. Barnes and Co., 1967. Intelligent, comprehensive discussion of Losey's work up to 1967, though thematic analysis is occasionally strained. Includes ample quotations from Losey about his own methods and intentions.

MILNE TOM, ed. *Losey on Losey.* New York: Doubleday, 1968. Lively, informal comments by Losey on each of his films up to and including *Accident.* Particular emphasis on visual preparation and intention; clearly shows Losey's emphasis on mise-en-scène.

In addition to these two books in English on Losey's work, there are two critical discussions in French: *Losey* by Pierre Rissient in the Editions Universitaires series (1966) and *Joseph Losey* by Christian Ledieu in the Cinema d'Aujourd'hui series(1964).

2. Articles and Interviews

This is a highly selective listing; I have attempted to include only a representative sampling. *Sight and Sound* and *Cahiers du cinema* have the most complete coverage of Losey's work, though both journals tend to be biased in their discussions; those in the British journal are often negatively slanted while those in the French publication are extravagantly lavish in their praise.

CALLENBACH, ERNEST. "The Servant." *Film Quarterly* 18: i (Fall 1964): 36–38. One of the most persuasive anti-Losey pieces. Attacks the film's allegorical pretensions.

COMBS, RICHARD. "Losey, Galileo, and the Romantic Englishwoman." *Sight and Sound* 44: iii (Summer 1975): 138–43. Especially significant for the quotations from Losey on his approach to filming *Galileo.*

DURGNAT, RAYMOND. "Puritan Maids," in two parts. *Films and Filming,* April and May 1966, pp. 26–36; pp. 28–33. At times incoherent, but on the whole a challenging and highly idiosyncratic reading that stress-

es the moral complexities of Losey's work, with particular reference to *Eve* and *Modesty Blaise*.

GREENSPUN, ROGER. "Secret Ceremony." *New York Times,* November 17, 1968 Brilliant discussion of Losey's mise-en-scène; among the most sympathetic of American reactions to Losey.

JACOB, GILLES. "Joseph Losey; or the Camera Calls." *Sight and Sound* 35:2 (Spring 1966): 62–67. Fine overview of Losey's characteristic visual style.

LOSEY, JOSEPH. "Entretiens." *Cahiers du Cinema* 111(September 1960): 2–7. One of the best of Losey's interviews in this journal. Stresses the Hollywood phase of his career.

———. "Entretiens." *Positif* 104(1969): 8; 128(1971): 32. Good comments by Losey on his collaboration with Pinter.

———. "L'oeil du maitre." *Cahiers du Cinema* 114(October 1961): 21–22, 27. Losey discusses Brecht's style and influence on his own work.

STRICK, PHILIP. "The Mice in the Milk." *Sight and Sound* 38:2 (Spring 1969): 78–79. Excellent discussion of Losey's imagery, with particular reference to *Boom* and *Secret Ceremony*.

Filmography

1. Early Short Films

PETE ROLEUM AND HIS COUSINS (Petroleum Industries Exhibition Inc., 1939)
Produced and scripted by Joseph Losey
Director of Photography (Technicolor and 3-D): Harold Muller
Music: Hanns Eisler, Oscar Levant
Narrator: Hiram Sherman
Running time: 20 minutes
[A film with Howard Bay's puppets shown at the petroleum industry exhibit at the New York World's Fair, 1939–40]

A CHILD WENT FORTH (National Association of Nursery Educators, 1941)
Producers: Joseph Losey, John Ferno
Script: Joseph Losey
Director of Photography: John Ferno
Music: Hanns Eisler
Narrator: Munro Leaf
Running time: 18 minutes

YOUTH GETS A BREAK (National Youth Administration, 1941)
Script: Joseph Losey
Directors of Photography: Willard van Dyke, Ralph Steiner, John Ferno
Running time: 20 minutes

A GUN IN HIS HAND (M-G-M, "Crime Does Not Pay" series, 1945)
Script: Charles Francis Royal, from a story by Richard Landau
Director of Photography: Jackson Rose
Music: Max Terr

Cast: Anthony Caruso (Pinky), Richard Gaines (Inspector Dana), Ray Teal (O'Neill)
Running time: 19 minutes

2. Feature Films

THE BOY WITH GREEN HAIR (RKO-Radio, 1948)
Producer: Adrian Scott, replaced by Stephen Ames
Production Manager: Ruby Rosenberg
Assistant Director: James Lane
Script: Ben Barzman, Alfred Lewis Levitt, from a story by Betsy Beaton
Director of Photography (Technicolor): George Barnes
Editor: Frank Doyle
Art Directors: Albert S. D'Agostino, Ralph Berger
Music: Leigh Harline (Song, "Nature Boy" by Eden Ahbez)
Costumes: Adele Balkan
Cast: Dean Stockwell (Peter Frye), Pat O'Brien (Gramp), Robert Ryan (Dr. Evans), Barbara Hale (Miss Brand), Samuel S. Hinds (Dr. Knudson), Walter Catlett (The King), Regis Toomey (Mr. Davis), Dwayne Hickman (Joey)
Running time: 82 minutes
U.S. release date: January 8, 1949
16mm. rental and lease: Films, Inc., 1144 Wilmette Ave., Wilmette, IL 60091

THE LAWLESS (British title, **THE DIVIDING LINE**) (Paramount, 1949)
Producers: William H. Pine, William C. Thomas
Script: Geoffrey Homes [pseud. Daniel Mainwaring], from his novel *The Voice of Stephen Wilder*
Director of Photography: Roy Hunt
Editor: Howard Smith
Art Director: Lewis H. Creber
Music: Mahlon Merrick
Cast: MacDonald Carey (Larry Wilder), Gail Russell (Sunny Garcia), Lalo Rios (Paul Rodriguez), John Sands (Joe Ferguson), Lee Patrick (Jan Dawson), Pedro de Cordoba (Mr. Garcia)
Running time: 83 minutes
New York premiere: June 22, 1950
16mm. rental: Select Films, 115 West 31st St., New York, NY 10001

THE PROWLER (Horizon Pictures, 1951)
Producer: S. P. Eagle (Sam Spiegel)
Production Manager: Joseph Nadel
Assistant Director: Robert Aldrich
Script: Dalton Trumbo and Hugo Butler, from an original story by Robert

Thoeren and Hans Wilhelm
Director of Photography: Arthur Miller
Editor: Paul Weatherwax
Art Director: Boris Leven
Music: Lyn Murray (Song "Baby" by Murray and Dick Mack, sung by Bob Carroll)
Costumes: Maria Donovan
Cast: Van Heflin (Webb Garwood), Evelyn Keyes (Susan Gilvray), John Maxwell (Bud Crocker), Katherine Warren (Mrs. Crocker), Emerson Treacy (William Gilvray)
Running time: 92 minutes
New York premiere: July 1, 1951
Not available for rental

M (Columbia, 1951)
Producer: Seymour Nebenzal
Production Manager: Ben Hersh
Assistant Director: Robert Aldrich
Script: Norman Reilly Raine and Leo Katcher, based on an original script (1932) by Thea von Harbou and Fritz Lang
Additional Dialogue: Waldo Salt
Director of Photography: Ernest Laszlo
Editor: Edward Mann
Art Director: Martin Obzina
Music: Michel Michelet
Cast: David Wayne (Martin Harrow), Howard da Silva (Carney), Luther Adler (Langley), Martin Gabel (Marshall), Steve Brodie (Lt. Becker), Raymond Burr (Pottsy), Glenn Anders (Riggert), Karen Morley (Mrs. Coster), John Miljan (Blind Vendor), Jim Backus (The Mayor), Janine Perreau (Intended Victim)
Running time: 88 minutes
New York premiere: July 10, 1951
Withdrawn from circulation

THE BIG NIGHT (Philip Waxman, distributed by United Artists, 1951)
Producer: Philip A. Waxman
Assistant Director: Ivan Volkman
Script: Hugo Butler, Ring Lardner, Jr., Stanley Ellin and Joseph Losey, based on Ellin's novel *Dreadful Summer*
Director of Photography: Hal Mohr
Editor: Edward Mann
Art Director: Nicholas Remisoff
Special Effects: Ray Mercer, Lee Zavitz
Music: Lyn Murray

Costumes: Joseph King
Cast: John Barrymore, Jr. (Georgy La Main), Preston Foster (Andy La
    Main), Howard Chamberlin (Flanagan), Howard St. John (Al Judge),
    Dorothy Comingore (Julie Rostina)
Running time: 75 minutes
New York premiere: March 19, 1952
16mm. rental: United Artists 16, 729 7th Avenue, New York, NY 10019
STRANGER ON THE PROWL (Consorzio Produttori Cinematografici
    Tirrenia/Riviera Film, Inc., distributed by United Artists, 1952)
Producer: Noel Calef
Script: Andrea Forzano (pseud. Ben Barzman), from a story by Noel Calef
Director of Photography: Henri Alekan
Editor: Thelma Connell
Art Director: Antonio Valente
Music: G. C. Sonzogno
Cast: Paul Muni (The Man), Joan Lorring (Angela), Vittorio Manunta (Gia-
    como Fontana), Luisa Rossi (Giacomo's mother), Noel Calef (flute-player)
Running time: 100 minutes, cut to 82 minutes for U.S. release
New York premiere: November 9, 1953
16mm. rental: Ivy Films 16, 165 West 46th St., New York, NY 10036
Note: Losey signed this picture with the pseudonym Andrea Forzano. Its
    Italian title is *Imbarco a Mezzanotte*, and its British title is *Encounter*.

THE SLEEPING TIGER (Insignia, 1954)
Producer: Victor Hanbury
Assistant Director: Denis Johnson
Script: Derek Frye (pseud. Harold Buchman and Carl Foreman), from the
    novel by Maurice Moiseiwitsch
Director of Photography: Harry Waxman
Editor: Reginald Mills
Art Director: John Stoll
Music: Malcolm Arnold
Cast: Dirk Bogarde (Frank Clements), Alexis Smith (Glenda Esmond),
    Alexander Knox (Dr. Clive Esmond), Hugh Griffith (Inspector Simmons),
Running time: 89 minutes
London premiere: June 24, 1954; New York premiere, October 8, 1954.
Not available for rental
Note: Losey signed this picture with the producer's name, Victor Hanbury.

A MAN ON THE BEACH (Hammer Films, 1955)
Producer: Anthony Hinds
Production Manager: Michael Delamar
Assistant Director: Denis Bertera
Script: Jimmy Sangster, based on Victor Canning's story "Chance at the
    Wheel"

Director of Photography (Cinepanorama and Eastman Color): Wilkie Cooper (location photography by Len Harris)
Editor: Henry Richardson
Art Director: Edward Marshall
Cast: Donald Wolfit (Carter), Michael Medwin (Max), Michael Ripper (chauffeur), Alex de Gallier (casino manager)
Running time: 29 minutes
No sale or rental information available

FINGER OF GUILT (British title, **THE INTIMATE STRANGER**) (Anglo Guild, distributed in U.S. by RKO-Radio, 1956)
Producer: Alec S. Snowden
Production Manager: Jim O'Connolly
Assistant Director: Bill Shore
Script: Peter Howard (pseud. Howard Koch)
Director of Photography: Gerald Gibbs
Editor: Geoffrey Muller
Art Director: Wilfred Arnold
Music: Trevor Duncan
Costumes: Alice McLaren
Cast: Richard Basehart (Reggie Wilson), Mary Murphy (Evelyn Smith), Constance Cummings (Kay Wallace), Roger Livesey (Ben Case)
Running time: 91 minutes (cut to 71 minutes in U.S.)
London premiere, May 25, 1956; released in U.S. in October
16mm. rental and lease: Video Communications, Inc., 6555 E. Skelly Drive, Tulsa, OK. 74145

TIME WITHOUT PITY (A Harlequin Production, 1957)
Producers: John Arnold and Anthony Simmons
Production Manager: Leigh Aman
Assistant Directors: Adrian Pryce-Jones, Colin Brewer
Script: Ben Barzman, from the play *Someone Waiting* by Emlyn Williams
Director of Photography: Freddie Francis
Editor: Alan Osbiston
Art Director: Bernard Sarron
Music: Tristram Cary
Cast: Michael Redgrave (David Graham), Ann Todd (Honor Stanford), Leo McKern (Robert Stanford), Peter Cushing (Jeremy Clayton), Alec McCowen (Alec Graham), Joan Plowright (Agnes Cole)
Running time: 88 minutes
London premiere, March 21, 1957; New York premiere, November 22
Not available for rental

THE GYPSY AND THE GENTLEMAN (J. Arthur Rank, 1957)
Producer: Maurice Cowan
Assistant Director: Robert Asher
Script: Janet Green, from the novel *Darkness I Leave You* by Nina Warner Hooke
Director of Photography: Jack Hildyard
Editor: Reginald Beck
Art Director: Ralph Brinton
Music: Hans May
Costumes: Julie Harris
Historical adviser: Vyvyan Holland
Cast: Melina Mercouri (Belle), Keith Mitchell (Sir Paul Deverill), Patrick McGoohan (Jess), June Laverick (Sarah Deverill), Flora Robson (Mrs. Haggard)
Running time: 107 minutes (cut to 90 minutes in U.S.)
London premiere, February 2, 1958; released in U.S. in August, not shown in a major New York theater
Apparently withdrawn from circulation

CHANCE MEETING (original title, **BLIND DATE**) (Independent Artists. A Julian Wintle-Leslie Parkyn Production, distributed in U.S. by Paramount, 1959)
Producer: David Deutsch
Assistant Director: René Dupont
Script: Ben Barzman and Millard Lampell, from the novel by Leigh Howard
Director of Photography: Christopher Challis
Art Director: Harry Pottle
Music: Richard Bennett
Costumes: Morris Angel
Cast: Hardy Krüger (Jan Van Rooyen), Stanley Baker (Inspector Morgan), Micheline Presle (Lady Fenton called Jacqueline Cousteau), Robert Flemyng (Sir Brian Lewis)
Running time: 95 minutes
London premiere, August 20, 1959; New York premiere, October 26, 1960
16mm. rental: Films, Inc.

THE CONCRETE JUNGLE (original British title, **THE CRIMINAL**) (Merton Park Studios, 1960)
Producer: Jack Greenwood
Assistant Director: Buddy Booth
Script: Alun Owen, from an original story by Jimmy Sangster
Director of Photography: Robert Krasker
Editor: Reginald Mills
Art Director: Scott Macgregor

Music: Johnny Dankworth ("Prison Blues" sung by Cleo Laine)
Cast: Stanley Baker (Johnny Bannion), Sam Wanamaker (Mike Carter), Margit Saad (Suzanne), Patrick Magee (Chief Warder Barrowes)
Running time: 97 minutes, cut to 86 in U.S.
Premiered at the Edinburgh Festival, August 28, 1960: released in U.S., May 1962, not shown at a major New York theater
16mm. rental: Corinth Films, 410 East 62nd St., New York, NY 10021

THESE ARE THE DAMNED (original British title, **THE DAMNED**) (Hammer/Swallow, distributed in U.S. by Columbia, 1962)
Producer: Anthony Hinds
Assistant Director: John Peverall
Script: Evan Jones, from H. L. Lawrence's novel *The Children of Light*
Director of Photography: Arthur Grant
Editor: Reginald Mills
Art Director: Don Mingaye
Music: James Bernard (Song "Black Leather Rock" by Bernard and Evan Jones)
Costumes: Mollie Arbuthnot
Cast: MacDonald Carey (Simon Wells), Shirley Ann Field (Joan), Viveca Lindfors (Freya Neilson), Alexander Knox (Bernard), Oliver Reed (King), Walter Gotell (Major Holland), James Villiers (Captain Gregory)
Running time: 87 minutes, cut to 77 in the U. S.
London premiere, May 1963; New York premiere, July 8, 1965.
16mm. rental: Corinth films (see entry for *The Concrete Jungle* above)

EVE (Paris Film/Interopa Film—Rome, distributed in U.S. by Times Film Corporation, 1962)
Producers: Robert and Raymond Hakim
Assistant Director: Guidarino Guidi
Script: Hugo Butler and Evan Jones, based on the novel by James Hadley Chase
Director of Photography: Gianni Di Venanzo
Editors: Reginald Beck, Franca Silvi
Art Directors: Richard MacDonald, Luigi Scaccianoce
Music: Michel Legrand (Songs "Willow Weep for Me" and "Loveless Love" sung by Billie Holiday)
Jeanne Moreau's costumes: Pierre Cardin
Cast: Jeanne Moreau (Eve Olivier), Stanley Baker (Tyvian Jones), Virna Lisi (Francesca Ferrara), Giorgio Albertazzi (Branco Mallona), James Villiers (Arthur McCormick), appearances by Peggy Guggenheim, Gilda Dahlberg, Vittorio De Sica, and Joseph Losey
Running time: 115 minutes (U.S.), cut from 155 minutes as originally edited.

Paris premiere, October 3, 1962 (100-minute version); New York premiere, June 5, 1965

16mm. rental: Available under Italian title EVA from MacMillan/Audio-Brandon, 34 McQueston Parkway S, Mt. Vernon, NY 10550

THE SERVANT (Springbok/Elstree, 1963)
Producers: Joseph Losey, Norman Priggen
Production Manager: Teresa Bolland
Assistant Director: Roy Stevens
Script: Harold Pinter, from the novel by Robin Maugham
Director of Photography: Douglas Slocombe
Editor: Reginald Mills
Art Director: Ted Clements
Music: John Dankworth ("All Gone" sung by Cleo Laine)
Costumes: Beatrice Dawson
Cast: Dirk Bogarde (Hugo Barrett), James Fox (Tony), Wendy Craig (Susan), Sarah Miles (Vera), Catherine Lacey (Lady Mounset), Richard Vernon (Lord Mounset), Harold Pinter (young man in restaurant)
Running time: 115 minutes
Premiere, Venice Film Festival, September 3, 1963; American premiere, New York Film Festival, September 16, 1963. General U.S. release in March, 1964
16mm. rental: Janus Films, 745 Fifth Avenue, New York, NY 10022

KING AND COUNTRY (B.H.E. Productions, distributed in U.S. by Allied Artists, 1964)
Producers: Joseph Losey, Norman Priggen
Production Manager: Richard Goodwin
Assistant Director: Scott Wodehouse
Script: Evan Jones, from the play *Hamp* by John Wilson, based on a story by James Lansdale Hodson
Director of Photography: Denys Coop
Editor: Reginald Mills
Art Director: Peter Mullins
Music: Larry Adler
Costumes: Roy Ponting
Cast: Dirk Bogarde (Capt. Hargreaves), Tom Courtenay (Pvt. Hamp), Leo McKern (Capt. O'Sullivan), Barry Foster (Lt. Webb), James Villiers (Capt. Midgley), Peter Copley (Colonel)
Running time: 86 minutes
Premiere: Venice Film Festival, September 5, 1964; American premiere, New York Film Festival, September 23, 1964; general U.S. release, September, 1965
16mm. rental: Ivy Films 16; MacMillan/Audio-Brandon

MODESTY BLAISE (Modesty Blaise, Ltd., distributed by 20th Century–Fox, 1966)

Producer: Joseph Janni

Assistant Directors: Gavrick Losey, Claude Watson

Script: Evan Jones, based on the comic strip created by Peter O'Donnell and Jim Holdaway

Director of Photography (Technicolor): Jack Hildyard (with location photography in Amsterdam by David Boulton)

Editor: Reginald Beck

Art Director: Jack Shampan

Music: John Dankworth (songs by Benny Green and Evan Jones)

Costumes: Beatrice Dawson

Cast: Monica Vitti (Modesty Blaise), Terence Stamp (Willie Garvin), Dirk Bogarde (Gabriel), Harry Andrews (Sir Gerald Tarrant), Michael Craig (Paul Hagan), Scilla Gabel (Melina), Tina Marquand (Nicole), Clive Revill (McWhirter and Sheikh Abu Tahir)

Running time: 119 minutes

London premiere: May 5, 1966; New York premiere, August 11, 1966.

16mm. rental: Films, Inc.

ACCIDENT (Royal Avenue Chelsea, distributed in U.S. by Cinema V. 1967)

Producers: Joseph Losey, Norman Priggen

Production supervisor: Geoffrey Haine

Assistant Director: Richard Dalton

Script: Harold Pinter, from a story by Nicholas Mosley

Director of photography (Eastman color): Gerry Fisher

Editor: Reginald Beck

Music: John Dankworth

Costumes: Beatrice Dawson

Cast: Dirk Bogarde (Stephen), Stanley Baker (Charley), Jacqueline Sassard (Anna), Michael York (William), Vivien Merchant (Rosalind), Delphine Seyrig (Francesca), Alexander Knox (The Provost), Harold Pinter (Mr. Bell), Freddie Jones (frantic man at TV studio), Nicholas Mosely (a don)

Running time: 105 minutes

London premiere: February 9, 1967; New York premiere, April 18, 1967

16mm. rental: Swank Films, 201 S. Jefferson Ave., St. Louis, Mo. 63166

BOOM! (World Film Services—Moonlake Productions, distributed by Universal, 1968)

Producers: John Heyman, Norman Priggen

Assistant Director: Carlo Lastricate

Script: Tennessee Williams, from his play *The Milk Train Doesn't Stop Here Any More*

Director of photography (Technicolor): Douglas Slocombe
Editor: Reginald Beck
Art Director: Richard MacDonald
Music: John Barry (with Indian sitar music by Nazirali Jairazbhoy and Viram
    Jasanic); song "Hideaway" by John Dartmouth and Don Black, sung by
    Georgie Fame
Miss Taylor's wardrobe by Tiziani of Rome
Cast: Elizabeth Taylor (Flora Goforth), Richard Burton (Chris Flanders),
    Noel Coward (The Witch of Capri), Joanna Shimkus (Bladie), Michael
    Dunn (Rudy), Romolo Valli (Dr. Lully)
Running time: 110 minutes
New York premiere, August 10, 1968
16mm. rental: Universal-16, 445 Park Ave., New York, NY 10022

SECRET CEREMONY (Universal Pictures–World Film Service, 1968)
Producers: John Heyman, Norman Priggen
Assistant Director: Richard Dalton
Script: George Taloris from a story in Spanish by Marco Denevi
Director of Photography (Technicolor): Gerry Fisher
Art Director: John Clark
Editor: Reginald Beck
Music: Richard Rodney Bennett
Costumes: Sue Yelland (Miss Taylor's wardrobe by Marc Bohan and Chris-
    tian Dior)
Cast: Elizabeth Taylor (Leonora), Mia Farrow (Cenci), Robert Mitchum
    (Albert), Peggy Ashcroft (Hannah), Pamela Brom (Hilda)
Running time: 109 minutes
New York premiere: December 2, 1968
16mm. rental: Universal-16

FIGURES IN A LANDSCAPE (Cinema Center Films, distributed by
    National General Pictures, 1970)
Producer: John Kohn
Script: Robert Shaw, from a novel by Barry English
Director of photography: Henri Alekan
Music: Richard Rodney Bennett
Cast: Robert Shaw (MacConnachie), Malcolm McDowell (Anell), Henry
    Woolf (helicopter pilot), Pamela Brom (widow)
Running time: 118 minutes
New York premiere: July 18, 1971
Not available for sale or rental

THE GO-BETWEEN (EMI/World Film Service, distributed by Columbia,
    1970)

Producers: John Heyman, Norman Priggen
Script: Harold Pinter, from the novel by L. P. Hartley
Director of photography (Technicolor): Geoffrey Fisher
Music: Michel Legrand
Cast: Julie Christie (Maria), Alan Bates (Ted Burgess), Michael Redgrave
    (Leo Colston, as a man), Dominic Guard (Leo as a boy), Edward Fox
    (Hugh Trimingham), Margaret Leighton (Mrs. Maudsley), Michael Gogh
    (Mr. Maudsley)
Running time: 116 minutes
Premiere: Cannes Film Festival, May, 1970 (Grand Prize Winner); U. S.
    Premiere, 68th St. Playhouse, New York, July 29, 1970
16mm. rental: MacMillan/Audio-Brandon; Swank; and others

THE ASSASSINATION OF TROTSKY (Dino de Laurentiis/Josef Shaf-
ter/Cinetel, distributed by Cinerama Releasing Corporation, 1972)
Producers: Joseph Losey, Norman Priggen
Script: Nicholas Mosley and Masolin d'Amico
Director of Photography: Pasquale de Santis
Editor: Reginald Beck
Music: Egisto Macchi
Cast: Richard Burton (Leon Trotsky), Alain Delon (Jessen), Romy Schneider
    (Gita), Valentina Cortese (Natasha), Enrico Maria Salerno (Salazar), Luis
    Vangucchi (Ruiz), Dullio del Prete (Felipe)
Running time: 103 minutes
New York premiere: New York Film Festival, October 13, 1972
16mm. rental: Swank

A DOLL'S HOUSE (World Film Service, shown in U.S. on ABC-TV, 1973)
Producer: Joseph Losey
Script: David Mercer from Michael Meyer's English translation of Henrik
    Ibsen's play.
Director of Photography: Gerry Fisher
Editor: Reginald Beck
Music: Michel Legrand
Art Director: Elleen Diss
Costumes: John Furniss
Cast: Jane Fonda (Nora), David Warner (Torvald), Trevor Howard (Dr.
    Rank), Delphine Seyrig (Kristine Linde), Edward Fox (Krogstad)
Running time: 106 minutes
New York premiere: New York Film Festival, October 1, 1973
16mm. rental: Contemporary Films–McGraw Hill and others; lease, Learn-
    ing Corporation of America, 1350 Avenue of the Americas, New York,
    NY 10019

GALILEO (Cinevision, distributed in U.S. by American Film Theater, 1975)
Producer: Ely Landau
Script: Barbara Bray and Joseph Losey from Charles Laughton's English version of Bertolt Brecht's German play
Director of photography: Michael Reed
Editor: Reginald Beck
Music: Hans Eisler
Cast: Topol (Galileo Galilei), Edward Fox (Cardinal Inquisitor), Colin Blakeley (Priuli), Clive Revill and Georgia Brown (ballad singer and his wife), Margaret Leighton (Court lady), John Gielgud (aging cardinal), Michael Lonsdale (Cardinal Barberini/Pope)
Running time: 145 minutes
Shown simultaneously at several hundred theaters across the country on January 27–28, 1975, as part of the uncompleted second-year program of the American Film Theater and not re-released commercially
16mm. rental: Paramount Non-Theatrical Division, 5451 Marathon St., Hollywood, CA 90038

THE ROMANTIC ENGLISHWOMAN (Dial/Meric-Matalon, distributed by New World Pictures, 1975)
Producer: Daniel M. Angel
Script: Tom Stoppard and Thomas Wiseman from Wiseman's novel
Director of Photography: Gerry Fisher
Editor: Reginald Beck
Music: Richard Hartley
Cast: Glenda Jackson (Elizabeth Fielding), Michael Caine (Lewis Fielding), Helmut Berger (Thomas), Kate Nellinan (Isabel), Rene Kolldenhoff (Herman), Michael Lonsdale (Simon)
Running time: 117 minutes
New York premiere: November 26, 1975
16mm. rental: Films, Inc.

MR. KLEIN (Basil Films, distributed by Quartet Films, 1977)
In French with English subtitles
Producer: Raymond Danon
Script: Franco Solinas
Director of Photography: Gerry Fisher
Music: Egisto Macchi and Pierre Porte
Cast: Alain Delon (Mr. Klein), Jeanne Moreau (Florence), Michael Lonsdale (Pierre), Juliet Berto (Janne), Suzanne Flon (concierge)
Running time: 122 minutes
New York premiere: November 6, 1977
Not available for rental

NOTE ON *DON GIOVANNI*

(American premiere'' New York, November 10, 1979.)

Following his adaptations of *A Doll's House* and *Galileo*, *Don Giovanni* is Losey's third recent attempt to find a fluid film style for material deeply rooted in theatrical conventions. Unlike Ingmar Bergman, who gives his film of *The Magic Flute* a realistic framework by presenting it as a staged performance, Losey moves opera out into the real world, photographing *Don Giovanni* primarily in the rooms and on the grounds of a glorious Palladian villa. But his transformations of physical reality throughout the film provide much the same kind of aesthetic distance, the same kind of framework for the music, as the performance motif in Bergman's adaptation.

The film's strange and mystical prologue, in which Don Giovanni and an entourage journey by boat to visit a Venetian glass-blowing factory, is typical of Losey's dramatic use of real settings. Moving from the brilliant daylight on Venetian waterways to the cavernous darkness of the factory, the passage has an eerie, otherworldly quality; we seem to be observers of an exotic ritual. In choosing his backgrounds, and then in the way that he films them, Losey's concern has been to establish a visual field within which to sound the cadences of Mozart's sublime music. If the world he creates is too real, the clash between setting and action—between a realistic film style and operatic theatricality—is likely to be jarring; if the film's atmosphere is patently artificial, it might have the cramped, flattened look of filmed theater that Losey wanted to be sure to avoid. Respecting the requirements of both film and opera, Losey harmonizes his decor with the music; beautifully filmed and beautifully sung, his *Don Giovanni* is a rare blend, as filmic openness and variety enhance material conceived for the fixed space of the opera stage.

Losey chose an ideal setting for the grandest of Mozart's grand operas, a heroic Palladian villa near Vicenza. The villa has the striking dramatic presence of houses in many Losey films, though in its diversity of textures and its monumentality it is without equal in the canon. Setting scenes in galleries as well as grand salons, in porticoed corridors, bedrooms, in a bathroom and in the kitchen, Losey makes generous use of Palladian architecture. The great house is regal and detached, yet like the houses in all of Losey's work, it too offers a comment on its owner, reflecting Don Giovanni's love of opulence, his grandiosity and theatricality. Through lighting, angles, furniture, as well as the kind of activity that takes place within them, Losey endows Palladio's magnificent rooms with a surprising range of personality. At times, they are aglow with a festival spirit; at other times, metamorphosed from palace to church, from place of revelry to a mausoleum, they radiate funereal gloom.

Losey also guards against the intrusion of neutral physical reality in his choice of exterior locations. Scenes of gondolas on Venetian waterways and

Don Giovanni and his entourage on their way to a glass-blowing factory.

The thick Palladian column divides the enigmatic valet from the three masked figures. Sharp contrasts between light and dark add to the eerie, fateful ambience of the scene.

on canals that cut through the flat, spare countryside near the villa have a surreal quality; the film's real landscapes look almost like painted backdrops. But a few outdoor scenes lack the degree of visual transformation that Losey maintains for most of the film, and for a few isolated moments, film reality and opera collide. As Don Ottavio strolls on the great lawn, with no evident destination in sight, kicking peasants who lie sleeping in carefully posed groups, real settings and stylized action clash in strained juxtaposition.

Losey's stylized compositions employ columns, doorways, arches, corridors, and mirrors to provide frames within frames that underscore the alienation and entrapment of the characters. (One scene, in which the action is observed in and framed by a mirror may well be the most elegant mirror shot in Losey's work—a self-homage in the form of a visual grace note.) The grand architectural details seem sometimes to weigh down on the characters, imprisoning them within ovals, squares, circles, rectangles. Losey discovers many images of enclosure within the grand spaces of Palladian architecture. But the film is not simply a procession of closed frames, and many expansive long shots convey the vastness of the villa and its grounds. In alternating closed images with open ones, Losey provides visual equivalents for the shifting moods, the rosy tints and dark undercurrents, of Mozart's score.

Like Mozart as well, Losey "paints" his scenes in contrasting tones of light and dark. The film at times is flooded with glorious light, the wide expanses of the Palladian lawn illuminated with a joyous sparkle that recalls an impressionist landscape. Some of the interior scenes have the stark chiaroscuro of a painting by de la Tour, as a central source of light throws shadows over faces and decor. Throughout, figures costumed in severe black and white are set off from the marbled rooms and vernal landscape. For the stunning Act I climax, bolts of lightning and thunder and the flickering light of many torches provide a bravura display of chiaroscuro effects.

Like other Losey houses, the villa is filled with works of art. Frescoes, tapestries, and statuary portray scenes of both pagan and Christian themes, thereby pointing up the dominant conflict in the opera between pagan sensuality and indulgence on the one hand and Christian retribution on the other. Echoing the style of many different artists and historical periods, from medieval to Renaissance to neoclassical, to baroque and rococo, from Michelangelo and Da Vinci to Poussin and David, the paintings and sculpture enclose the action in an extraordinary textural richness. The aura of great art—of master paintings—that surrounds the action is carried directly into some of Losey's compositions. Rustic scenes evoke Breughel's packed canvases; one image of a seated peasant woman bathed in light from a nearby window is right out of Vermeer; an early morning scene in the country has the pearly grey tones of a Corot landscape; formally composed

Losey's symmetrical compositions match the balance and grandeur of neoclassical architecture and statuary.

group scenes within the great house have the studied grandeur and mon-umentality of a Piranesi print; while lighter romantic episodes have the charm of Watteau or Fragonard. The range of style indicates the film's visual lushness, its grand painterly manner.

In an attempt to find visual equivalents of Palladio's immaculate neo-classical balance, Losey's camera work and editing are notably sedate. Losey composes the film in long takes and deep focus, with panoramic vistas glimpsed through windows and swirls of activity visible at the ends of labyrinthine corridors. His use of perspective echoes that found in Ren-aissance drawings and stage design and also recalls Olivier's rendering of the Castle at Elsinore, in his film of *Hamlet*, as a place of endlessly receding hallways. And Olivier used long takes for the same reason that Losey does, to allow his performers an uninterrupted flow of feeling. Tracking slowly and gracefully through the palatial rooms, the camera movement sustains the film's measured rhythm. Sometimes, the camera remains stationary for long passages, as if the action is being performed within the fixed space of the stage; and sometimes Losey overcompensates by using too much movement. One of Donna Elvira's impassioned arias is filmed in one dar-ingly long tracking shot, as the character moves through the corridors of the villa. The continuous movement of both subject and camera begins to seem a studied way of avoiding theatrical stasis.

Losey's images are sometimes simplified to the point of abstraction, and sometimes burst with the multiple activity of a dense Breughel painting. For long scenes, Losey attains neoclassical balance and stillness, his camera remaining in place as characters are framed by columns, or grouped sym-metrically against spare backgrounds. But maintaining such a calm, stolid manner throughout the opera would betray its powerful conflicts and radical shifts of mood. Losey therefore counterpoints scenes of neoclassical serenity with images that evoke Romantic energy; there is a long, marvelously orchestrated passage leading up to the dance in which the frame is loaded with activity, as peasants, in the rear of the image, rush back and forth on errands as the masters prepare themselves for the evening festivities. The cross-cutting between events above stairs and below points up a social contrast that Losey discovers in the opera, while adding touches of daily life that are charming in and for themselves. The crowded deep focus compositions and the roving camera (which recall Renoir's mise en scène for the house party in *The Rules of the Game*) capture the lighthearted spirit of the rustic characters and help give variety to the film's pace.

The shifts of rhythm, texture, and mood that mark Losey's style serve the opera's essential ambivalence. In her vigorous study, *Mozart the Dram-atist*, Brigid Brophy suggests that *Don Giovanni* reveals the tensions felt by Mozart as a man of feeling in the Age of Reason. She argues that the opera's central ambivalence issues from Mozart's struggle to reconcile his desire to celebrate the Don as a true revolutionary with a conflicting impulse

to punish him for his sexual excess. The opera's view of the legendary libertine and anarchist is thus double-edged. Musically and dramatically, *Don Giovanni* is a mixture of light and dark tones, as Mozartian verve is shadowed by Christian guilt.

Though there are fleeting moments of Mozartian gaiety and elation, Losey directs the opera as high drama rather than darting comedy, stressing its negative, unromantic aspects. This is a singularly dark reading of the Don Juan legend. Losey's cavalier is not a heroic rebel against stifling tradition, nor a lighthearted hedonist, a celebrant of the body and the sun, but a sexual neurotic caught by his own inner compulsions. The character's sexuality is joyless, his endless conquests less a matter of choice, a daring invocation of freedom, than an addiction. More sexual victim than sexual tyrant, Losey's Don is only intermittently a commanding master of the revels, seizing sexual opportunity from every chance encounter. Ruggero Raimondi is a scowling, heavy-hearted Don, his frozen face and stiff movements recalling Donald Sutherland's Casanova, in Fellini's recent portrait of another cold and desiccated seducer. A number of critics complained that Raimondi looks as if he belongs on the opera stage rather than in a film, yet his unromantic appearance is necessary to Losey's interpretation. Raimondi sings the role powerfully, but there is no exaltation in this compulsive womanizer, no true heroism or freedom. He seems bored by his lust, continuing his quests because that is the fate to which he has resigned himself.

Losey introduces a homosexual undertone, providing the Don with a handsome young valet who opens and closes windows and doors, who strums the guitar to accompany the Don's serenades, and who stands by dutifully, observing his master with deadly concentration. Is he lover or nemesis? A symptom of the Don's omnivorous sexual interests or a reminder, since he is dressed in black and looks severe, of the Don's inevitable rendezvous with death and damnation? The homosexual ambience complies with readings of the legend which suggest that the character's voracious sexual appetite comes not from an overabundance of feeling for women but from a basic hostility, reflected in his objectification of sexual partners, his rampant promiscuity, his fear of involvement.

The film is not entirely one-sided in its view of the Don. There is a marvelous moment when the Don stares at a young woman bathing herself by the river; the girl seems to materialize out of the bright air like a Joycean epiphany. The libertine gazes at her sadly, as at an idealized figure destined to remain beyond the scope of his conquests. Briefly, in scenes with Zerlina, Don Giovanni approaches the game of love with a zest and abandon that make it look like fun.

Donna Anna and Donna Elvira, in Losey's version, are as neurotic as the Don. Donna Anna has such an overpowering attachment to her father that she denies her husband, while Donna Elvira, too naive to survive in

a worldly eighteenth century society, carries a sickly aura of the convent from which she comes and to which she returns at the end. Both characters, as sexually tainted and as obsessive as the Don, seem to fester in morbid anxiety, bewailing their fate in displays of voluptuous masochism. Losey casts the roles with two beautiful women (Edda Moser as Anna, Kiri Te Kanawa as Elvira), exceptional singers as well as actresses, whose physical resemblance to each other is enhanced by the fact that both appear often in black—in mourning for their lives—and wear gray wigs.

All the aristocratic characters, then, are in some way neurotically stalled; only the lower class figures—Giovanni's servant Leporello (Jose Van Dam) and Zerlina (Teresa Berganza, the only performer who conveys a full, unguilty pleasure in sexual indulgence)—are allowed vitality. Leporello unrolling Don Giovanni's list of conquests—1003 in Spain alone!—to a thunderstruck Donna Elvira is one of the few scenes Losey plays for comedy. The contrast between classes—peasant earthiness and common sense pivoted against aristocratic lassitude—evokes memories of symbolic class struggles in other Losey films. *Don Giovanni* opens with an epigraph from Marxist Antonio Gramsci: ". . . the old order is dying and the new cannot be born; in this interregnum, a great variety of morbid symptoms appears." The statement underlines Losey's view of Giovanni as a man of a particular social class, a depleted aristocrat attracting women more by the power of his social position than by his sexual attractiveness. In stressing the class conflict, Losey very much downplays the opera's religious and supernatural elements. In operatic performances, the meeting in the cemetery between the Don and the Commendatore, and the fateful dinner at which the statue is a guest, are normally spectacular high points, moments which test directorial ingenuity as well as display the budget. Reversing theatrical convention, Losey handles these two confrontations without any fanfare, the brief, modest hellfire sequence little more than a visual echo of the visit to the glass-blowing factory in the prologue. Losey reserves his big moment for the end of Act I, as the party guests, led by the three sinister masqueraders, turn against Don Giovanni with a force that signals a social upheaval.

In the libretto, the implications of the statue are ambiguous: is he an agent of divine retribution, the voice of Christian conscience come to punish the blasphemer? Or is he, as Brigid Brophy suggests in her Freudian reading of the opera, a father figure come to exact payment from his errant son? Or does he simply represent a social force which expels the Don in order to insure the health of the society? Whatever the symbolic import of the supernatural agent—whether religious, or oedipal, or social—Losey severely underplays it. In his dark interpretation, the Commendatore is perhaps more than anything a liberator who releases the Don from his compulsive revelry, his macabre sexual dance.

The Don's expulsion, though, does not heal the society. The film ends

with images of division rather than resolution, the characters separated from each other by the thick Palladian columns, or, observed from an uncomfortable high angle, isolated on gondolas in separate groupings that underline the class tension that has run throughout the film. The last image is one of retreat and seclusion as the valet closes the heavy doors of the villa. There is no triumph here, either religious or social; the morbid symptoms announced in the epigraph continue; the interregnum endures.

As in many of his earlier films, Losey is both attracted to and critical of a life of sensual extravagance. He is clearly delighted by the surroundings in which the Don lives; the dinner feast, the Don's last supper, is presented with an elegance and abundance that evoke sighs of pleasure from the audience. The camera caresses the piled fruits, the heaping vegetables and meat and poultry, the luscious desserts, endowing the sensuous life, here as throughout the film, with a kind of magical appeal. The marbled floors and walls that surround the golden table, the rich brocades and satins worn by the revelers, the warm glow cast by the tapers, and the swelling music create an aura of unimaginable sumptuousness. And yet it is just this kind of excess that, on one level at least, the opera condemns.

Losey's opulent decor matches the triumphal and celebratory quality of the music. The heroic music and mise en-scène overpower the libretto's dark theme and its unheroic protagonist, sweeping away everything but their own magnificence. And the overall effect of the film, as of the opera on stage, is one of triumph and exaltation, as form conflicts with and to some extent reverses theme. Mozart's music, finally, is greater, more noble, than its story or its characters or the moral that it dramatizes; like Losey's film, it is to be savored for its own richness, quite apart from any statements that may be embedded within it.

Losey begins and ends the film in a silence that is punctuated only by the sound of breaking waves. It is a surprising and personal touch (the boom of the ocean's roar figures as an aural motif in many Losey films) that indicates the importance of extra-musical sound effects throughout the film: the steady patter of rain in the opening fight between the Don and the Commendatore; echoing footsteps; the rustle of garments; the clop of horses' hooves.

Don Giovanni is a major achievement that opened with more fanfare in America than any of Losey's other films. Widely interviewed and fêted, and given prominent billing (the film was advertised as the Mozart-Losey *Don Giovanni*), the expatriate director finally seemed to be receiving the kind of recognition in America that he has long enjoyed in England and France. In early 1980, Losey began shooting his first film in America since he was blacklisted nearly thirty years ago. Certainly *Don Giovanni* contains questionable directorial choices (the most dubious is surely a scene in the Don's bedroom as he and Leporello argue while a nude suntanned woman reclines face down on the bed, looking, Vincent Canby suggested, as if she

couldn't sing a note!); but in its painterly richness, its array of textures, its compositional elegance and variety, its graceful use of movement, and its dramatic force, the film attests to Losey's continued authority. At seventy, he is still experimenting with the possibilities of his medium. The film suggests again his suitability as a director of Proust; but even if he doesn't get the chance to realize that long-contemplated project, *Don Giovanni* makes clear the thrilling visual and dramatic power of which he is capable.

Index